CW00405092

THE T-SHIRT BOOK

© 2002 Assouline Publishing, Inc.
601 West 26th Street
18th floor
New York, NY 10001
USA
Tel.: 212 989-6810 Fax: 212 647-0005
www.assouline.com

ISBN: 2 84323 346 1

Color separation: Gravor (Switzerland)
Printed by SNP Leefung Printers Limited China

Translated from the French by Simon Pleasance and Fronza Woods.

Copyediting: Jennifer Ditsler

All rights reserved.
No part of this publication may be reproduced,
stored in a retrieval system, or transmitted in
any form or by any means, electronic, mechanical,
photocopying, recording, or otherwise, without prior
consent from the publisher.

THE T-SHIRT BOOK

CHARLOTTE BRUNEL

FOREWORD BRUNO COLLIN

ASSOULINE

BOB
MARLEY
The Trooper
CHE
seamos realistas,
exijamos lo
POSITIVE VIBRATION
HONDA
mom
bad
HOT CHILI PE

Contents

Foreword

Bruno Collin

The T-shirt phenomenon is today's sequel (and complement) to the sneaker phenomenon. Urban fashion has evolved and now has its own sought-after brands. Like all nascent trends, it is often over the top. In 1994, many a brand went gung-ho for the street attitude. Kids wore their jeans too big and this baggy look was refashioned season after season. Then the shape became slimmer. To begin with, leading brands called the shots, but today the market is in the hands of their challengers. People are nowadays learning how to successfully mix and match products and styles, so that everyone can reinvent their own image. In the past few years, sneaker

Opposite: Pièce à conviction T-shirt (www.pieceaconviction.com).

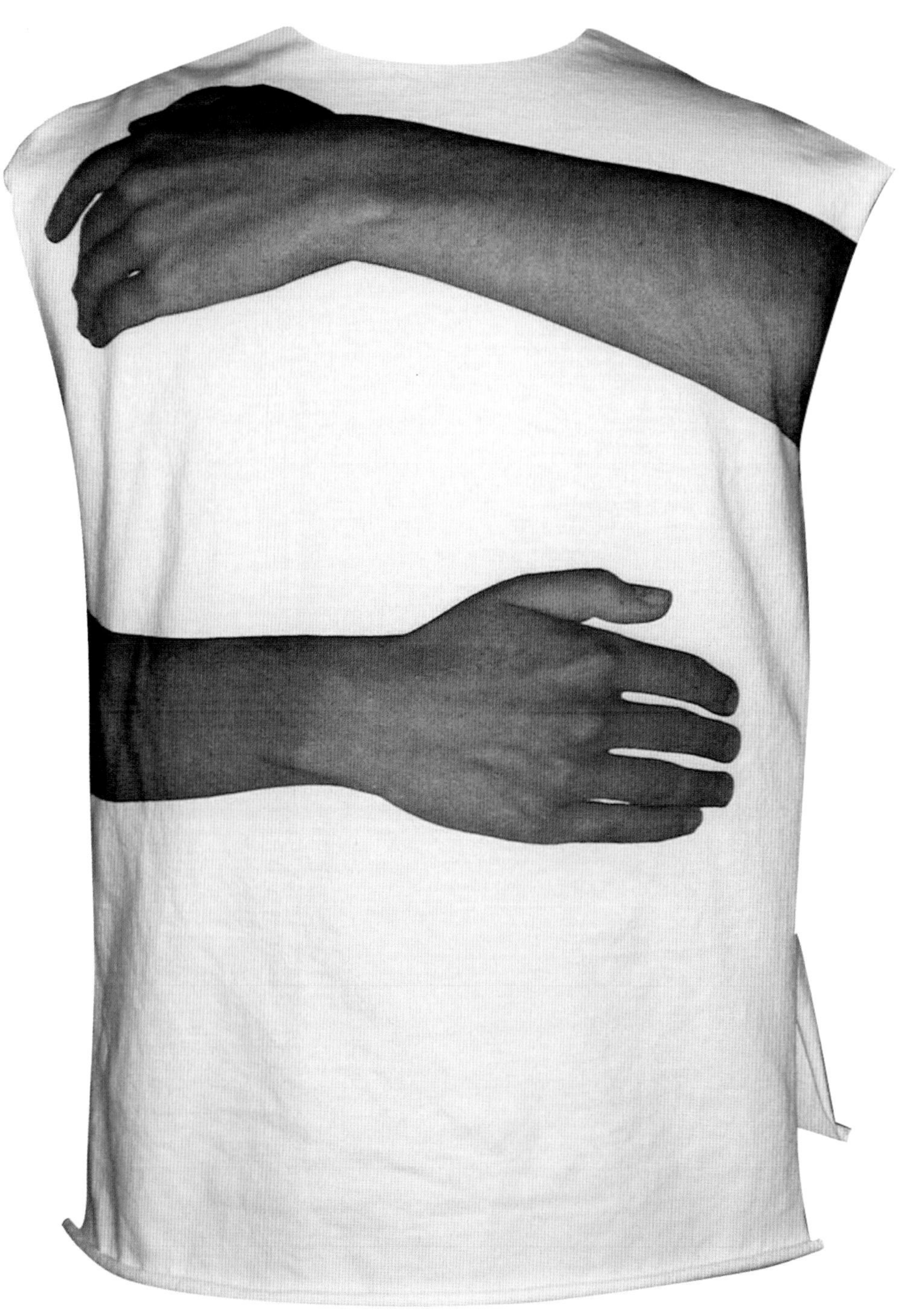

mania has embodied these new desires: limited editions, exclusive colors, collectors' items, originals. For the last three seasons, this trend—still very much on the upward curve—has been combined with a special T-shirt craze. The T-shirt is now a way of expressing oneself. It can put the finishing touch—often at very low cost—on a look that remains classic. James Dean's white T-shirt has spawned colored versions. To keep it trendy, its sleeves are often ripped off. But don't be fooled: this doesn't turn it into an athletic shirt. Because we are in the midst of an age of customization, it is the cut that gives it its different styles. Things have to be personalized. Even in Dior ads you see the words "J'adore Dior." Because the T-shirt's been upgraded, it features in every kind of collection, including the most prestigious (living proof being those

Galliano T-shirts). Couturiers are customizing them and turning them into collectors' items. People go bargain-hunting for them in flea markets, and buy secondhand models at Kiliwatch. Alternatively, they resurrect T-shirts they wore many moons ago. "Hey, mom, you know that old Dunlop T-shirt I never got rid of... d'you know where it is?" The T-shirt is something emotional. It embodies memories of a torrid trip to Ibiza or time spent at a university. After its "second skin" or extreme XXL phase, the T-shirt has come back down to size. It is worn fairly tight or sometimes a bit big. Exclusive, but affordable, its success comes hot on the heels of the sneaker. "I love T-shirts."

≠

Bruno Collin has one of the most impressive T-shirt collections of the world. He is the editor in chief of *WAD* magazine.

16

Introduction

Just like jeans, T-shirts became one of the 20th century's most universal and mythical items of clothing—with more than two billion a year sold worldwide. An extraordinary fate for this unassuming cotton tube shaped like a T that began its career in the men's underwear department. In the 1970s, *Elle* magazine announced that the T-shirt would become "a basic item of clothing that will never go out of fashion because it's already beyond fashion." The wager was won, because the T-shirt has been admitted to that hallowed pantheon of basics, alongside the trench coat and the little black number. Yet nothing seemed to preordain the T-shirt's exalted status as a worldwide, unisex uniform not only of relaxation, but of elegance, too. Before being displayed on chests of every shape and size, the T-shirt began its career in the secrecy of the men's underwear department.

At the end of the 19th century, this shirt learnt the ropes in the U.S. Navy well before it won the hearts of sportsmen and workers alike, with its twin virtues of comfort and hygiene. When those GIs who showed off their T-shirts during the Second World War in the sweltering heat of the Tropics returned home, their shirts were as heroic as they were. And the new gods of Hollywood, going by such names as Marlon Brando and James Dean, gave the T-shirt its rebel cachet and showed the whole world just how erotic it could be. In the 1960s, with the development of silkscreen inks, the T-shirt became the universal, unisex medium for proclaiming—or just sending—messages. Whether delivering the peace-and-love message of the hippies or the "Fuck You" message of the Punks, or even as a walking billboard for multinational corporations, this symbol of consumer society has turned into a kind of portable modern medium; one both affective and demanding. It is also a work of art that embodies new democratic ideals. In a word, the T-shirt is to clothing what the blank sheet of paper is to writing—a surface for imagination and free expression to run wild. Be it in chic plain colors or a gaudy print; adorned with a message on the front or the back, the T-shirt sends out certain signals. Printed with the Rolling Stones' tongue or the name of

Britney Spears, embellished with the crest of a favorite team, this undershirt juggles with every manner of identifying sign among all the many tribes and clans in the world of youth. The official fashion world, often influenced by the eye-catching styles of the street, got its hands on the T-shirt so that it could meet the new desire for luxurious relaxation. Enhanced by shape-hugging Lycra, cashmere or 100% silk, pop designer or logomaniac, the T-shirt has little by little betrayed its democratic origins, and turned into a luxury article. Henceforth, well-removed from political manifestos, brands are involved with both mass customization and limited editions, turning this basic garment into the fleeting reflection of the wearer's personality.

A long way from universalized fashion, the T-shirt also plays hooky and can be adapted to anyone's personal whim or wish. As a result of new computer software and stores offering personalized transfers, the T-shirt can be made to measure or to commemorate the big moments of everyday life. Life stories can now be told on T-shirts. And the story of the T-shirt, which fashion historians have hitherto turned their noses up at, is nowadays trying to unfold in words and pictures.

CHAPTER 1

Birth of a myth

Origins of the T-shirt

"The piece of clothing that emancipated America's top half" reads a T-shirt ad from the 1970s. Just like its fellow American, jeans, to which legs and bottoms are every bit as indebted, the T-shirt enjoys the status of a national hero in the United States. Work of art, political mouthpiece, advertising billboard, fashion fetish, in less than 50 years the T-shirt has become a kind of textile chameleon. There are times when its multifaceted personality disguises what it really and truly is—a simple item of clothing or, more accurately, underclothing. Before it came out as the unisex uniform for casual wear, the T-shaped white cotton undershirt had already begun its career in the hidden realm of men's underwear. These intimate beginnings helped to initiate its reputation as something comfortable to wear. In its private contact with the skin was the origin of this revolutionary piece of underwear's future success. The soft, cotton fabric, with its elastic texture both hugged the body and at the same time allowed it the freedom to move. The color white—symbol of cleanliness and purity—is still the T-shirt's most popular color today. And, finally, the simplicity of its T-shaped form—hence its name—insured its popularity and staying power.

In 1925 Japanese-born, French painter Fujita (1886-1968) posed in a ribbed undershirt—the famous French *marcel*—in his studio. As an ideal piece of clothing, which allowed great freedom of movement, this item of underwear would subsequently be adopted by many other artists.

The shirt proper took several centuries before it could hold its own as a fully-fledged piece of clothing; the T-shirt was a lot luckier. It was adopted as an undershirt in the 1930s, and twenty years later, started to

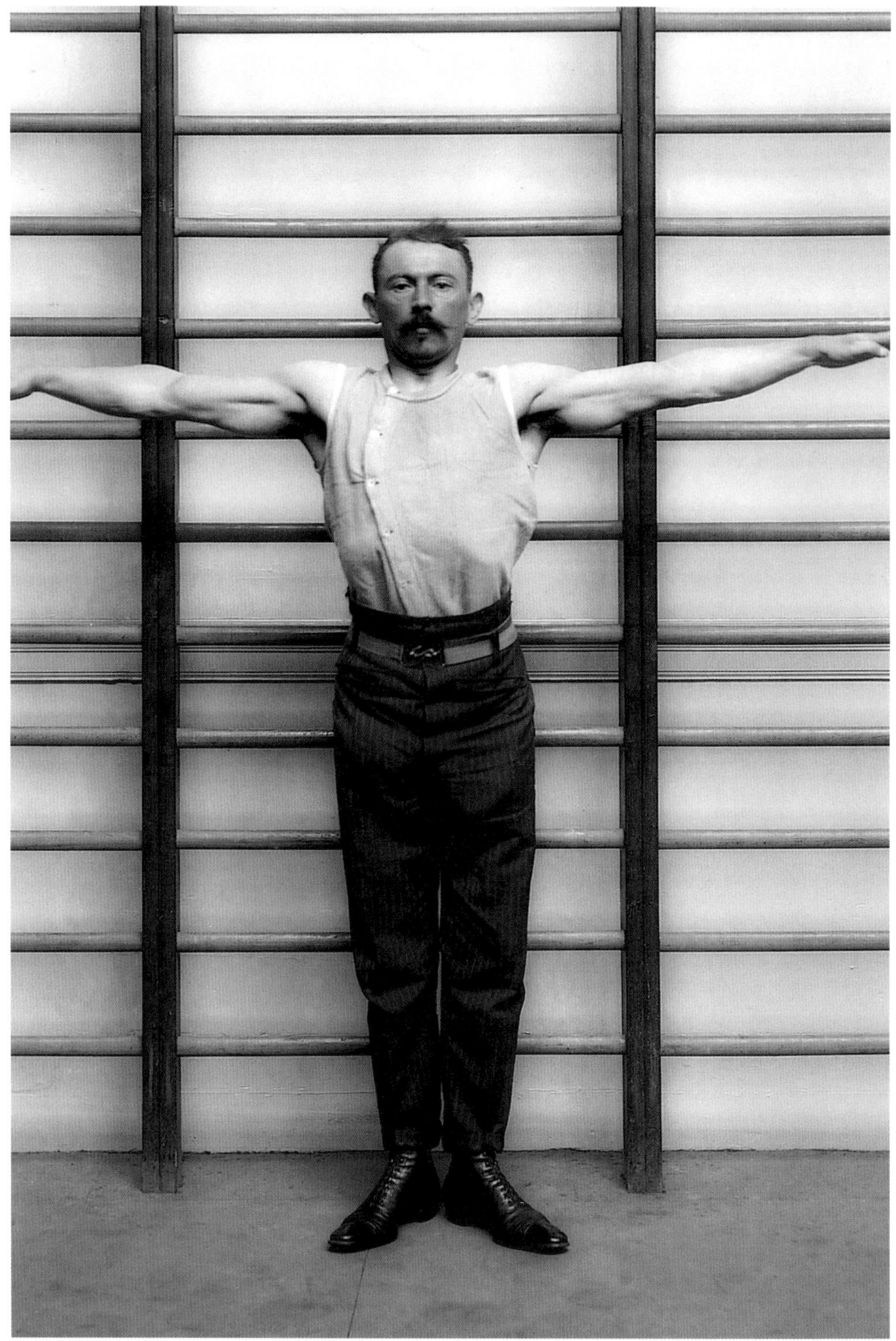

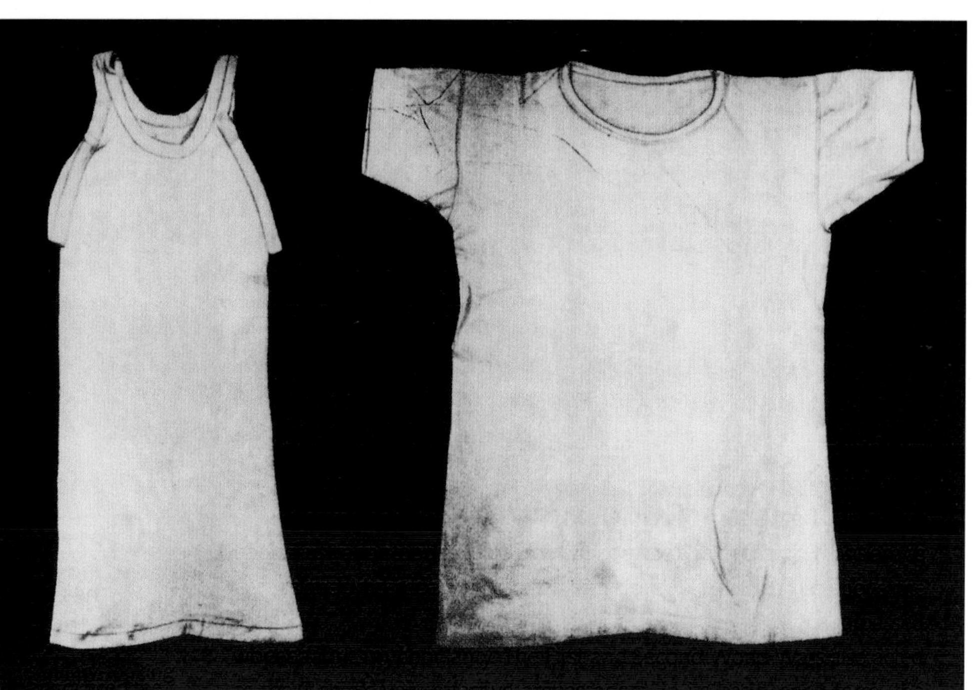

**Above:
U.S. Navy
underwear.**

**Opposite:
1910, gymnasts made clean and sanitary-looking athletic shirts their training uniform. On the eve of the First World War, people started showing off their muscles in gyms and stadiums. The forebears of the T-shirt announced the emancipation of the body.**

defy the postwar years of decorum by being displayed over the tattooed biceps of rockers and bikers. The speed of its rise to fame offers a pretty good illustration of that particular day and age; a time when hosiery in general enjoyed a dazzling boom, as did jersey (another name for knitted fabric), which at the turn of the century had gradually surpassed woven fabrics in popularity. The First and Second World Wars also acted as the T-shirt's very effective ambassadors. In its basic, early form, the T-shirt cut its teeth, so to speak, in the U.S. Navy, then gained a firm foothold as the official underwear of the U.S. Army immediately after the Second World War. All the same, its precise origins are still somewhat shrouded in mystery, and many theories jostle each other for position, as if bent on further fueling the T-shirt myth.

The sailor myth

Like many recent products and technologies—for instance, the first buttoned shorts, designed during the Great War with American soldiers in mind—men's underclothes were revolutionized at wartime. But the link between war and underwear goes back a lot further than 1914. As long ago as the Middle Ages, soldiers were covering their bodies above the

Opposite:
1930, actor Carlo Aldini flexes his biceps on the deck of a ship in the German movie *Kampf gegen die Unterwelt.* From the end of the 19th century, the athletic shirt revealed the attractive anatomies of seafaring men for all to see.

waist with linen shirts made of flax, not so much for protection from the cold as to spare the skin from being chaffed by the heavy armor then worn by troops. This linen clothing was subsequently adopted by noblemen, who wore it to prevent their fine and costly garments from becoming stained from direct contact with the skin. With the introduction of hose and breeches—the forbears of trousers—the long tails of these shirts, packed between the legs, also served as underpants or drawers. The shirt, which was first and foremost a functional piece of clothing, acted as men's underwear up until the 1830s, a decade that freed it from its utilitarian status and turned it into an item that was, for a middle-class gentleman, an integral part of the dress code. In Victorian times, when propriety declared the words "underpants," "bloomers" and "pantaloons" indecent because they conjured up images of naked male legs, sailors were the first to offer official glimpses of the whiteness of their underclothes.

In about 1880, the uniform of the U.S. Navy actually revealed in the V-neck of its pullover-like jerseys a loose-fitting, cotton flannel—called "flannelette"—shirt with a square neck and buttons on the neckline. This could well be the T-shirt's ancestor. Such, in any event, is the thesis advanced by Alice Harris in her book *The White-T.* Along with the famous flared white trousers, this official undergarment was

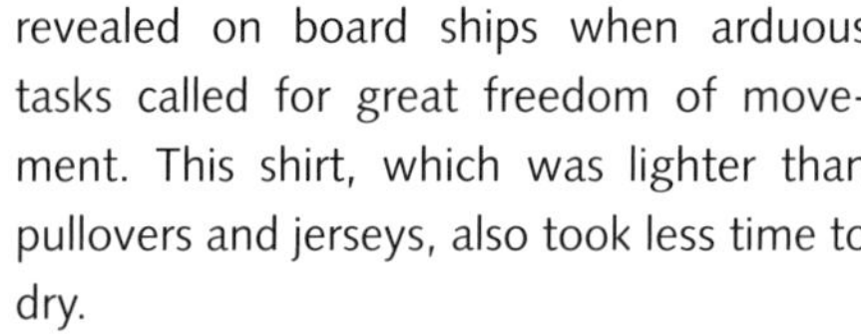

revealed on board ships when arduous tasks called for great freedom of movement. This shirt, which was lighter than pullovers and jerseys, also took less time to dry.

"There's one good thing about the sea/that every sailor knows./It's why he doesn't have to wear/mud-colored army clothes./The winds may blow/and the waves run free,/and the ship may get all rusty...," runs an American poem (*A Very Clean Poem* by G.M; *Our Navy*). The fairly casual uniform was earmarked just for grand occasions and shore leave. In a period conspicuous for starched collars, people looked a bit askance at bared necks. A British theory also connected with the world of the sea, offers another explanation

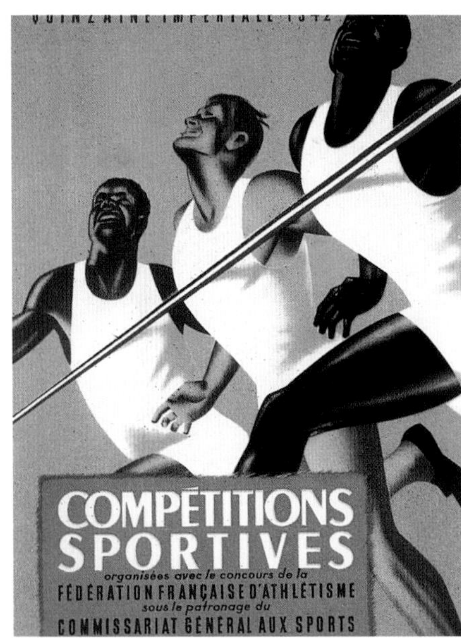
COMPÉTITIONS
SPORTIVES
organisées avec le concours de la
FÉDÉRATION FRANÇAISE D'ATHLÉTISME
sous le patronage du
COMMISSARIAT GÉNÉRAL AUX SPORTS

Below:
A propaganda poster for the French fascist government of Vichy, 1942.

90

Above: In 1942, sailors in the U.S. Navy stand to attention in shorts and close-fitting white T-shirts, waiting to be inspected. The T-shirt has been part of the uniform of the American fleet since 1913.

Opposite: A poster for the American Library Association, November 1918.

of the T-shirt's birth. Even in the latter years of the 19th century, sailors in the Royal Navy took to wearing under their blue uniforms a sleeveless, woolen undergarment which closely resembled the athletic shirt. One day, a member of the royal family (legend has it that it was Queen Victoria herself) announced that they would be making a surprise inspection of the fleet. The chief officer immediately drew up his troops and inspected his men one by one. Noting that these undershirts in no way concealed a sailor's hirsute manliness—nor, for that matter, his tattoos—he ordered the sailors to sew on sleeves, thus sparing the royal gaze the impropriety of such exposure. Whatever the T-shirt's true origins, in 1913 the U.S. Navy officially adopted "the short-sleeved, crewneck (i.e., collarless) version of the T-shirt to cover the chests of its old salts," explains Alice Harris. At first made of wool, this undershirt began to be made of knitted cotton during the First World War. The damp, cold conditions of the trenches were more than enough to persuade sailors that the light, faster-drying fiber used to make the underclothing of French soldiers had its distinct advantages. It was practical, too, because the wide slit at its neck—henceforth known as the "American armhole"—meant that it was easy to slip over the head.

These sea-dog origins contributed greatly to the T-shirt's popularity. This cowboy of the waves, sporting his combination of freedom and

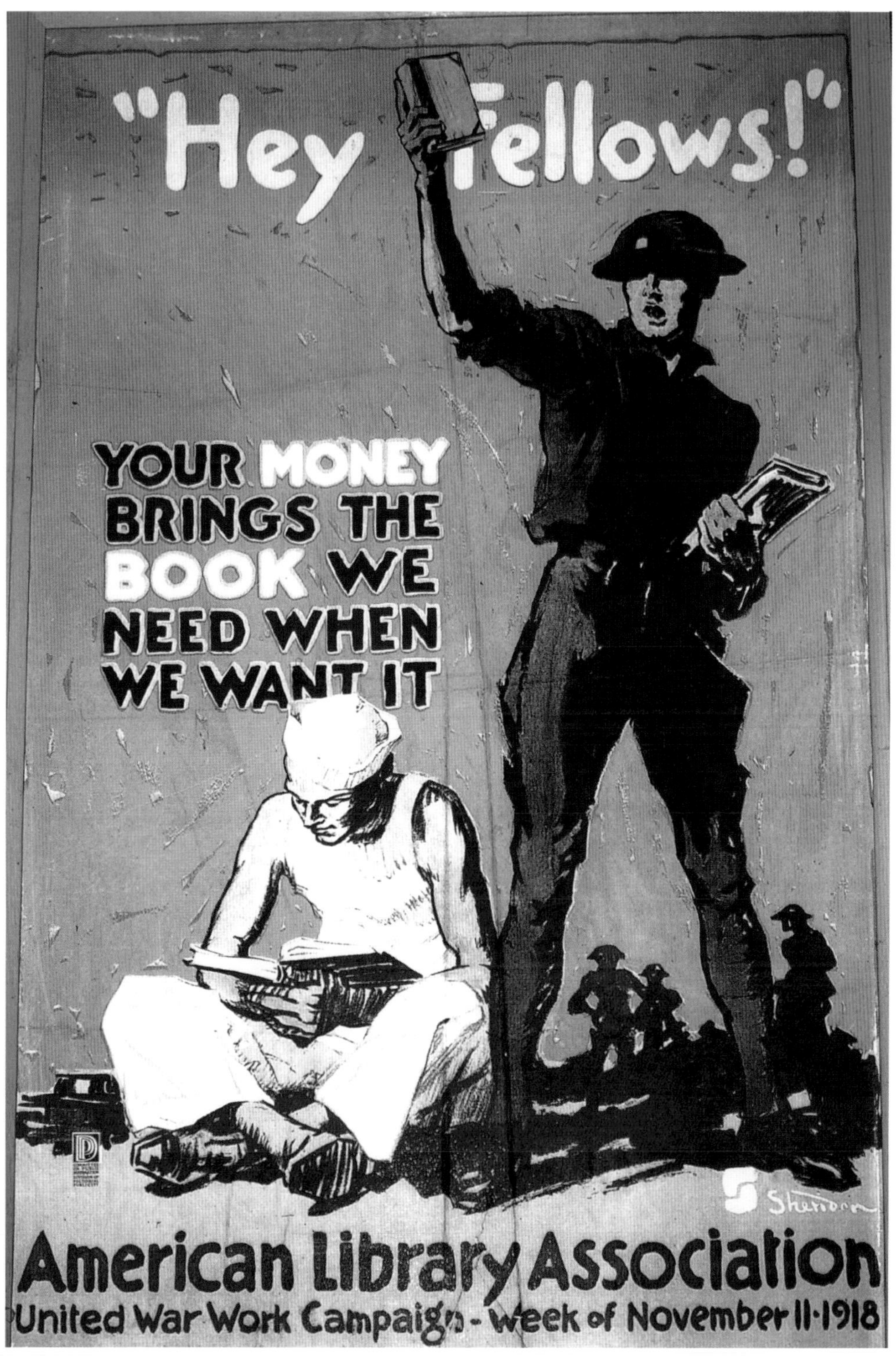
"Hey Fellows!"
YOUR MONEY BRINGS THE BOOK WE NEED WHEN WE WANT IT
Sheridan
American Library Association
United War Work Campaign - Week of November 11-1918

individualism, bravery and cunning, has always been a source of fascination. For the working classes, the world of the sea offered dreams of glory and social advancement. The young, handsome, smiling sailor, with his tattooed biceps and his buttocks sharply delineated in his tight white trousers, embodied a wholesome but steamy eroticism. In the 1940s, an advertisement for Coca-Cola depicted a sailor beside a girl clearly not immune to his charms, with the three-word slogan: "That Extra Something." The sailor's uniform has always had a certain allure, and the prestige implicit in it has been a crucial factor in U.S. Navy recruitment drives. At the end of the 19th century the sailor's striped shirt even found its way into women's wardrobes.

The underwear age

Romantic origins aside, the T-shirt owes its existence above all else to a period when the hosiery boom, coupled with notions of hygiene and comfort, turned the world of men's underwear upside down, not to mention inside out. In Europe, physical and mental health were one of the obsessions of the "philanthropic" middle classes of the 19th century. As the chosen target for these health-oriented concerns, underclothes were finally deemed to be worthy of interest (though it was not until the 1920s that taking regular baths and changing underwear on a weekly basis became an accepted habit in France). Woolen flannel was thought to be an effective weapon against colds and rheumatism, and was worn in the form of long underwear and undershirts buttoned right up to the neck and aptly named "health cardigans."

Doctors and physicians looked learnedly into the matter of underclothes, and even launched their own brands. One such proponent was the celebrated Dr. Jaegger, a fierce champion of wool, and in his wake came Drs. Breton and Rasurel, vying for public popularity in their underwear crusade. In the mid-19th century, the hosiery industry underwent major expansion with the modernization of production and distribution. The manufacture of clothing veered away from cottage industries toward the mass-production of apparels which soon became accessible to a much broader public. This mass-produced clothing was particularly attractive to working men and women whose ever-increasing numbers were causing the demand for cotton jersey to explode. From then on, underclothes were no longer luxury items. As a result of the cotton circular knitting

Charlie Chaplin in *Modern Times*.

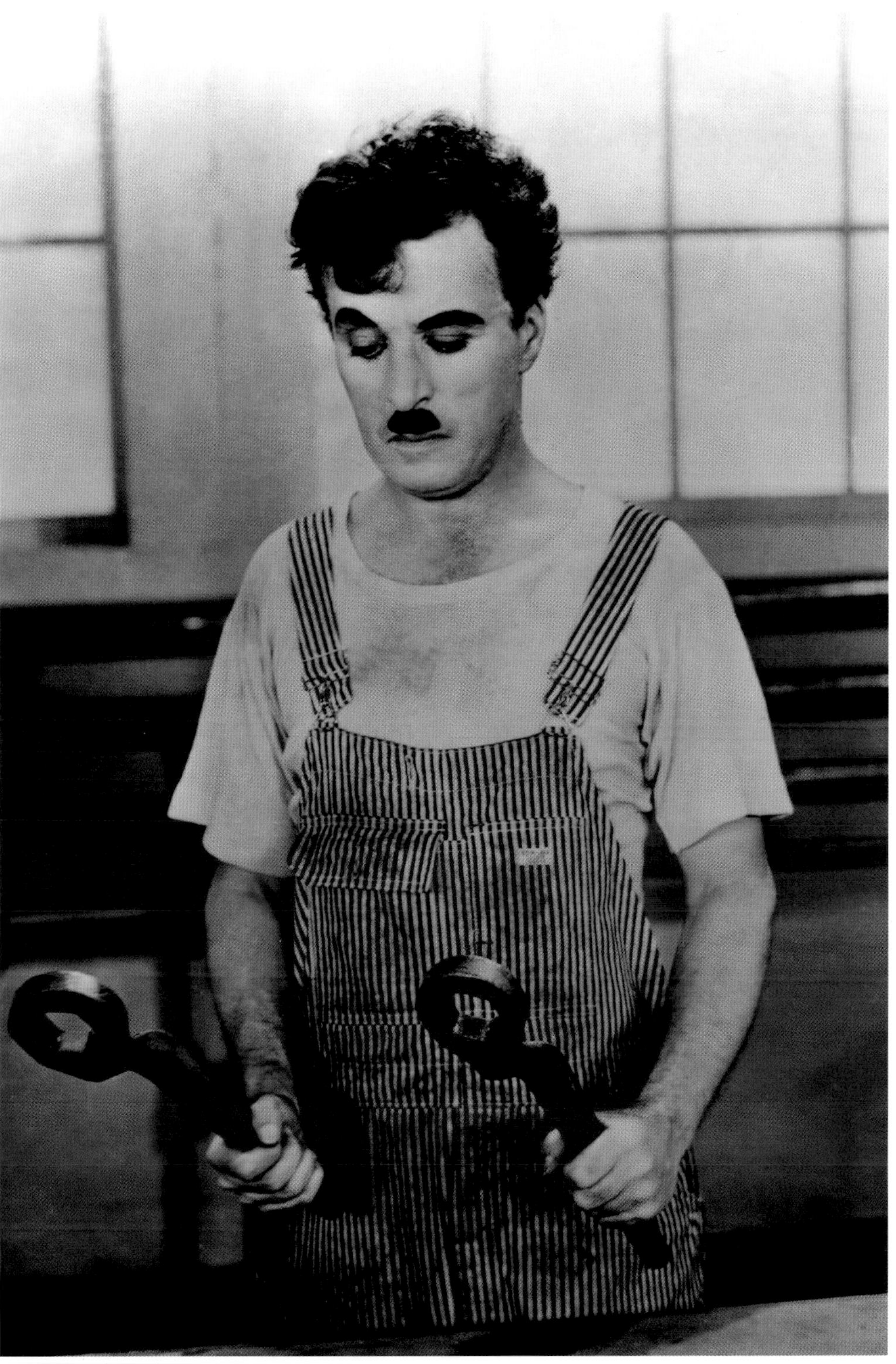

loom (patented in 1863), knitted jersey surpassed woven fabrics, which vanished altogether from the underwear sector by the end of the century. A new concept of comfort came into being. Hosiery factories located mainly in the Carolinas and New England, produced in less than one hour items that previously would have required three working days. Wool nevertheless remained much in demand on account of its luxury and warmth, but from the early 20th century on, cotton was eminently suitable for summer wear, because of its lightness and coolness. So underwear, too, began to follow the rhythm of the seasons.

At that time, it was sports that triggered a desire for comfort and gave rise to new forms of clothing. Paul Poiret cashed in on this development and gave women's waists a bit more breathing space by lightening corsets, and Coco Chanel became the very first apostle of this fashion by using knitwear which in that day and age was deemed "unseemly, too meagre, too flimsy, just about good enough for underclothes" (Edmonde Charles-Roux, *Le temps Chanel*).

Swimming in the sea—which had shed its purely therapeutic function—had given the body a taste of freedom, and capsized the rules of decorum and propriety. The man's swimsuit, a long woolen garment reaching halfway down the thigh with straps over the shoulders, was inspired by the kind of sleeveless one-piece costume that wrestlers and acrobats wore. It was espoused by sports teams of the day, and gradually accustomed the eye to the sight of underclothes, thus blazing the trail for its successor, the T-shirt. For in the 1920s, declared French columnist Armand Lanoux, "...the only revolution was sport. The year 1900 witnessed the bicycle, horses and riding, and the first car races; the 1920s ushered in athletics, boxing and the stadium..." In France, the 1930s was also the decade of the Popular Front and paid vacations, which encouraged casualness. Leisure activities began to blur differences between social classes, and the middle class began to sport the kind of clothes that before only working-class people had worn, like the cap and the athletic shirt. In the United States the range of underwear broadened and a new kind of elegance was introduced. The Union Suit was a comfortable one-piece garment consisting of a sleeveless undershirt attached to a pair of underpants by a button-hole, and it was all the rage. As early as 1916, an advertisement for a New York underwear firm called the BVD Co. vaunted its "modern" aspect. The ad featured a father, graying at the temples, dancing a crazy waltz with a teenager, a bunch of amused

Opposite: In the late 1930s, Gabrielle "Coco" Chanel poses in a sailor's T-shirt and men's trousers at her villa on the French Riviera. In so doing, she launched a fashion at once elegant and casual, which would usher in the birth of sportswear in France.

Next page: August 6, 1945, the American crew of the B-29 bomber Enola Gay poses for the camera a few moments before taking off for Hiroshima to drop the first atomic bomb. This tragic act, duplicated at Nagasaki, would signify the end of the Second World War.

youngsters looking on. "He had old-fashioned notions about underwear, until the boys went out, bought BVDs and made him put them on. Look at him! Now, Pa joins right in the young folks' fun, because he's cool." Soldiers returning from the war also nudged this burgeoning athletic style along. Boasting a buttonhole and short sleeves with an elastic hem like a polo shirt, this cotton sports shirt, which could be found at the time in Sears, Roebuck & Co. mail-order catalogues, cost barely 50 cents, and was a harbinger of the T-shirt. In about 1930, it cropped up again with the Hanes company, manufacturers of underwear (at a later date, under the trade name Fruit of the Loom, this became the number one T-shirt), which gave it the name "gob shirt," to emphasize its naval origins. The shirt, designed expressly for sports and leisure, had quite simply turned into the T-shirt!

T-shirt as hero

In 1941, a catalogue ran an ad for its "Army Style T-shirt." For in the meantime the U.S. Navy, which was readying itself for another war, had designed a new version of the T-shirt—a round-necked 100% cotton shirt, shaped like a T. Sears, Roebuck and Co. made the most of this design and launched a new, attention-grabbing slogan: "You needn't be a soldier to have your own personal T-shirt." The army image did actually contribute greatly to the popularity of the T-shirt among civilians. This undergarment, aligned with the qualities of bravery and manhood, managed to get the message across that its practical

OLA
GAY

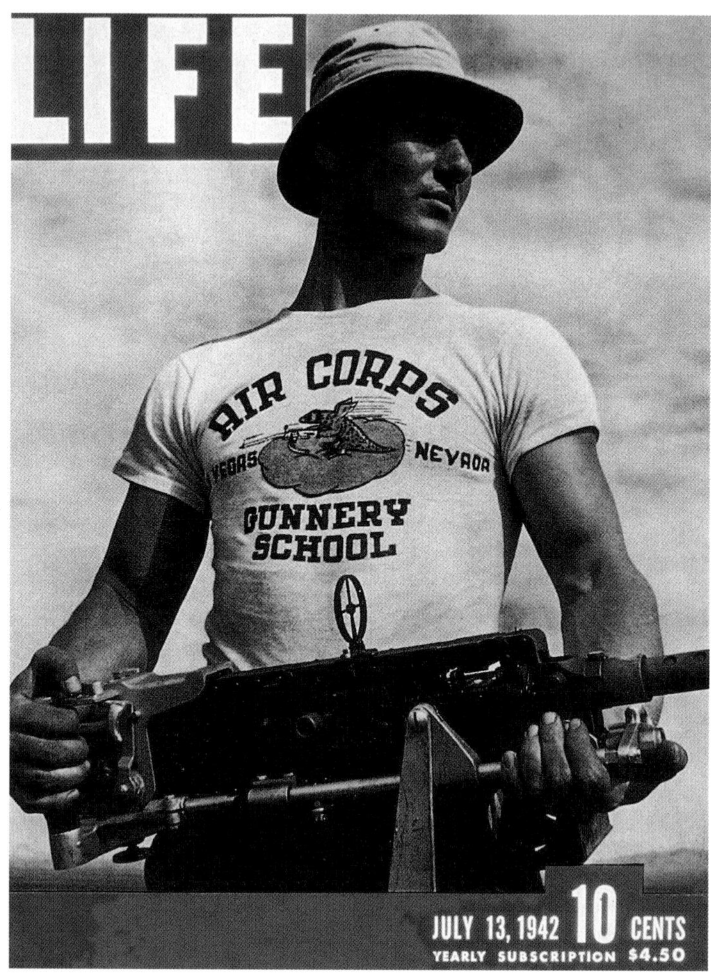

LIFE
AIR CORPS
VEGAS NEVADA
GUNNERY
SCHOOL
JULY 13, 1942 10 CENTS
YEARLY SUBSCRIPTION $4.50

A photo of Eliot Elisofon makes the cover of *Life* magazine in July 1942. The United States had entered the war, and was glorifying its fighting men.

comfort and relative propriety put it somewhere beyond the narrow confines of underwear and sports garments. At war in the Pacific, the hot and humid tropical climate made wearing a shirt out of the question. Major Galen Jones, an officer in a decontamination unit in the Philippines, described his uniform at the war's end thus: a pair of combat boots, khaki chinos, a T-shirt and a pith helmet. The historian Philip Katcher (*The U.S. Army 1941–1945*) adds that, quite possibly, "the extreme filth of war and the horrible terrain where it was conducted (and the apparent lack of interest among the Japanese in what they wore) contributed to the general victory of comfort over crap in the Pacific." Under these extreme conditions, the T-shirt flaunted its many different qualities and uses. Towel, smoke mask, hat, or, if necessary, white flag.

It was equally adept at being unobtrusive and could be rolled up into a tiny ball weighing just an ounce or two. Because of its whiteness, however, it was an easy target for the enemy. So it was dyed khaki, the better to blend into the lush and verdant landscape of the tropics.

That war, with all its media coverage, helped turn the T-shirt into a military icon, displayed on *Life* magazine covers and in newsreels. Before the war was over, the T-shirt was already identified with the hero's outfit. Throughout Europe, it appeared like a liberator, gracing GI chests and symbolizing modern America, along with chewing gum and nylon stockings. Hitherto worn by the Marines, the was coveted by the other fighting forces, envious of the comfort of this second skin. But they had to wait until 1948 before they got its new and final version, with three-quarter length sleeves. This is the T-shirt we know today. Worn by all ranks, the T-shirt managed to do away with social hierarchies and come across as a symbol of democracy. As worn upon returning from the front by the likes of Elvis Presley, John F. Kennedy as well as the working man, this item of underwear finally became an item of overwear.

1952, under the torrid sun of Central America, Yves Montand and Charles Vanel sport the trucker's traditional undershirt. In the film *The Wages of Fear*, the two actors immortalized this garment in the history of French cinema.

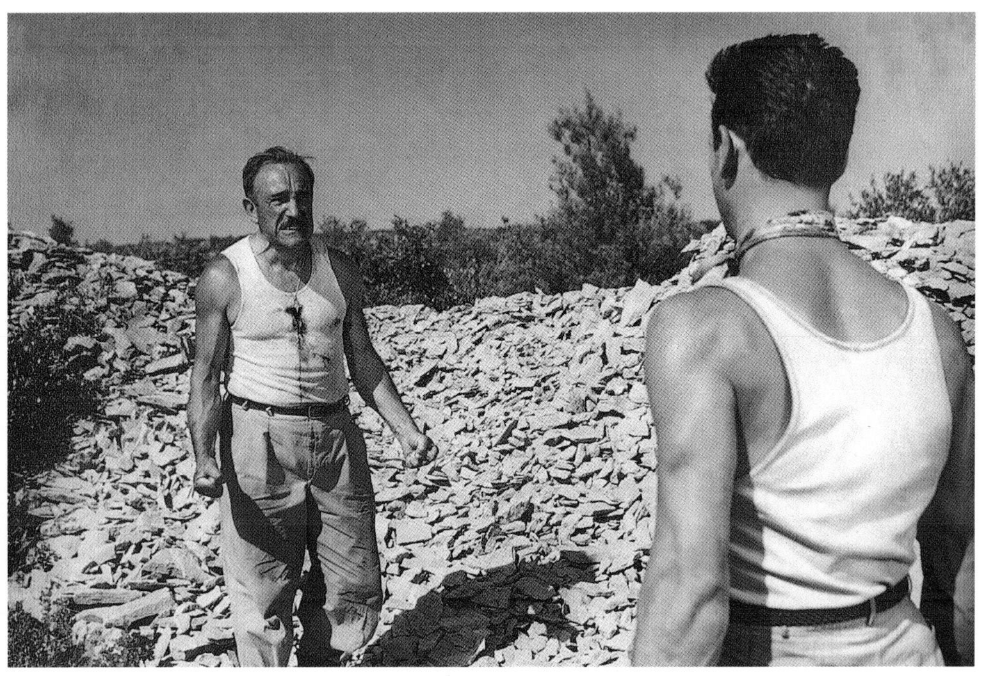

CHAPTER 2

Cotton saga

100% cotton

Cotton has freed our skins from the rough stiffness of flax and linen, soothed them after being scratched by wool, and absorbed the sweat of hardworking bodies. Even nowadays, these outstanding qualities make cotton the most widely used natural fiber in the world. Synthetic materials may sometimes be used as a substitute, but the T-shirt generally remains faithful to its "100% cotton" origins, which have kept it at the top of the comfortable-clothing charts for half a century. A formula that to this day is still a success, since its largest producer—the United States—usually uses these plant fibers to mass produce it.

Cotton is as light as air, but a heavyweight contender, nonetheless, in the world economy. Each year, tens of thousands of tons of it (20,000 for 1998-1999) find their way not only into the textile industry, but also into the food-processing industry and agribusiness, in the form of oils and flours made from cottonseed. Cotton is also a born democratic commodity, inasmuch as it is picked and harvested in the arid regions of 70 tropical and subtropical countries. In the early 20th century, the United States held total sway over the production of cotton. A century later, however, the cotton king is China, which controls a quarter of the global market. The United States has been relegated to second rank with a host of Asian countries—including India, Pakistan, Uzbekistan, Turkey, and some African states (Egypt, and French-speaking nations)—in its wake.

Opposite: Cheap, light, easy to wash, cotton is the ideal underwear material. (Design by Tim Fletcher)

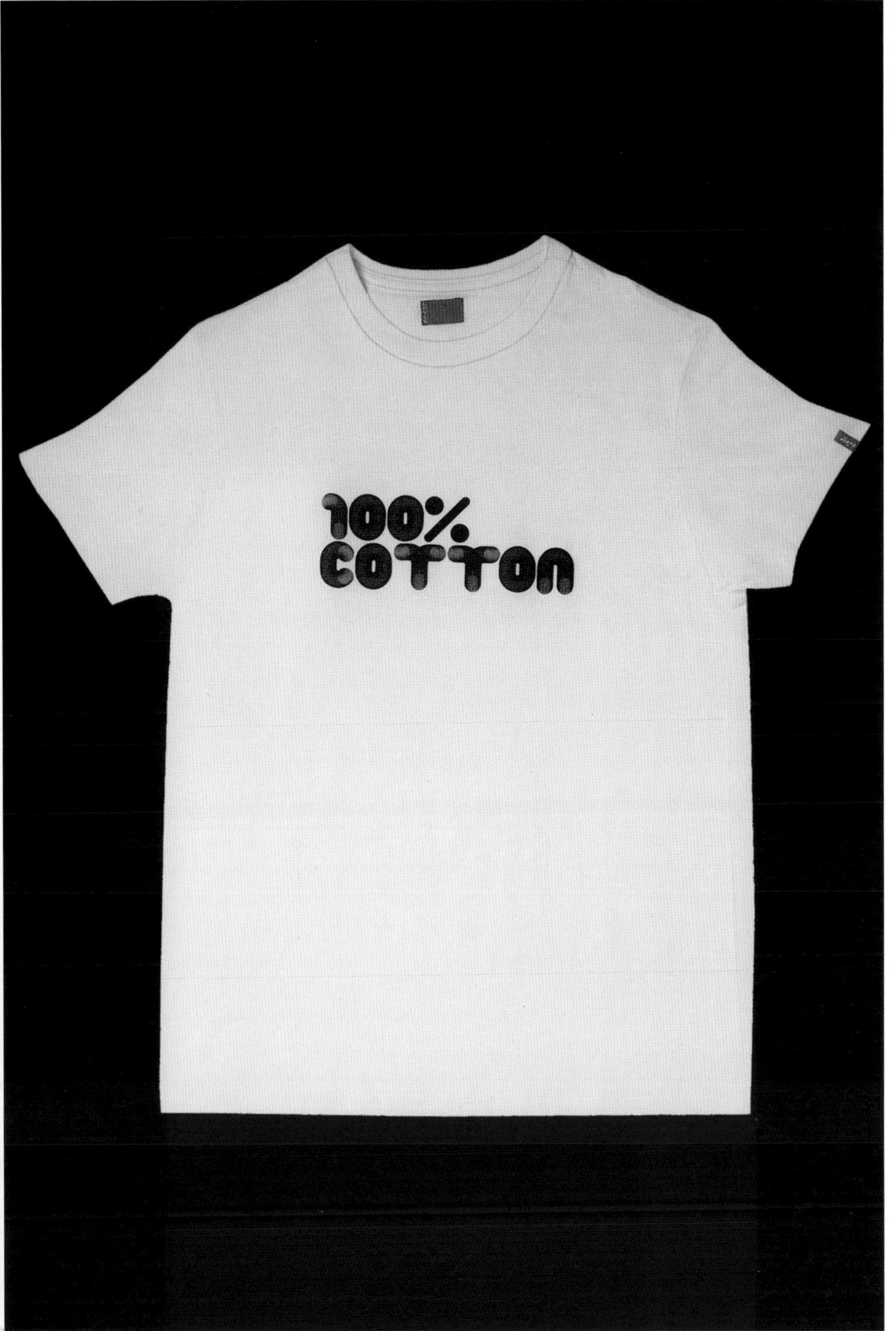
100%
COTTON

THE COTTON FLOWER

Cotton, strictly speaking, is the long cellulose hairs that swathe the seeds of the cotton plant inside a capsular fruit. This extremely prolific shrub is a member of the family *Malvaceae* (hibiscus, mallow, etc.). There are some twenty major species, the most widely cultivated being *Gossypium barbadense* (originating from Barbados in the Caribbean) and *G. hirsutum*, the commonest of them all. After flowering, the fruit of the cotton plant grows to maturity in about 50 days, providing the seeds and the husk around them, from which derives the fibrous, downy cotton. When the seeds burst open it is time for the harvest to begin. This usually occurs in the autumn, and cannot be put off.

AN AGE-OLD FIBER

In 3,000 B.C., cotton was already being used to clothe the inhabitants of the Indus Valley; and 500 years later, cotton clothing was being worn by the peoples of northern Peru. Since then, cotton has been permanently on the move, gradually fanning out to all five continents. From very early on in the Christian era, it was transported westward in caravans coming overland from India, to flourish along the shores of the Red Sea, eventually reaching all the way to Spain, in the 8th century A.D., with Moorish horsemen. In the Americas, it was used from the earliest days as currency in the Aztec Empire. Finally, European settlers adapted these plant species in Virginia, the Carolinas and Georgia.

Opposite: The cotton flower is picked by hand, using cheap labor. In 1954, in the plantations of Arkansas, a young boy repeats the same movements as his forebears, former slaves owned by Southern landowners.

Next pages: In Argentina, laborers—*indios*—beat cotton flowers to remove the seeds. This operation is carried out before the flowers are packaged in tight and heavy bales which are then sent to spinning mills.

AMERICAN COTTON AND SLAVERY

To keep the mechanical looms spinning back in Britain, the colonies of the New World, where the pace of production was being slowed down by a dearth of labor, called upon the services of slave traders, who set sail for the shores of Africa in quest of "human ebony." Hundreds of thousands of Africans were brought to the Americas to slave their lives away in the cotton fields. "The lovely pink and flame-red hues with which our ladies clad themselves, the cotton with which they pad their skirts, the sugar, coffee and chocolate they have for their luncheon [...], all these things are prepared for them by the hands of wretched Blacks. You women, with your sensibilities, you weep over tragedies, while what is served up for your pleasure is drenched with the tears of men and tinged with their blood." So railed the author of *Paul and Virginia*, Bernardin de Saint-Pierre, in *Voyage à l'Isle de France et à l'Isle Bourbon*.

9 FT

In a French cotton mill, impressive machines produce reels holding several miles of yarn. To obtain this thread, the cotton fibers are passed through a spinneret which calculates the gauge.

After the Civil War (1861-1865), cotton was still grown by black wage earners and white sharecroppers. Today, the great American cotton belt stretches from the Atlantic seaboard west to the Mississippi Valley, Oklahoma and Texas, Arizona, New Mexico and Southern California.

The making of a T-shirt

For almost five decades, the Petit Bateau company has been producing its T-shirts—from their knitting to their packaging in simple cardboard boxes—at Troyes, the hub of France's hosiery industry. Every day more than 1,000 Egyptian cotton T-shirts (one of the best quality cottons, along with Sea Island) leave their factories to fill the wardrobes of children and grown-ups alike.

KNITTING AND DYEING

Wound on gigantic bobbins—two pounds of spun cotton reach a length of nearly eight miles—the drawn and twisted threads are first put through a series of stress tests in the laboratory. Only the strongest are eligible to proceed to the knitting plant. Here, threaded onto dozens of needles arranged in circles, they are unwound at the hectic pace of the machinery, as row upon row, they knit a flimsy jersey tube. It takes

Above: A 1999 Issey Miyake creation.

Next pages: The various manufacturing stages for a long-sleeved A-POC T-shirt designed by Issey Miyake.

around six miles of yarn to make one T-shirt. Once formed, the knitted tubes are then placed in huge washing machines where they are dyed with the house colors.

CUTTING

In a tube form, the lengths of fabric are laid one on top of the other like colossal layers of puff pastry, a hundred or so in all, some of which may reach a length of 55 yards. At this stage, the computer then works out the precise positioning of the different parts of the T-shirt, no matter what size. This virtual pattern is then fed into the automatic cutting machine, and guides the saws which, down to the nearest millimeter, cut dozens of sandwich panels made up of sleeves, backs and fronts. In this kit form, the T-shirts-to-be are then sorted and arranged by size in trays to speed up the seamstresses' task.

PUTTING IT ALL TOGETHER

Meanwhile, other hands are busily preparing the neckline trim which will add a bit of pizzazz to the T-shirt's otherwise rather austere simplicity. In a matter of minutes, yards of tape, made with the same fabric—thus avoiding inconsistencies in color—parade perilously past, beneath the needles of the machines, and emerge sporting the famous

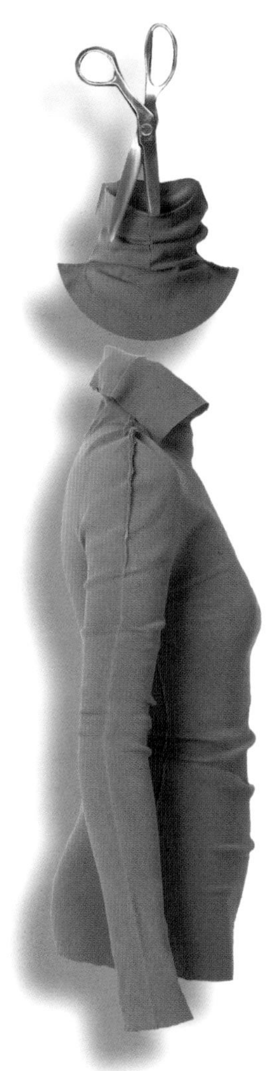

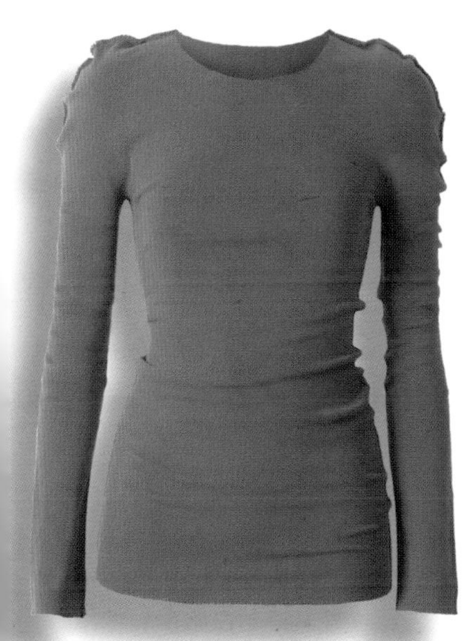

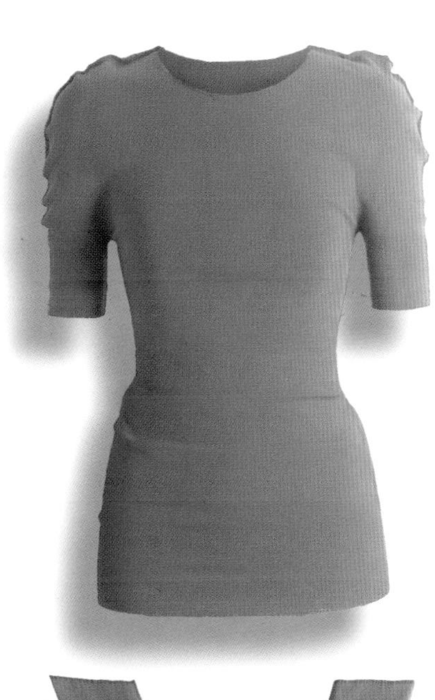

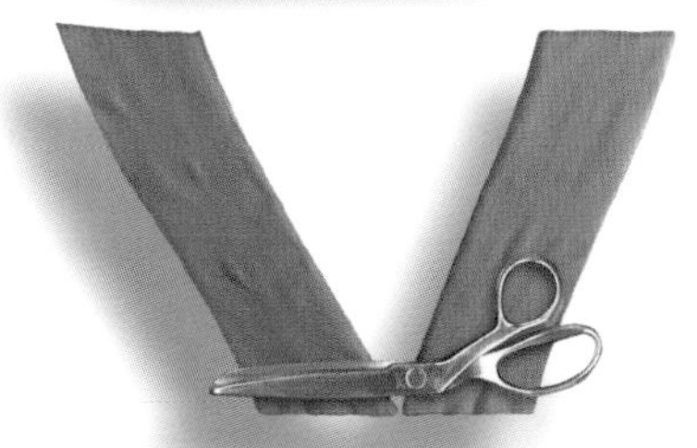

The Petit Bateau brand of children's underwear reproduced the initial version of its undershirt for more adult bodies. The success of this T-shirt is undiminished. It is now worn by all generations.

perforated, half-moon topstitch. The time has finally come to put the pieces of this textile puzzle together. At this point, the fronts are still being diverted so they can be embellished with silkscreened motifs and embroidery, while others are delivered to the skillful hands of the seamstresses and their sewing machines, grouped together in small workshops. The T-shirts are assembled with a series of very precise operations on the assembly line. Working at two machines, one worker puts the front and the back together by sewing the first shoulder, trims the neckline with the topstitch, then finishes the second shoulder. The T-shirt-to-be—still looking like a poncho—is then united with its sleeves by another worker. Once stitched together, these two tubes are then assembled in a circle on the shoulders. All that remains to do now is assemble the sides, and sew a hem around the bottom, so that all the pieces finally come together complete. A final check involves the finished shirt being drawn like a stocking over a metal form, where all its seams are inspected. Now it's time to pack it in its yellow-and-blue-striped cardboard box.

PETIT BATEAU

CHAPTER 3

Decorative techniques

Ever since the T-shirt found its voice, it has been increasing its graphic vocabulary in step with the various technological innovations that have occurred over the years. From the old-fashioned stencil to digital printing by way of transfers, this chatty piece of clothing, which is never at a loss for words, offers everybody a way to express what they want to say.

Printing

American singer Mariah Carey, a fan of tight mini-tank tops, wears a rainbow model. The graded effect is achieved by the flocking technique which gives the top its velvety look.

Next pages: A souvenir T-shirt sold at the Eiffel Tower in Paris.

SILKSCREEN PRINTING. Silkscreen printing, known technically as serigraphy (from the Latin *sericum*, meaning silk, and Greek *graphein*, to write) is one of the oldest of textile printing techniques, derived from the stencil principle. This process consists of drawing a motif on a silk or nylon screen with ink, which is then covered with a waterproof blocking solution made of glues or protective paints. Once dry, this design is then removed with a solvent. The printing inks are spread with a squeegee over the screen, thus finding their way through the now easily penetrated mesh to print onto the fabric. The number of colors used can be varied ad infinitum by changing the screens.

TEXTURES. Silkscreen printing can also offer a variety of textural effects. Glazing paper hot-pressed on the print gives the motif a glossy or shiny

My

Top
mode

Gaugui
Milkfed
BABS & BUNTY
EMOTION
LOVE
IL FÛT UN TEMPS ... 1979
MUSIC THERAPIE
DES HALLES
1979/1999

look. Other popular effects are spangled, scented, luminescent, phosphorescent, heat-sensitive and reflective. Nowadays, silkscreen inks make any fantasy possible.

Opposite: Flock printing: with this technique it is possible to create relief patterns and designs. The fabric is coated with glue which is then dusted with microscopic colored fibers. These fibers are attracted by an electrostatic field, and cling perpendicularly to the surface of the fabric until they take on a velvety look.

Next pages, left: A unique piece signed by fashion designer Irina Volkonskii. On a sleeveless T-shirt, two gigantic embroidered raspberries studded with sequins are set at breast height.

Next pages, right: Photography provides a new arena of expression. An agnès b. T-shirt features a landscape which shows the navel to best advantage.

Hot processes

THE TRANSFER. The hot transfer technique, introduced in 1963, is easier and faster to use. All you do is draw or print the motif of your choice with a felt-tip or marker, using silkscreening ink on special paper which is applied on the underside of the fabric; apply heat (a simple iron will suffice) and pressure, and the motif becomes fixed on the fibers, just like a transfer or decal.

DIGITAL. These days, thanks to computers, we can print T-shirts ourselves in a thoroughly professional way. All you need to do is devise or reproduce motifs using graphics software, print them on transfer paper, and apply them to the fabric using a hot iron.

Embossing processes

FLOCK PRINTING. With this technique it is possible to create relief patterns and designs. The fabric is coated with glue which is then dusted with microscopic colored fibers. These fibers are attracted by an electrostatic field, and cling perpendicularly to the surface of the fabric until they take on a velvety look.

BUBBLE COATING. With this process it is possible to make embossed motifs. The fabric is coated with glue and sprinkled with microscopic colored fibers. These fibers are attracted by an electrostatic field and flattened perpendicular to the fabric's surface, where they will take on a velvety appearance.

EMBROIDERY. Like any other fabric, the T-shirt can also be embroidered. Whether decorated mechanically or manually, it can be enhanced by gold thread, beads, spangles, sequins or feathers. On an emblem, the embroidery, known as thermobrod, is either applied by iron or sewn on to the fabric.

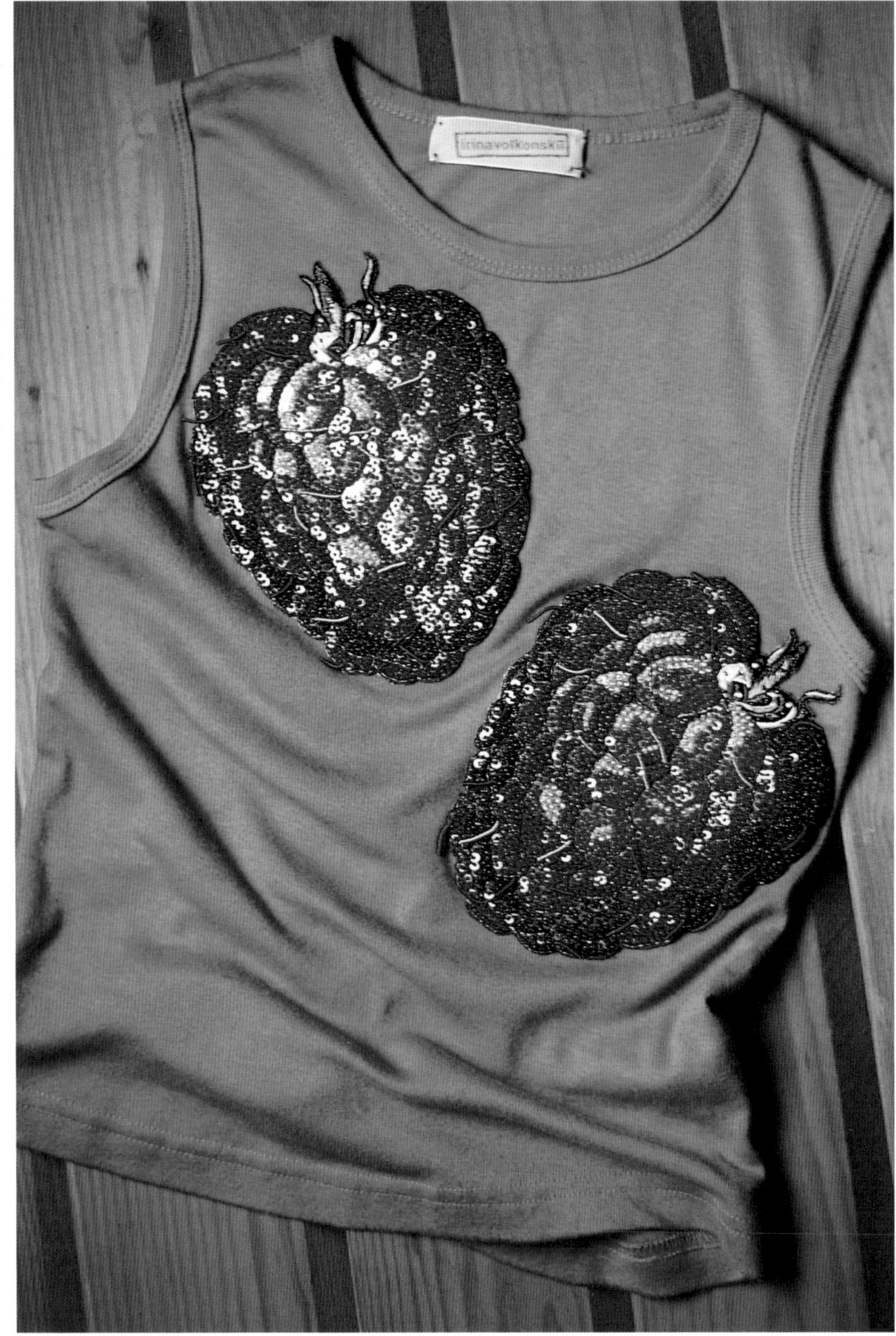

CHAPTER 4

Underwear comes out on top

Emancipation of the T-shirt

After the war, the T-shirt became emblematic of a victorious America. This intimate fabric of heroes, which so faithfully served the national cause, clearly earned its status as something above and beyond a mere undergarment. In the puritanical and conformist America of the 1950s, showing your T-shirt outside the privacy of your own home, or anywhere other than in stadiums, was still considered bad taste. Together with blue jeans, this item of underwear was for a long time the uniform of the working-classes. If worn for physical labor, or beneath a checked Chambray shirt, it absorbed the worker's noble sweat as it had the sailor's in earlier times. In order to become the mythical piece of clothing that we know so well, it needed soul and style. And this is what the "rebellious" young, in search of an identity to call their own, would bring to the T-shirt. They made up that new social class which would become more and more important over the years. The T-shirt, now inseparable from blue jeans and leather or denim jackets, foreshadowed the anti-fashion trends of the 1960s. Hollywood's rising stars would swiftly promote it to the rank of icon. In those Cold War years, Europe's eyes were riveted on the United States, fascinated as everyone was by that new economic and cultural model. Young people on the other side of the Atlantic were quick to appropriate those new images being shown at the movies. Be it torn open

Elvis Presley, wearing the U.S. Army uniform in 1958 during his military service, is hounded by the press. GI Presley rolled up the sleeves of his T-shirt, thus turning this standard-issue garment into a rebel icon.

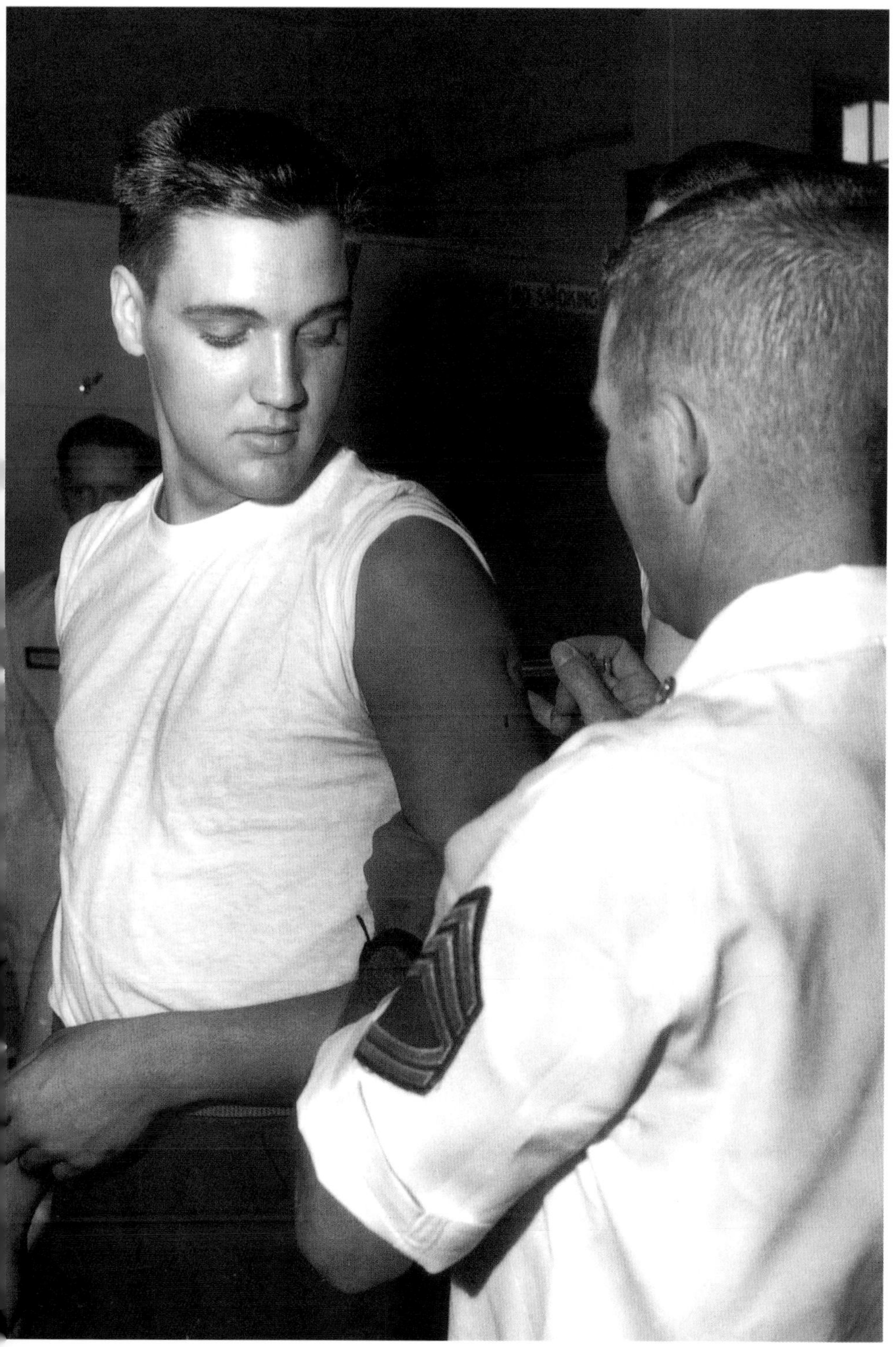

That mythical baseball team, the New York Giants, during a match against the Brooklyn Dodgers in the 1950s. Sports teams were the first to print the player's number, and sometimes his name, on their T-shirts.

on Marlon Brando's torso in Elia Kazan's *A Streetcar Named Desire*, or peeping out, dazzlingly white, from under James Dean's red jacket in *Rebel Without a Cause*, the T-shirt flaunted its sexuality and emanated the sweet smell of revolt. It would be the banner of rebellion for a whole generation. The T-shirt had finally found its way into the history of fashion and was there to stay.

Birth of teenage style

Fifties' teenagers born during the postwar baby boom (between 1946 and 1957, there were almost 35-million births in the United States), accounted for a large part of the U.S. population. Their parents had been marked by their war experiences and had flung themselves headlong into the new prosperity that was dazzling Europe and Japan, both in ruins. Many women who had tasted the responsibilities of work outside the home during the war years, had returned to their homes which were being transformed by the progress fairy into household cocoons with all the mod cons: fridge, mixer, vacuum cleaner and television. The appearance of new synthetic fibers, the expansion of the clothing industry and the mushrooming of department stores, made the lifestyle of the privileged

In the 1950s, American universities started to create their own T-shirts. This item of clothing would replace the crests decorating students' blazers in Old England.

few accessible to many, signaling the arrival of the new middle class. The consumer society had been born, and newness now dictated its tyrannical pace. As model wives, women followed the rules of "good taste" to the letter, as dictated by women's magazines which had become so plentiful. She matched her clothes to each different moment of the day; she became infatuated with the New Look launched in France by Christian Dior, who once again fettered the body in the famous "hourglass" line. In *Wife Dressing*, the American fashion designer Anne Fogary extolled the virtues of refinement, banning the wearing of jeans, even for housework. The cult of elegance and consumerism created a deep chasm between generations—that famous gap.

At the same time, the concept of adolescence was changing. The adolescent who up until the 1950s had just blended into the microcosm of the family, and whose rite of passage into the adult world was usually marked by his/her first paying job, was to find a new identity and attain a new freedom. United by a craving for the novel and untried, teenagers began to have a shared culture beyond social boundaries. They soon became the advertising agencies' target of choice. With the appearance of 45-rpm records, music became much more accessible, and in 1954 record sales were four times higher

The writer Truman Capote, at age 23, photographed by Henri Cartier-Bresson in New Orleans.

than in the prewar years. Rock 'n' roll would become the rallying cry of a whole new generation. Bill Haley and the Comets' *Rock Around the Clock*, with sales of more than 16 million disks worldwide, served as a revolutionary chant. And "Elvis the Pelvis," whose gyrating hips were considered incredibly lewd at the time, brought the new sound, appropriated from the forceful and insistent rhythm of black American blues, into the homes of white America, where, to the consternation of many a parent, it became the bomb for mostly white teenagers. The "angry young man" look was born. The T-shirt had its ticket to fame. The rest is history.

Rebel triple-bill: T-shirt, jeans, leather jacket

Challenging and protesting against the old order was what bound together the generation that rejected "the vision of a whole nation that had espoused a standardized haircut, a little house furnished with standardized appliances and standardized cars, kids and even dogs" (Mick Farren, *The Black Leather Jacket*). Clothing style thus became an identifying sign. It was the beginning of teenage gangs, young people banding together in a shared malaise with a thirst for

John F. Kennedy and a friend photographed in casual clothes in Charleston, South Carolina. In that same year (December 1941), the future president would enlist in the U.S. Navy.

freedom. They rejected outright the new, permanent-press suit that confined grown-ups within their conventional cut. English Teddy boys had a preference for Edwardian elegance in their long jackets, drainpipe trousers and bow ties. Conversely, American teenagers opted for the blue-collar casualness of T-shirts and jeans. In the United States, where teenage style came into being, the school system, more flexible than in Britain, rarely demanded that pupils wear uniforms, and this left them fairly free to express themselves through their dress. In the late 1940s, it was still bodacious to show glimpses of a white T-shirt under your checked shirt, and the jean "look" didn't exactly go unnoticed either. These clothes were usually relegated to leisure activities—drinking a Coke with friends at the snack bar, going to the movies or dancing to rock 'n' roll at one of the "in" spots. It wasn't until the mid-1950s that the T-shirt became a fashion phenomenon. Teenagers uniformly adopted this article of clothing which from then on was no longer considered underwear. This was when the white T-shirt became the personal billboard of choice to advertise one's membership and support of this or that group: high schools and colleges proudly displayed their teams' insignias and colors on T-shirts. "Once the T-shirt became acceptable

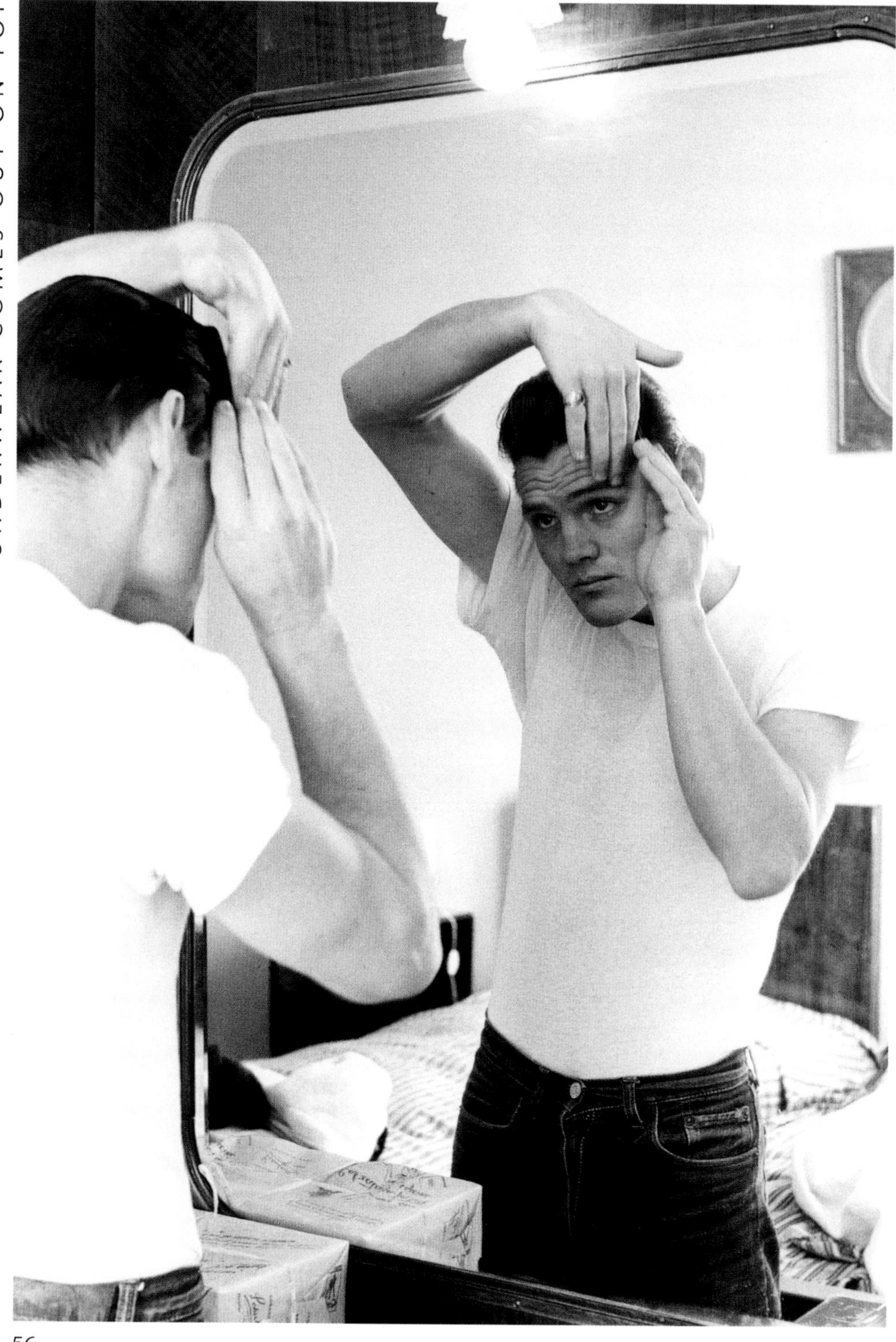

Above: In 1954, Marlon Brando brought animal magnetism to his portrayal of Johnny, in *The Wild Ones*. Wearing his biker's jacket, jeans and white T, he terrified and fascinated a still conventional American society. The T-shirt as icon was born.

Opposite: Jazz trumpeter Chet Baker. In 1961, the white T-shirt and jeans look came in as the uniform of mutinous youth. It is now a classic style.

outerwear, its size, shape, cut and decoration became a reliable badge of the wearer's identity. The greasers were the first to adopt the tight white T-shirt as a uniform, usually with a pack of filterless smokes rolled up in one sleeve. The tight white T-shirt has been a macho symbol..." explains American fashion designer Tommy Hilfiger in his book *All Americans: A Style Book by Tommy Hilfiger*. The T-shirt, jeans and leather jacket became synonymous with social protest and were very threatening to a society in the thick of the McCarthy witch-hunting years, when every effort was being made to stifle the class struggle which McCarthyites linked to the dreaded Communism. In the late 1950s, schools launched a campaign ordering "bad boys" to wear appropriate clothing. "I couldn't wear a T-shirt to school. I remember in 1969 I wore a dyed-purple Wallace Beery Henley, one of those old-fashioned undershirts, to school once. They took one look at me and said: "You've got an undershirt on. Go home," recalls Tommy Hilfiger. It was not until the 1970s that the T-shirt was finally allowed in schools and was worn by teenagers from middle-class families and poor families alike. By now it was confusing the issue and escaping from its ignominy to invent a whole new language: the lingo of equality. Be it as gang uniform or badge of consensus, it helped people express their individuality.

The Actors Studio and Hollywood

The Hollywood machine was already a master at mythmaking. Now it put its weight behind the youth phenomenon. In no time at all, the major studios would provide tormented young people with their first idols.

The T-shirt, jeans and leather jacket triple bill took over from the suit-and-tie uniform worn by prewar stars like Cary Grant and Humphrey Bogart. "You've gotta live fast, die young and make a beautiful corpse," this retort from *Rebel Without a Cause* served as a manifesto for a whole generation. James Dean, star of Nicholas Ray's movie, immortalized his generation better than anyone else by involving his very own destiny in the equation—in October 1955, four days before the film was released, he died at age 24 behind the wheel of his sports car. A teenage icon had been born; he would be the first of many. American and European adolescents alike were quick to identify with Dean, and changed their way of dressing as a result. Red or leather jacket, bright white T-shirt, Levis and biker boots—this now famous style had become synonymous with the actor. Photos taken back then capture him beside his racing car, sporting a V-necked or striped T-shirt. Like the good student of the Actors Studio he was, the actor merged with the characters he played. James Dean said: "I went and hung out with teenage kids in Los Angeles before making the movie...they wear leather jackets and go driving about looking for somebody to beat up" (*James Dean, In*

His Own Words, Crescent Books, 1991). Marlon Brando occasionally criticized Dean for mimicking the jeans and T-shirt slob look which Brando had immortalized in the cult movie *The Wild Ones* (1953). In that film he played Johnny the biker, who, with his gang, terrorizes a small town. Black biker jacket with gleaming zippers and studs, army hat, white T-shirt with black-trimmed collar, short sleeves with a tight hold on the tough-guy biceps, blue jeans and biker boots, all represented the virile attributes of this wonderful, charismatic hoodlum who ended up, year after year, pinned up on the wall in the bedrooms of young fans. For ten years the film was banned in Great Britain—the censors citing its violence. But it had a profound effect on its day and age, and influenced the way those who considered themselves non-conformists dressed. Many of those dropout bikers, blasting their way across the wide open spaces of California astride their Harley Davidsons and their Triumphs were former soldiers. Back home from the war, they were confronted with a postwar consumer society that was meaningless to them, and they had trouble fitting in. That "deranged youth turned primitive" would find its counterpart in France. In the late 1950s, the "blousons noirs" borrowed the gear worn by their American counterparts and mentors, the Hell's Angels. By this time the T-shirt, brought over to Europe by GIs during the war, had spawned a few imitators and was starting to be manufactured in France. In the suburbs, some 50,000 teenagers openly displayed their anger and their boredom; gangs readily wrecked Johnny Halliday and Bill Haley concerts. In 1960, some 30,000 acts of juvenile delinquency were committed in France.

But the T-shirt's real hour of glory came in *A Streetcar Named Desire* (1950). This Tennessee Williams play, later adapted to the screen by Elia Kazan, brought the house down on Broadway night after night. Through the character of Stanley Kowalski, played by Marlon Brando, the T-shirt finally revealed its full sexual potency. "Brando's got brashness, cruelty and sadism, and at the same time there's something incredibly attractive about him. Blanche Dubois—his half-crazy sister-in-law—plays affectionately with an animal who's going to kill her. She rebukes him for being brash and depraved, but at the same time she's seduced by that same brashness and depravity," explained Kazan. The T-shirt managed to get this ambiguity across more effectively than flesh. Stanley was from working-class roots

Previous pages: James Dean in *Rebel Without a Cause* embodies the American youth of the 1950s.

Opposite: In 1950, Marlon Brando played Stanley Kowalski, a brutal, sensual working man in *A Streetcar Named Desire*. The sexual power of his character was transmitted via his sweat-soaked T-shirt.

and at home he wore his T-shirt alone, both for comfort and coolness in New Orleans' notoriously sultry weather. Men digging trenches in a Manhattan street inspired the costume designer Lucinda Ballard to come up with this henceforth mythical garment. "Their clothes were so filthy that they clung to their bodies. It was the sweat that did it, of course, but they looked like statues. I said to myself: 'that's what I want... that animal quality'", she recalls. The T-shirt of the day was quite full with elbow-length sleeves, but on Brando's torso it would become skintight. The costume designer went to work putting her own touches to half a dozen athletic shirts, giving them a faded red color, and then ripping them over the left shoulder to suggest scratches from Stanley's wife, Stella. In the same creative spirit, she came up with the first pair of jeans specially fitted to the body by a tailor. To make it completely anatomical, Brando insisted that the fitting should be done without any underclothes. Like a second skin, the T-shirt clung perfectly to the musculature the actor had developed for the part. It also conveyed the violence of the play's relationships: ripped and torn by Stella's desire for Stanley, drenched by Stanley's inner ferment, object of both fascination and repulsion for Blanche. The expressive, erotic power of Brando's T-shirt fired the imagination of all America and earned it a secure place in the pantheon of legendary clothes. In 1966, Marlon Brando commented, with a touch of cynicism: "I could have sold torn T-shirts with my name on them... they would have sold a million."

Yet there was nothing coincidental about the fact that Brando and Dean turned the T-shirt into an icon of rebellion. Both actors were products of the Actors Studio, the acting school-cum-theater workshop founded in 1947 by Elia Kazan, Cheryl Crawford and Robert Lewis, and subsequently run by Lee Strasberg. That revolutionary acting style, which in due course became a real tradition in the United States, was inspired by the Stanislavsky method, and encouraged the development of the actors' hidden sensitivity, imagination, spontaneity and power. Movements were more natural, and, once freed up, the body became the mirror of emotions wrenched from the subconscious. The T-shirt was the ideal piece of clothing for this kind of work. In photos from that time, you can see Elia Kazan sporting one among his students. Marlon Brando, Paul Newman, Montgomery Clift, Faye Dunaway...the list of actors who wore

Previous pages: Rebellious teenage gangs were brought to the big screen in 1957, via the mighty Hollywood machine, in the mythical film *West Side Story*. The sexy, virile white T-shirt was perfectly suited to its rumble dances.

Opposite: In his white T-shirt, jeans, biker jacket and boots, the Fonz, a loveable rocker, embodied the toned-down version of the 1950s biker in the cult series *Happy Days*. By the mid-1970s, the rebel's gear was nothing if not hackneyed.

9625N8
DRIVE SAFELY

T-shirts for their rehearsals is a lengthy one. And the list of those who wore T-shirts on screen to play the role of the outsider or the dropout is every bit as long.

T-shirts for movie's misfits

Opposite: In 1967, Warner Bros. came up with their glamorous version of the rebel in Arthur Penn's film *Bonnie & Clyde*. Warren Beatty and Faye Dunaway played a pair of young criminals on the run. The athletic shirt stretched tight over Beatty's powerful musculature suggests the subversive force of a character who is defiantly breaking away from accepted codes of conduct.

Next pages: Matt Dillon in Francis Ford Coppola's movie *Rumble Fish*. The actor plays an alienated teenage hoodlum who lives in the shadow of his older brother.

As far back as the movie *Modern Times* (1936), Charlie Chaplin embodied a worker who was incapable of complying with assembly-line work. Surrounded by conveyor-belts and machinery with outsize cogs, Charlie has to keep up—even during his lunch break—with their breakneck pace, which finally ends up unhinging him. In this film, the white T-shirt-striped dungaree combination—which would later be adopted by the French comic, Coluche, with a yellow T-shirt—depicts the worker's standardized uniform. In the south of France, in 1938, Raimu, in his singlet and denim trousers, wove a metaphor between love of food and love in *The Baker's Wife*, a picturesque film directed by Marcel Pagnol. For *The Wages of Fear* (Henri-George Clouzot), four adventurers—including Yves Montand and Charles Vanel—are singed by the Central American sun as they carefully transport a cargo of nitroglycerin for 300 miles, their undershirts dripping with sweat. In the 1950s Broadway musical turned film, *West Side Story*, it was the Puerto Rican gang the Sharks that became the new role model for yet another generation of teens. In the film version, George Chakiris, leader of the Sharks, does a pre-rumble dance to Leonard Bernstein's electrifying score, sporting the essential symbol of the "Tuff guys"—the white T-shirt. The 1950s would make another nostalgic appearance later on with George Lucas's cult film, *American Graffiti* (1973), a comedy about youngsters coming of age after high school. Wearing leather jackets and T-shirts was part of the rite of passage, as was hanging out in snack bars and drive-ins, doing the twist and playing rock 'n' roll; a light-hearted, carefree atmosphere reminiscent of the TV series *Happy Days*, where the Fonz, a friendly rocker ever ready to pull out his comb, mesmerized the girls with his leather jacket and dazzling T-shirt.

Peter Fonda, another rebel, sported the more up-to-date form of the T-shirt, worn by his father, Henry, in John Huston's film *The Grapes of Wrath*. In *The Wild Angels*, Peter plays the part of a biker clad in a black leather jacket and black T-shirt. This character foreshadowed

the powerful cult figure he played in *Easy Rider*. This film, made in 1969 by Dennis Hopper and situated somewhere between the road movie and the psychedelic trip, depicts two long-haired California hippies who, as they cross the country on motorcycles in search of the "real America," come up against the hostility of redneck countryfolk. "An ironical, bitter lampoon against the prejudice, stupidity and violence of small-town America" (*Cinema Characters*), in which Jack Nicholson, playing an alcoholic lawyer just released from jail, dressed in his varsity jacket and black T-shirt, acts as a foil to the hippies' Indian shirts and Stetsons.

Whether white or khaki, this film costume would crop up time and again in war movies as a stand-in for a uniform. In the 1980s, several American filmmakers took a close look at the Vietnam war, and, in so doing violated the myth of the soldier-hero. Films from that decade were soul-searching treatises on an unjust war, complete with guilty consciences and disillusionment. In *Full Metal Jacket*, directed by Stanley Kubrick, young recruits standing to attention in their underpants and white T-shirts are inspected by a sadistic sergeant. Before long, in the heat and panic of battle, these undergarments lose their virginal whiteness and become stained with the colors of war—mud-brown and blood-red. In *Apocalypse Now*, Martin Sheen wears a khaki-colored variant, which seems to blend into the verdant green hell of the

Olivia Newton John and John Travolta in *Grease*, 1978.

STARFIX

-Pierre Jeunet
conte
buleux Destin
mélie Poulain

uiem
a Dream

orciste
ctor's cut

ilogie

aventurière
vient
formes !

• MARS/AVRIL 2001 • 29,00 FRANCS

Previous pages, left: Sylvester Stallone in 1985 in *Rambo II*. Previous pages, right: Lara Croft, her virtual female clone, with measurements to die for, in *Tomb Raider* with Angelina Jolie.

Right: Marilyn Monroe.

Opposite: The image of Jean Seberg making her way down the Champs-Elysées, wearing a T-shirt advertising the *New York Herald Tribune*, influenced a whole generation. In Jean-Luc Godard's film *Breathless* the T-shirt finally hit the screen in a feminized version.

Vietnamese jungle, which has already driven Colonel Kurtz mad. And then there is Rambo, far removed from matters of conscience. Instead, he has managed to spread the brutal image of the American hero to the world's four corners. This former GI, with his straightforward likes and dislikes, was one of the most notorious movie characters of the 1980s, even in China. Clad in a battle-torn black sleeveless T-shirt and red bandanna, he sports a modern guerrilla look.

The T-shirt, female version

Previously an exclusively male prop, the 1960s would see the T-shirt used to reveal the eroticism of a new generation of actresses. In the

The T-shirt, female version

early 1960s, Brigitte Bardot showed off her voluptuous curves in the French film *Babette Goes to War*. But it was Jean Seberg who would make film history in the pivotal French New Wave movie *Breathless* as Patricia, a young American selling the *Herald Tribune* on the Champs-Elysées. Roundly splashed across the front of her white T-shirt are the letters of her paper—an image that became hugely famous. As an embodiment of the new youth, embracing Lolita-like girls and androgynous seductresses, the T-shirt made its gradual contribution to "Girl Power" on view in moviehouses. Thelma and Louise turned it into the symbol of their fatal escapade to freedom, while Demi Moore used the T-shirt to display her perfectly muscled body, in *GI Jane*, as a statement of equality. With Lara Croft, the late 1990s ushered in the modern female warrior. Dressed in mini-shorts and black tank top, the heroine of Tomb Raider's videogame—played on the movie screen by Angelina Jolie—flaunted the ideal measurements of the contemporary pinup: 36-24-36.

Brigitte Bardot in 1958.

The Tank top

The athletic shirt, better known as the singlet in Britain and the tank top in the United States, was the virile clothing of amateur wrestlers; it was also essential classic vacationwear and, later on in tank top form, it became an identifying symbol for partying teenage girls. It has gradually shed its athletic and leisurewear image to become a fashion classic. This ancestor of the T-shirt, made its appearance among men's underwear items in the mid-19th century, then covered the torsos of lumberjacks and porters. In Hollywood, it clads the sexiest of torsos, from Paul Newman to Mickey Rourke, by way of the irresistible Clyde, played by the irresistible Warren Beatty. In the 1970s, women purloined this symbol of macho virility by wearing it in a variety of conspicuous ways. In the following decade, the athletic shirt became a clothing icon for gay men, who used it to show off their biceps. In 1992, the House of Chanel created quite a stir by introducing it into its fashion shows, bearing its signature double C on Naomi Campbell's voluptuous breasts. In a world filled with Parisian scamps and pretty Jean-Paul Gaultier kids, it has quite spontaneously found pride of place. In 1999, with the Nekt communications agency, it turned into nothing less than a stylistic exercise, entrusted to the imaginations of graphic artists (like Marc Atlan), fashion creators (Gilles Rosier, Pace...) and designers such as Ora-Ito, Jean-Marie Massaud, and Matali Crasset, the latter merely printing pouch-front briefs on it.

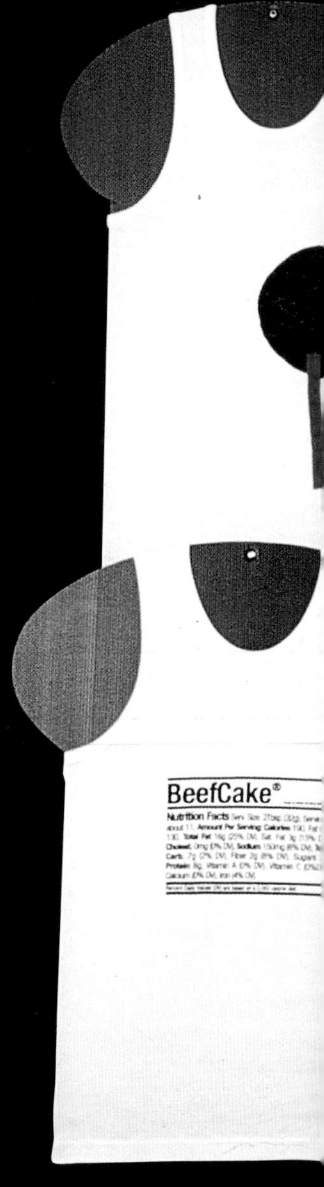

Creations by Marc Atlan, Matali Crasset, Norbert Fiddelers, Ora-Ito, Antonio Marras and Jean-Marie Massaud for Nekt, 1999.

marcel kangourou

MYTHOLOGY

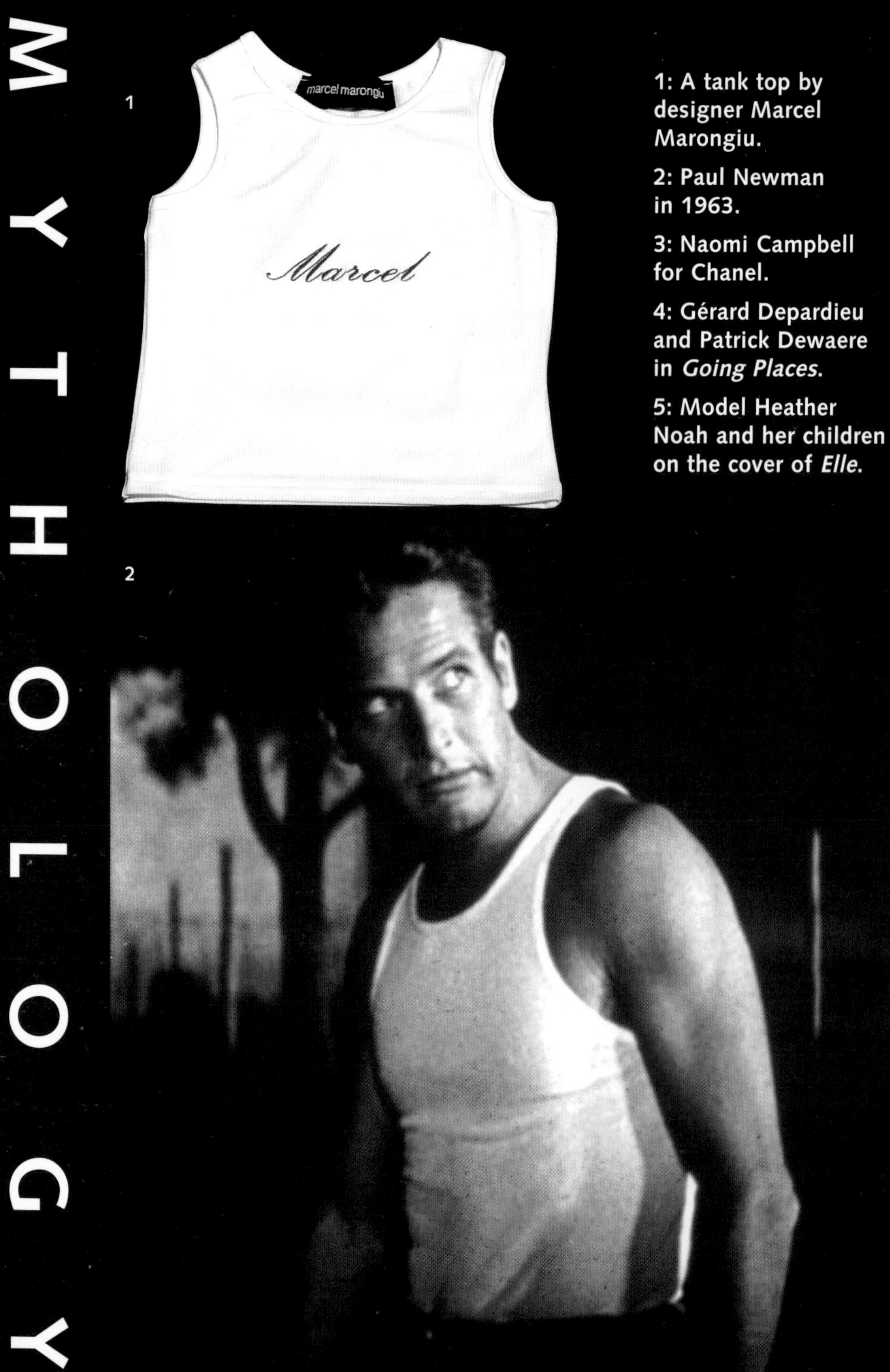

1: A tank top by designer Marcel Marongiu.

2: Paul Newman in 1963.

3: Naomi Campbell for Chanel.

4: Gérard Depardieu and Patrick Dewaere in *Going Places*.

5: Model Heather Noah and her children on the cover of *Elle*.

3

4

ELLE
LINGERIE
MODE
MAQUILLAGE
tout
est
rose !
XCLUSIF
près "Bridget
ones"
e nouveau
oman de
Helen Fielding
PSY
Commen
choisi
le bon
Heather
Noah
Secrets
de beauté
et recettes du
bonheur
HEBDOMADAIRE, 10 MAI 199
M 1648 - 2784 - 13,00 F

CHAPTER 5

The second skin

The T-shirt is the last layer of privacy, offering tantalizing glimpses of naked flesh, but it is also a kind of natural packaging. Cotton jersey is a thin and supple fabric that clings to the tiniest undulations of the body and leaves very little to the imagination, while still allowing for a decorum dictating that parts of the anatomy should be covered. Through a T-shirt, you can detect the line of a shoulder blade, the dip of "salt-cellars" in the collarbones, rippling abdominal muscles—and nipples. Not to mention those less appealing folds of flesh sported by the less body-conscious among us.

Opposite: The T-shirt enhances masculine eroticism. Photograph by Dale Durfee.

Next pages: Vitaminized T-shirts are overlaid like multi-colored *millefeuille* pastry on torsos that have spent a lot of time in bodybuilding gyms.
In 1986, the film *A Chorus Line* showed T-shirts paired with shiny leotards and pastel-colored leg warmers, all in a disco spirit.

Body liberation

The T-shirt revolutionized the concept of comfortable clothing. In the 1980s the heroes and heroines of the movies *Fame* and *Flashdance* leapt and bounded from studios to stages in T-shirts and leotards. Like a second skin, this elastic cotton hugs the body's form, no matter the shape or size, freely following every kind of movement, no matter how strenuous or extreme. It is also a highly absorbent material that can soak up the sweat produced by muscles taut from physical exertion, all the while letting the skin breathe. All it takes is a light breeze, and, in a matter of minutes, it is completely dry again. All these varied qualities established a place for the T-shirt and the athletic shirt in the realm of sport—so much so, in fact, that T-shirts and sport soon became inseparable. In the performance laboratory, they turned into the most

Above: Young dancers at the National Dance Institute in New York, 1998.

Opposite: As close as you can get to the body, the T-shirt becomes a second skin. Japanese fashion designer Issey Miyake invents a new clothing concept with the modifiable one-piece, christened A-POC—A Piece of Cloth.

state-of-the-art of high-tech mutants. In athletics, new fibers started to be used for athletic shirts, to gain a few precious hundredths of a second that would push a sprinter across the finishing line first. Thanks to Lycra, muscles came to be sheathed, and everything became streamlined. Coolmax developed the T-shirt's mechanical effectiveness by keeping it at a constant temperature. In sports, the T-shirt acted as a showcase for the machine-like body, goaded on by the cult of performance. Beyond that, it went on flaunting its fantastic power by inventing a language that was physical, erotic and sensual.

Erotic T-shirt

In the 1970s, the T-shirt took over from the shirt and the blouse and tied the knot with the human body. "Free Love," "Do your own thing" and "Let it all hang out" proclaimed the new sexual revolutionaries who, up until the advent of AIDS, would batter the conventions of propriety and decorum. Eager to be seen on equal terms, women appropriated the T-shirt—which had suddenly become very much the latest thing—and feminized this hitherto extremely virile item of clothing. Firm-breasted women took great delight in wearing T-shirts without bras. The 1970s pinup Farah Fawcett (one of the three original Charlie's

N
E
W
Y
O

Angels) was displayed, poster-like, on T-shirts, embodying the new feminine ideal. The T-shirt itself gave full rein to eroticism in its contours and its messages. One young woman boldly wore the key to her pleasure on her T-shirt: "Blow in my ear...and I'll follow you anywhere!" And in the time-honored tradition of self-promotion, another young woman emblazoned her T-shirt with the words "Squeeze in," written in letters that decreased in size between her breasts, giving the slogan a certain emphasis. Hugh Hefner, founding father of *Playboy*, had his famous cartoon Bunny depicted frolicking on T-shirts, and girls would add such come-hither plugs as: "Illinois Sex Instructor." Couples flaunted their lovemaking with such catchphrases as "Try it...you'll like it," on one partner's chest, while the other's torso replied "I tried it...and I like it." Risqué nudges and winks were couched in a bit of coy naiveté. One might see a T-shirt adorned with a bee and the words: "Be Healthy, Eat Your Honey," and another one stating: "Class of 69."

In due course, the punks discovered the mischevious provocativeness of the hippies before them, and spiced up their own erotic imagery with a zest for fetishism and pornography. Some of them ended up at Louise's, a lesbian club where the Kama sutra of kinky perversion was displayed loud and clear on the T-shirts worn by clubgoers. In the store called Sex, co-founded by Malcolm McLaren, there were vinyl T-shirts all ready, like so many breastplates, to cover chests and breasts with bits of mirror and wet effects. On one model, the McLaren-Vivienne Westwood partnership featured a somewhat

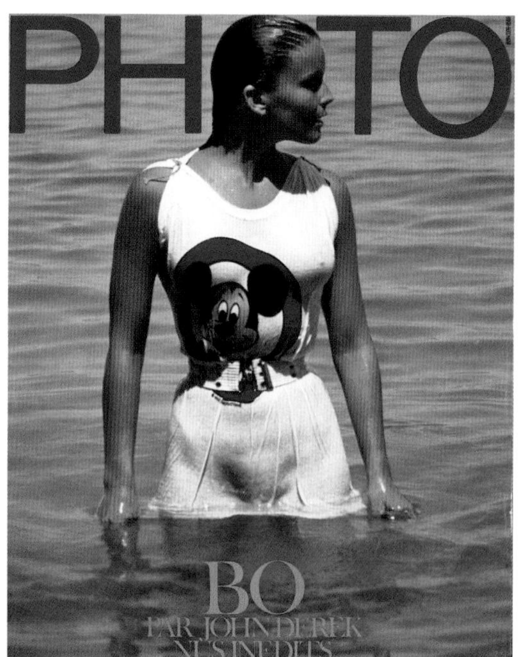

Above: Actress Bo Derek photographed by her husband John Derek.

Opposite: The wet-look T-shirt contest is all the rage among holiday-making starlets, poking fun at those overly academic official Miss-this and Miss-that beauty pageants.

X-rated parody of *Snow White and the Seven Dwarfs*. Their "Dance" T-shirt, depicting two bare-assed cowboys with their erect cocks almost clashing (a drawing signed by Tom of Finland, the Rubens of gay erotica), even stirred up a juicy scandal after a salesperson, one Alan Jones, was arrested by the police on a charge of offending public decency while wearing such a T-shirt. In court, the case put forth by the prosecution was based on the fact that the two penises were actually touching. But counsel for the defense proved them wrong with a ruler by measuring the gap between the two organs.

In the 1980s, the body became a cult object. It was sculpted like artwork in the rank sweatiness of gyms. As a key player in these narcissistic games, the T-shirt mopped up rivulets of perspiration and was an integral item from then on, growing larger and larger, until it reached the dimensions of a nightshirt. Needless to say, this bagginess only disguised the body's contours the better to make one wonder what was underneath. By the seaside, worn with a pair of swimming trunks to protect the upper body from the sun's fierce rays, the damp T-shirt stuck to various parts of the body, creating a sort of see-through effect which worked wonders for well-toned anatomies. In the United States, wet-look T-shirt competitions were held to elect Miss Beautiful Breasts, in a cheeky parody of those stiff and starchy official beauty contests. In the

Next pages: Be it on ordinary women or superstars (right, Pamela Anderson), T-shirts definitely invite reading. The message is made to fit chests and breasts and reflects a new kind of sexual freedom. Seduction strategies, be they for Girl Power or as sex objects, also come to us through T-shirts.

early 1990s, the nymphet T-shirt was photographed by Ellen von Unwerth, who captured the image of a famously sculpted Claudia Schiffer in her bath.

In the 1990s, the T-shirt's explicit eroticism took refuge in childishness. Forty-something women, benefiting from new skin-care products promising everlasting youth, rediscovered the innocence of their tender years by stealing their daughters' T-shirts. In a matter of just a few years, something like a gold rush occurred. The T-shirt was worn tight-fitting, body-hugging and very short, the better to show off a stomach now flattened by liposuction, rising up from low-waisted pants. Henceforth, the erotic zone was located just above the belt or waistband, at the level of the now pierced navel. The major brands couldn't possibly be outdone by such saucy—and profitable—upstarts thumbing their noses at fashion. Their very pride decreed otherwise. In the year 2000, Balmain plastered their T-shirt fronts with a very daring slogan for that period of zen-like passivity and inwardness: "J'aime les garçons"—I like boys. The following year, when French fashion was once again upstaging designers on the Italian peninsula, Dolce & Gabbana put the following inscription on a man's T-shirt: "Italians do it better." On her T-shirt, Madonna—true pro that she is—would then write the irreverent "Kiss My Ass," keen as ever to spice up her rockstar personae.

AMERICAN
GIRLS

A gay banner

Apart from those ancient times when pederasty was the order of the day, the male body has rarely been relegated to the status of sex object. When women were molding their figures with a whole raft of props and accessories—garter-belts, stockings, lace, embroidery, etc.—male underwear was confined to a functional role. Four centuries after the emblazoned codpieces of the Renaissance, men have nevertheless managed to chart new erotic terrain through the T-shirt. While Marlon Brando's T-shirt in *A Streetcar Named Desire* (based on the play by Tennessee Williams, a playwright from the South who never bothered to conceal his homosexuality) was throwing the fragile Blanche Dubois (played by Vivienne Leigh) into turmoil, James Dean's screen image was revealing a torso every bit as streamlined as the fast cars he loved so well. In an age of pinups, this was the logical culmination of a discreet trend towards fetishization introduced by "queers" and "fags"—as gay men were called—from the 1930s on.

It was from that period, explains Valerie Steele, that "the T-shirt [became] an important homosexual signifier [...], the fetish clothing of the gay imagination. It owes its virile dimension to the fact that it emphasizes the musculature and came into being among workers" (*Fashion and Eroticism*, 1985). It was in those same years that George Platt Lynes (1907-1955) photographed Carl Carlsen in an adjusted white T-shirt and jeans, with a chain round his neck, and a peaked cap on his head. Of all the gay fetishes photographed by Lynes, the T-shirt had pride of place. In *Identity: George Platt Lynes photographer of Carlsen*, an article published in 1955 in the magazine *Dress*, Richard Martin explains that "Carlsen's torso gains its impact from the fact that the many loose horizontal creases across the abdomen are surmounted right at the apex by the articulated forms of the pectoral, functioning almost as a kind of breastplate." Acting rather like sheaths, sleeves steered the eye toward flattering biceps. When striped like a sailor's shirt, the T-shirt would offer male desire other luxuriant shores. Jean Cocteau had checked all this out early on. So had Paul Cadmus in his drawings of cabin boys in deck pants and tight-fitting T-shirts, and, above all, Jean Genet's *Quarrel of Brest*, would firmly establish this fantasy. Rainer Fassbinder's film, *Querelle*, offered another gay icon in the form of Brad Davis wearing a sweat-soaked tank top clinging to his

Opposite: Sailor pants, ribbed T-shirt rolled up above the navel, scarf and boater... The banks of the river Marne, popular with working folk at play, were revisited at the famous Parisian cabaret The Lido in 1957, in a nothing if not ambiguous version that gave the artist Bruce Cartwright the limelight.

Next pages: Jean Genet's cult novel *The Quarrel of Brest* was adapted for the big screen by Rainer Fassbinder in 1982. The character of the sailor played by the American actor Brad Davis turned into an icon of the gay culture.

body, his crotch bulging in skintight trousers, his cap set at a jaunty angle, leaning against a streetlight in the pose of a permanent cruiser. Those gyrating sailors in song-and-dance numbers wear T-shirts with deep, plunging V-necks over the tightest of white trousers—a costume that focuses the attention on the mysteries of the navel, and offers glimpses of other steamy areas of promise—torsos and buttocks.

In men's fashion—where gay men represent the avant-garde of the clientele—the late Gianni Versace presented his young Adonises in striped T-shirts. Jean-Paul Gaultier—who was very involved in the coming-out phenomenon of the 1980s—turned this sailor's jersey into his personal emblem and presented it in many shapes and sizes which, as the years passed, became increasingly soft. His first perfume for men, a floral powdery Eastern scent created in 1995, was not content merely to be called "Le Mâle"; on top of that, Gaultier purloined Genêt's sailor as his icon. In the meantime, the pinup seaman (either smooth-jawed or sporting a moustache, depending on the fashion of the day), with his sundry charms considerably fleshed out by the artist Tom of Finland, had become the most irresistible of boy-traps, coming somewhere between GI Joe and Marilyn Monroe. In 1992, the same Tom—whose T-shirts had been all the rage for many years in backrooms—worked with Jean-Paul Gaultier for a collection called "Casanova in the Gym." As decoration, a jacket bore the drawing of an athletic shirt on suntanned skin, and a pair of minishorts from the pocket of which dangled an obscene bandanna (the color and position of the bandanna sent out signals proclaiming the wearer's degree of celibacy, his preferences, and so on). As the founding father of the new "male" eroticism, Tom of Finland was paid a major tribute by the American novelist Alan Hollinghurst, who has one of his characters dressed as follows: "...tonight, he was in a clean new denim and a Tom of Finland T-shirt; a bulging biker armlocked another across the shallow dip of his chest." For bikers—those outcasts whose virile poses invite every manner of

Opposite: ***Joli Voyou, José, 1996.*** **Since 1976, the camera of the art duo Pierre & Gilles has been snapping Parisian scamps, dishy hoodlums and various other pinup boys in a decidedly kitsch spirit.**

Below: A wide-mesh T-shirt reveals the torso.

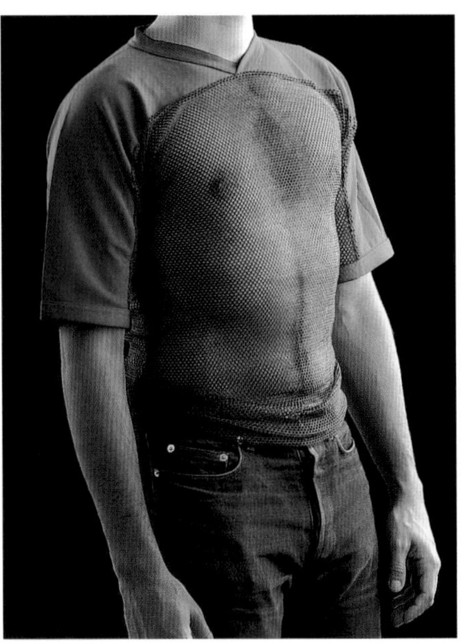

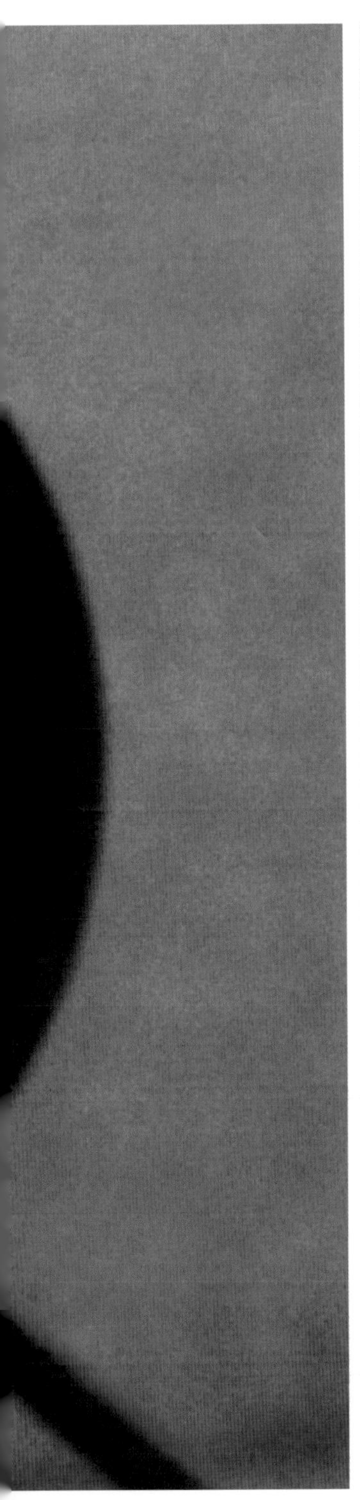

YAMAHA DX7

Previous pages and pages 104-105: In the early 1970s in San Francisco's Castro district, an image of male homosexuality in the days before HIV/AIDS.
Right, from top to bottom: Freddy Mercury of Queen, Marc Almond of Soft Cell and Jimmy Summerville of The Communards.

fantasy—have also become part of the gay iconography, which has become all the more strident and vociferous these days as the ever-present threat of AIDS also skulks and lurks within it. On the cover of their *Live And Sleazy* album, which was released in 1979, the Village People put a worker in jeans and white T-shirt alongside a biker sporting chains and a leather cap.

In this world of clones, French photographers Pierre and Gilles offered a French flavor by adding kitsch touches to their pretty hoodlums in tank tops, immortalized in front of a highly suggestive Eiffel Tower. By implicitly addressing its French customers—who signed the Civil Solidarity Pact [PACS], legalizing, among other things, homosexual relationships—by way of the gay magazine *Têtu* [literally: hard-headed], the Bouygues Telecom corporation would tread very carefully indeed to put across its new deal—two tank tops hanging out to dry on one and the same clothesline.

The gay community makes no bones about its codes, and, like other fashion-minded groups, has influenced the T-shirt with a wide range of perspectives. Homosexuals in the 1970s may have fantasized about scoop necks, but their kid brothers in the next decade would set their sights at physical perfection by making sure they had dream bodies,

Above, left: Be Gay, proclaims this T-shirt. From then on a political awareness had become included in the homosexual culture.
Above: T-shirts by the brand Kulte.

Page 106: Provocative T-shirt photographed by Allen Tannenbaum.
Page 107: In the 1960s, members of Lesbian awareness movements based their case on their differences. The tone was irreverant, and the messages unambiguous.

created in daily sweat sessions on body-building apparatus. In the 1980s, only really well-built guys and die-hard narcissists wore athletic shirts, while everybody else settled for less racy T-shirts, often worn three sizes too small, the better to hug the stomach muscles in what came to be called the "skinny" look. Between 1990 and 1995, mixtures of cotton and Lycra further highlighted the tight-fitting effect by adding accents of iridescent moiré patterns, creating the sexiest of designs. The mesh style also came into vogue in this period, but this style would only go with legendary torsos.

But in 1997, people started to become less and less prepared to suffer in order to be beautiful or handsome—exit sweaty Lycra, which, for years, had been turning dance-floors into Turkish baths. Now it was time for the comeback of 100% cotton. Having a little fun at the military's expense, T-shirts now either flaunted patriotic flags and eagles, or made playful allusions—one such being the Pink Panthera T-shirt by Dolce & Gabbana. A color, a fabric, a slogan, and it's all there, ready to get up people's noses as much as please them. The handsome guy in a tacky T-shirt will be the laughing stock of bikers and clones. Of the various T-shirts that are "to die for," purists single out the Mr. Clean model, and the sequined T-shirt, worn in places that don't measure up to it...

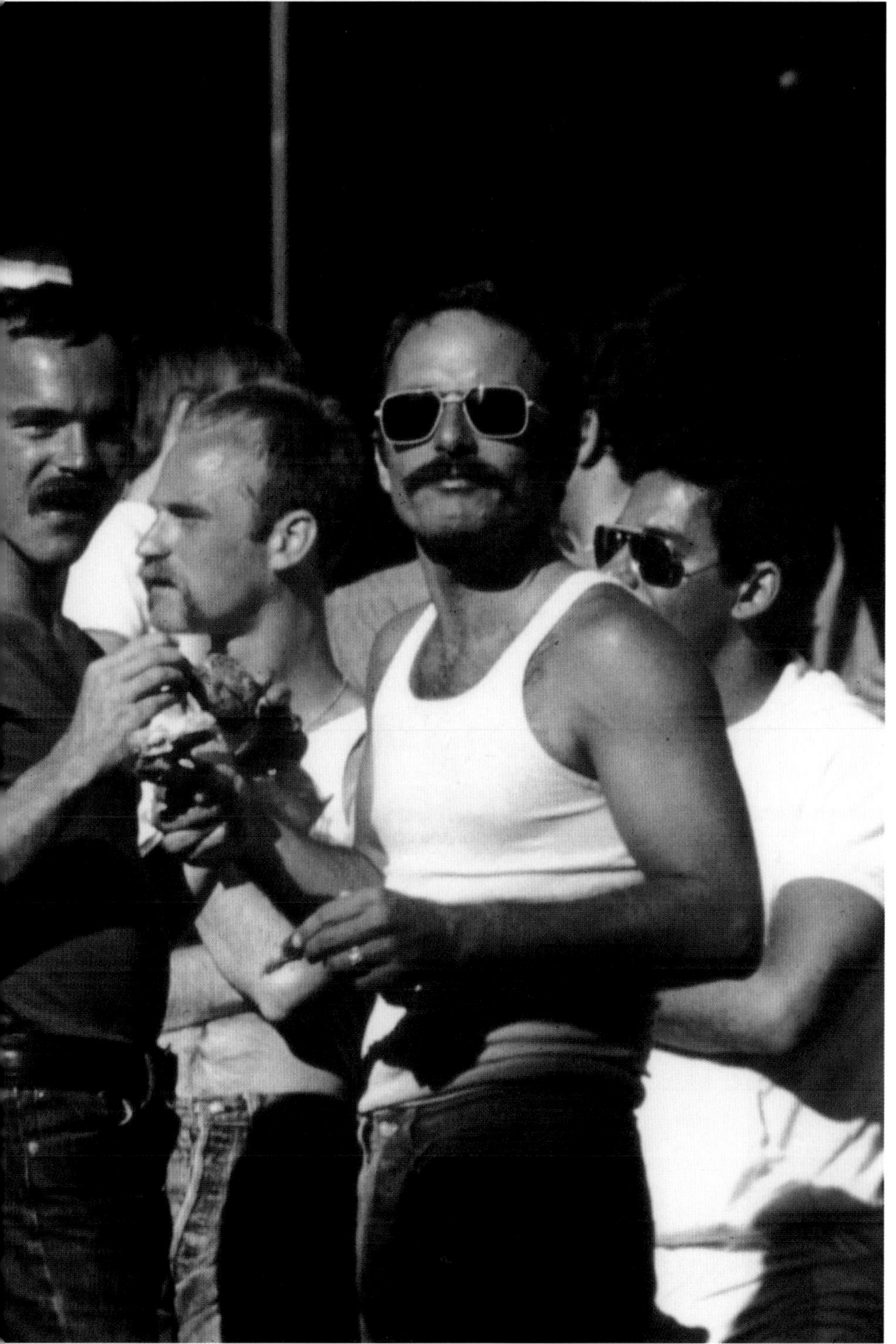

BEAT ME
BITE ME
WHIP ME
FUCK ME

MASTER
SLAVE

Che

Black beret sporting a star, black hair and black beard, handsome features set in defiance, eyes staring out at the faraway horizon...in March 1960 Alberto Korda's lens captured this classic portrait of Ernesto Guevara, better known as "El Che," and it has since seized the imagination of the world. His allure was such that it still crops up printed on millions of T-shirts, black on a Marxist red or guerrilla green background, underlined by the Cuban revolutionary's motto: "Hasta la Victoria siempre." Like holy shrouds, T-shirts have also immortalized Che's Christ-like corpse after he was killed by imperialist bullets in Bolivia. The man who Jean-Paul Sartre described as the most complete human being of his day has become in the collective mind the supreme icon of revolution, and his image has been worn as much by Marxist students as by Colombian guerrillas and anti-globalization demonstrators in Seattle and Genoa. The rock band Rage Against the Machine has even made Che its symbol, alongside T-shirts offering the recipe for making Molotov cocktails. Having become an icon, like Marilyn Monroe and Mao Ze-dong, the Cuban revolutionary has gradually shed his political dimension and turned into just one image among many of the international pop culture. A marketing tool, too. Printed on the labels of a fizzy drink, going by the name of "Revolution," bedecked with imitation jewelry on a glam rebel T-shirt, Che still has good box office draw.

Opposite: "Che Guevara" T-shirt featuring the famous photograph by Alberto Korda, one of the world's No 1 bestsellers...

100% COTON
PEIGNE
SIZE

MYTHOLOGY

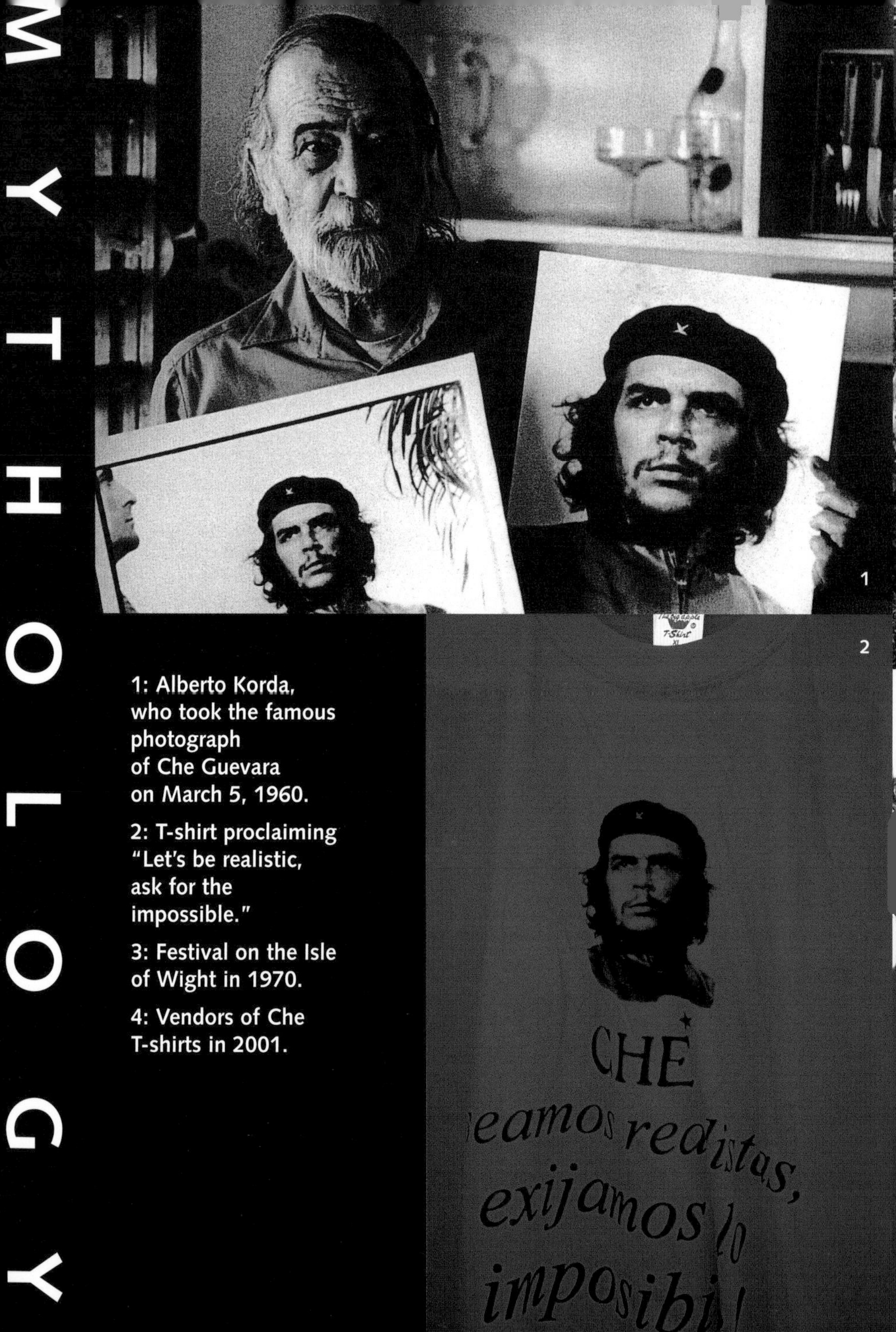

1: Alberto Korda, who took the famous photograph of Che Guevara on March 5, 1960.

2: T-shirt proclaiming "Let's be realistic, ask for the impossible."

3: Festival on the Isle of Wight in 1970.

4: Vendors of Che T-shirts in 2001.

3
CHE
4
E preciso
O ANALFABETO POLITICO

100%
Black Man
100%
ck Man

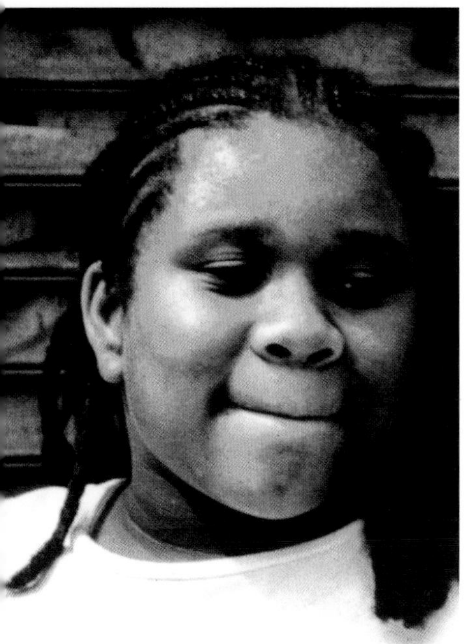

CHAPTER 6

Triumph of the slogan

A political banner

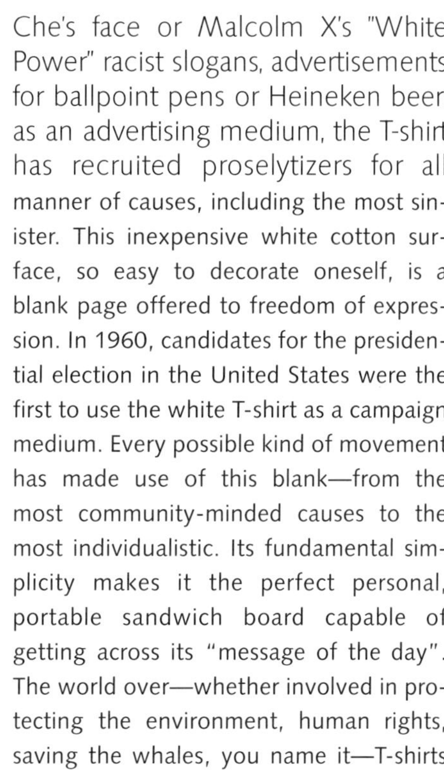

Che's face or Malcolm X's "White Power" racist slogans, advertisements for ballpoint pens or Heineken beer; as an advertising medium, the T-shirt has recruited proselytizers for all manner of causes, including the most sinister. This inexpensive white cotton surface, so easy to decorate oneself, is a blank page offered to freedom of expression. In 1960, candidates for the presidential election in the United States were the first to use the white T-shirt as a campaign medium. Every possible kind of movement has made use of this blank—from the most community-minded causes to the most individualistic. Its fundamental simplicity makes it the perfect personal, portable sandwich board capable of getting across its "message of the day". The world over—whether involved in protecting the environment, human rights, saving the whales, you name it—T-shirts

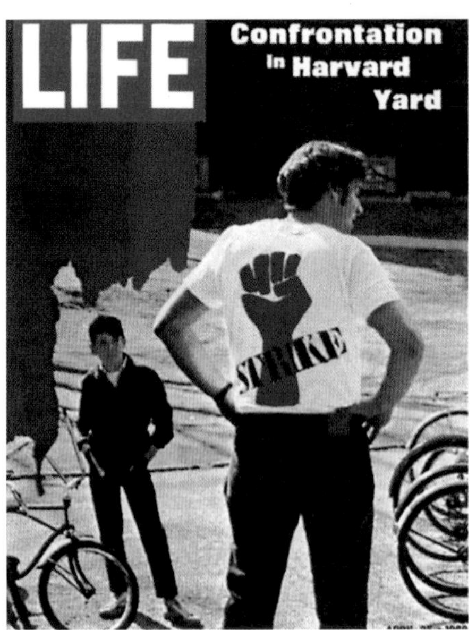

Previous pages: Million Man March, New York City, 1999.

Above: In the early 1960s, a British striker headlined his struggle on a T-shirt. Red fist clenched in a sign of anger, with the word "Strike" printed in black... This aesthetics calls to mind that of communist propaganda.

Opposite: American presidential candidates were the first to divert the T-shirt from its purely sartorial function and turn it into an electoral mouthpiece.

are an excellent means of identifying kindred spirits. And, in the universal language of imagery, it bypasses language barriers to identify political struggles and polarities, that nowadays so quickly become global.

The American "Wanted: bin Laden" T-shirt is instantly countered by the Afghan Taliban's T-shirt emblazoned with the face of Al Qaeda's leader, triggering a silent dialogue through the intermediary of television. The rise and rise of television has had the effect of a providential stepping stone for the protest T-shirt. The cause being championed doesn't have to pay the increasingly exorbitant sums of money that advertising space and radio or television spots cost. Thanks to the ingeniousness and/or boldness, not to say chutzpah of the person wearing it, the T-shirt weaves its way in front of camera lenses and delivers its message to millions of TV viewers without paying a cent. In a more marketing-oriented vein, T-shirts usually boost the reputation of major firms, who tattoo them with their advertisements, promulgating their corporate image absolutely free of charge. In bars and clubs, brands of Virginia tobacco cigarettes and alcoholic beverages—hamstrung by various laws governing their communications activities—have abandoned the famous publicity sunhat and cap in favor of the T-shirt. But this cheap and practical surface can also backfire on the advertiser distributing it. More so than ever since the September

Next pages, left: The T-shirt has embraced all manner of causes, from the loftiest to the most contemptible. On the left, a young skinhead uses this medium to trumpet his racist views. A neo-nazi at Rudolf Marsch in Roskilde Denmark, 1995. Next pages, right: In the streets of Harlem, a man offers an ironical list of the black community's history.

11th attacks in Manhattan and Washington, consumers have rekindled their role as citizens—and loving your country and your city comes down to the same thing as supporting the economy. So these new-style citizens are no longer just naïve and passive consumers. They may agree to act as a mobile surface advertising a particular brand, but they certainly don't shrink any longer from showing their acrimony, displeasure or political disapproval by twisting and distorting the slogans and logos of brands that have been using their personal belongings to squat in.

Every nuance of thought, every cause and brand name makes use of slogans in its attempt to hit the bull's-eye. But whatever the slogan's rhetorical impact may be, however original or thought-provoking or shocking by its very nature it reduces political ideas and projects to the visual equivalent of the sound bite. And it is one of the ironies of history that these slogans all become interchangeable—you can switch T-shirts as fast as you can turn your jacket inside out—or switch brands or political parties.

A political banner

AMNESTY
INTERNATIONAL

Amnesty International has been campaigning on behalf of basic human rights since 1961. The core of the movement's activities combines speaking out against violations of these rights, disseminating information, raising public awareness and getting the public to act. In this context, creating and producing products and backup materials, T-shirts, in particular, are a way of asserting a presence in everyday life. As a vehicle for imagery and a conveyor of the movement's concerns, the T-shirt, enables everyone to express their commitment to the values being championed by Amnesty International. At an individual level, the T-shirt has the effect of giving body and soul to a struggle aimed at creating a human community.

Pierre Huault

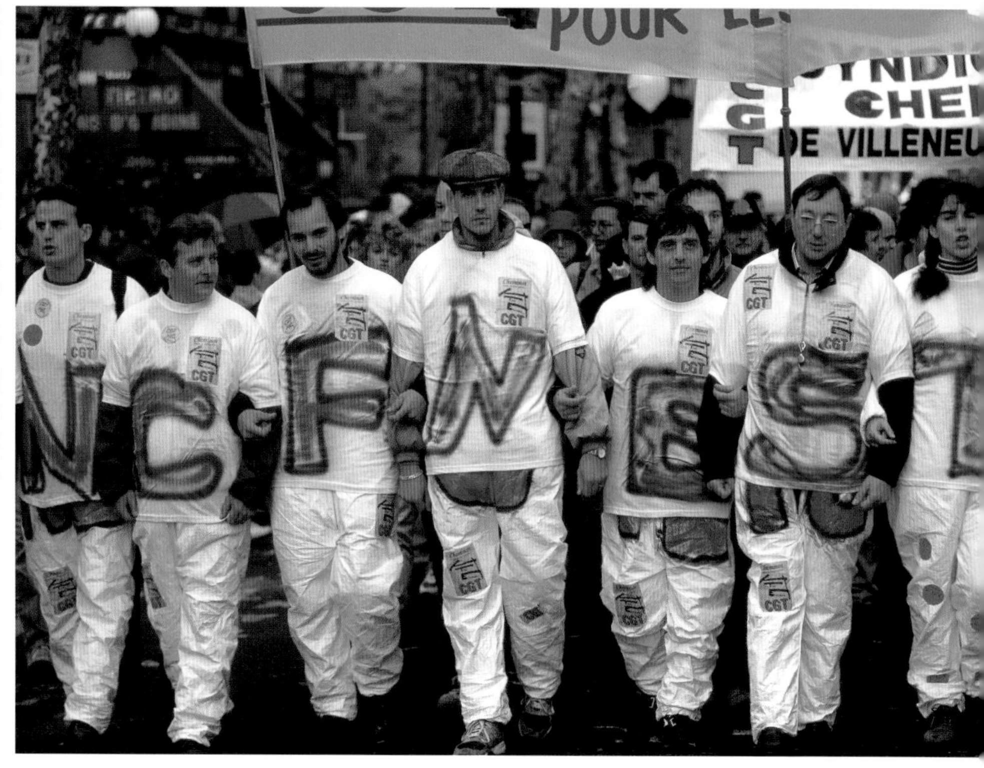

Above: T-shirts are also used to get messages across to the media. Here, on the front line, French railway workers have painted their movement's demands on white T-shirts.

Opposite: A Hong Kong demonstration celebrating the anniversary of the Tianenman Square student uprising in May 1989.

Battles and meetings

The T-shirt found its voice, so to speak, at a very early age. In the 1930s, jerseys and shirts worn by American sports teams had the number and name of the players stenciled on them. Taking things a step further, university teams added their crest. The T-shirt, thus decorated with graphic signs and numbers, was no longer just an item of clothing: the medium had become the message. The world of politics was quick to enlist the services of this inexpensive, easy-to-carry medium guaranteed to make an impact. During the party conventions—the grand finale of the American primaries—it is customary to use the T-shirt to display one's support for this or that candidate; it fits right in with the fanfare, the stars-and-stripes and the placards brandishing the candidate's face.

In 1948, Republican presidential candidate Thomas E. Dewey was the first to flaunt his slogan on a T-shirt: "Dew it with Dewey." The T-shirt may not have brought much luck to Thomas E. Dewey—he was beaten by Democrat Harry Truman—but his idea hit the bull's-eye and would be

反六四
“Fear is a habit.
I'm not afraid.”

FOR SILV
FUCK G8

adopted more or less systematically by all future presidential candidates. Along with the badge, the T-shirt has found its perch in the realm of political slogan-bearers. During the next presidential election, the Republican Dwight D. Eisenhower had has own picture printed on supporters' T-shirts, with the famous "I Like Ike" slogan. In 1960, against a backdrop of stars and stripes, candidate John F. Kennedy's campaign team printed a message that was as clear and direct as a right hook: "Kennedy for President." "The American T-shirt is a symbol of our egalitarian community; of our plain truthfulness; and even, in these instances, of our democratic responsibility," explained the curator of the "Vote" exhibition held in 1992 at the Fashion Institute of Technology in New York. The ballot may guarantee citizens their voting secrecy, but the T-shirt proclaims loud and clear the political views of its wearer. As such, in any forum or gathering, it prompts the discussion and debate that keep democracies alive.

Previous pages: Artist Gianni Motti's *Boomerang Girls* brings back to the collective memory bank the anti-globalization demonstrations in Genoa. As a political banner, the T-shirt fights injustice, campaigns for causes and brings people holding the same ideas together under the same flag.

Opposite: Mexico, 1994, members of the Party of Democratic Revolution [PRD] remember their hero Emiliano Zapata who brought victory to the revolutionary movement of peasants against large landowners.
This struggle pitting poor against rich is being carried on today in Chiapas, southern Mexico, under the leadership of Commandant Marcos.

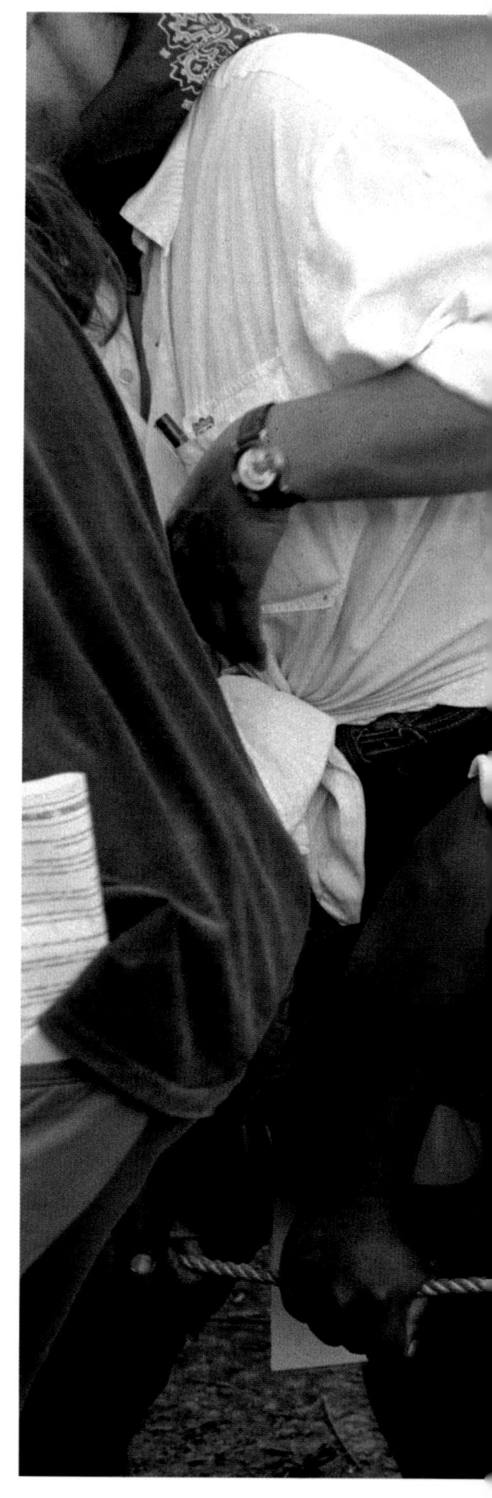

xcala
ZAPATA
VIVE
CND

I
LOVE
MY COUNTRY
I
HATE
APARTHEID

Previous pages, left: In front of the White House, a Muslim in an Ayatollah Khomeini T-shirt proclaims his support for Iranian protest movements against Saddam Hussein's government in Iraq.

Right: In 1990, a young South African celebrates Nelson Mandela's release from jail, wearing an anti-apartheid T-shirt.

Harbinger of a new world

In the 1960s, the Civil Rights Movement and the Vietnam War combined to make the American dream falter. The NAACP (National Association for the Advancement of Colored People) demonstrated, waving American flags and wearing T-shirts bearing the acronym of the organization set up to defend the civil rights of the African-American minority. In Washington, D.C., the reverend Martin Luther King Jr. delivered his famous "I Have a Dream" speech to a huge crowd that had flocked to the capital from all over the country to take part in the now historic March on Washington.

Whether proclaiming "Property of Utah Athletic Department" or "Harvard," the institutional T-shirts of colleges and universities were no longer fashionable or profitable. Students of the New Left, supporting progressive causes, preferred the seeming neutrality of plain T-shirts. Thus members of the Student Non-Violent Coordinating Committee or SNCC wore T-shirts with jeans as a sign of solidarity with the exploited working classes. The other great event of the 1960s—the Vietnam War—would add further rifts and divides to those brought to the fore by the Civil Rights Movement. The riposte of pacifist students to the

Above, left: Mao Ze-dong, "the Great Helmsman," has become a fashion icon. Above, right: The Soviet hammer and sickle as fun sticker.

patriotic slogan "My country, right or wrong" was "Make Love...Not War" and this phrase would be the cry of an entire generation. The young female student who was immortalized as she braved National Guard bayonets to slip a flower into a gun barrel recollects: "We were great, we knew how to rise up, we felt we were heroes. [...] We thought about what things happening meant, we thought about the whys and wherefores of life."

Peace march followed peace march, each successive demonstration looking more and more like a spectacular and provocative carnival. The "Peace and Love" symbols, which the hippies had borrowed from the anti-nuclear movement, was drawn on faces, jeans and T-shirts. And since it was in the realm of the counter-culture, everyone came up with their own personal touches. T-shirts were printed with homemade tie-dye patterns inspired by hallucinations glimpsed on LSD trips; that is when they weren't praising the beneficial effects of another popular drug—the cannabis leaf above the word "Enjoy," or even a reference to the varietal, "Smoke Colombian," for show-offs.

In this tidal wave of liberalism, it was not long before women started to make themselves heard. After Women's Lib, other feminist movements came along to demand equal rights for "the other half of humanity."

J'AIME TONTON
"J'aime tonton"
JAMES
TONTON
I Love tonton
J'aime tonton
TONTON tu t'entêtes et t'as RAISON!
MITTERAND
C'est ça ou rien
TonTon
Pour tout le monde!

With many women now financially independent (in 1968, 37% of American women were working) they had every intention of living free lives, in a climate of free love. Gone were the days of being tied down by marriage and, thanks in large part to the pill, of having unwanted babies. And while T-shirts and jeans were becoming the symbols of the new unisex phenomenon, feminist demonstrations were vying with one another to be the wittiest, most outrageous and provocative. During the 1968 Miss America Beauty Pageant in Atlantic City, some young women in the audience put a crown on a ewe and tossed their bras onto the "garbage can of freedom." Others wore the slogan "Feminist and Proud" on their T-shirts, and parodied military imagery by writing "U.S. Female" under the insignia of an eagle. The most brazen of all showed their disdain for the opposite sex by declaring on their chests: "A woman needs a man like a fish needs a bicycle."

Opposite: In 1981, François Mitterrand was elected President of the French Republic. In the Place de la Bastille his supporters recorded that historic moment for posterity.

Next pages, left: As media figures, stars have often used their image to support political struggles. The actress Susan Sarandon, with her husband Tim Robbins, holds a T-shirt printed with a slogan backing striking members of the actors' union.
Right: In 2000, actor Johnny Depp poses with a T-shirt from the Native Americans movement.

PROUD
UNION
ACTOR
ACTORS ON STRIKE
FOR A FAIR CONTRACT

AMERICAN INDIAN MOVEMENT
STILL
STRONG

Fight crime; buy a gun.
THIS IS A PUBLIC SERVICE ANNOUNCEMENT BROUGHT TO YOU BY fuct

Above: The brand Fuct uses the slogan of the defensors of the second Amendment.

Opposite: The Holy Face in an international version.

Next pages: While Americans reacted to 9/11 attacks by producing T-shirts like"Evil will be Punished," in a Bangkok mosque Thai Muslims wearing T-shirts with the image of Osama bin Laden showed their support for Afghanistan.

A worldwide medium

The 1970s witnessed the exponential rise of the power of the media. Carried away by the speed with which news was being generated, *Life* photographers and the first television news reporters were regaling the planet with live reports. A burning issue in one country soon became headline news in all the rest. Here, there and everywhere was a proliferation of human rights issues and great causes, all helping to galvanize "humanist" consciousness. In 1970, black militant Angela Davis was imprisoned in the United States during her campaign for African-American rights. In a flash, there were "Free Angela" T-shirts all over the world. Writ large, in every language under the sun, there were also T-shirts demanding "Free Nelson Mandela." Organizations like Amnesty International have called on the services of the T-shirt, too. Amnesty produces a special T-shirt for each of its campaigns (usually about eight a year), which contributes greatly to its running costs. Even in China, the T-shirt has gone to battle for "the people" or democracy, depending on what's in fashion. First, it displayed the sayings of Mao, as Great Helmsman; later, in the 1980s, the simple characters "min-zhu," meaning democracy, like so many cotton *dazibao* (those news sheets pasted on walls) sold under the counter.

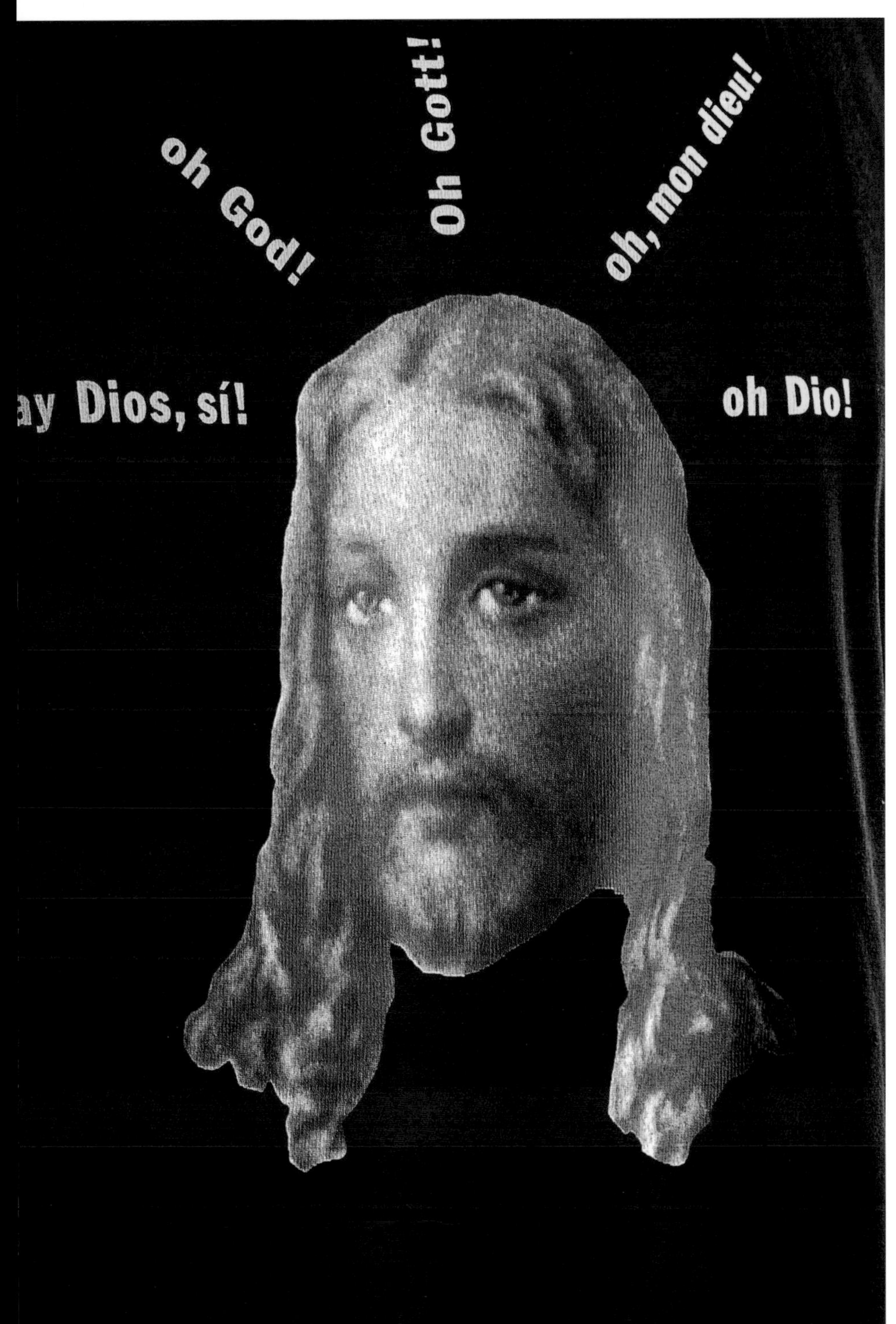
oh God!
Oh Gott!
oh, mon dieu!
ay Dios, sí!
oh Dio!

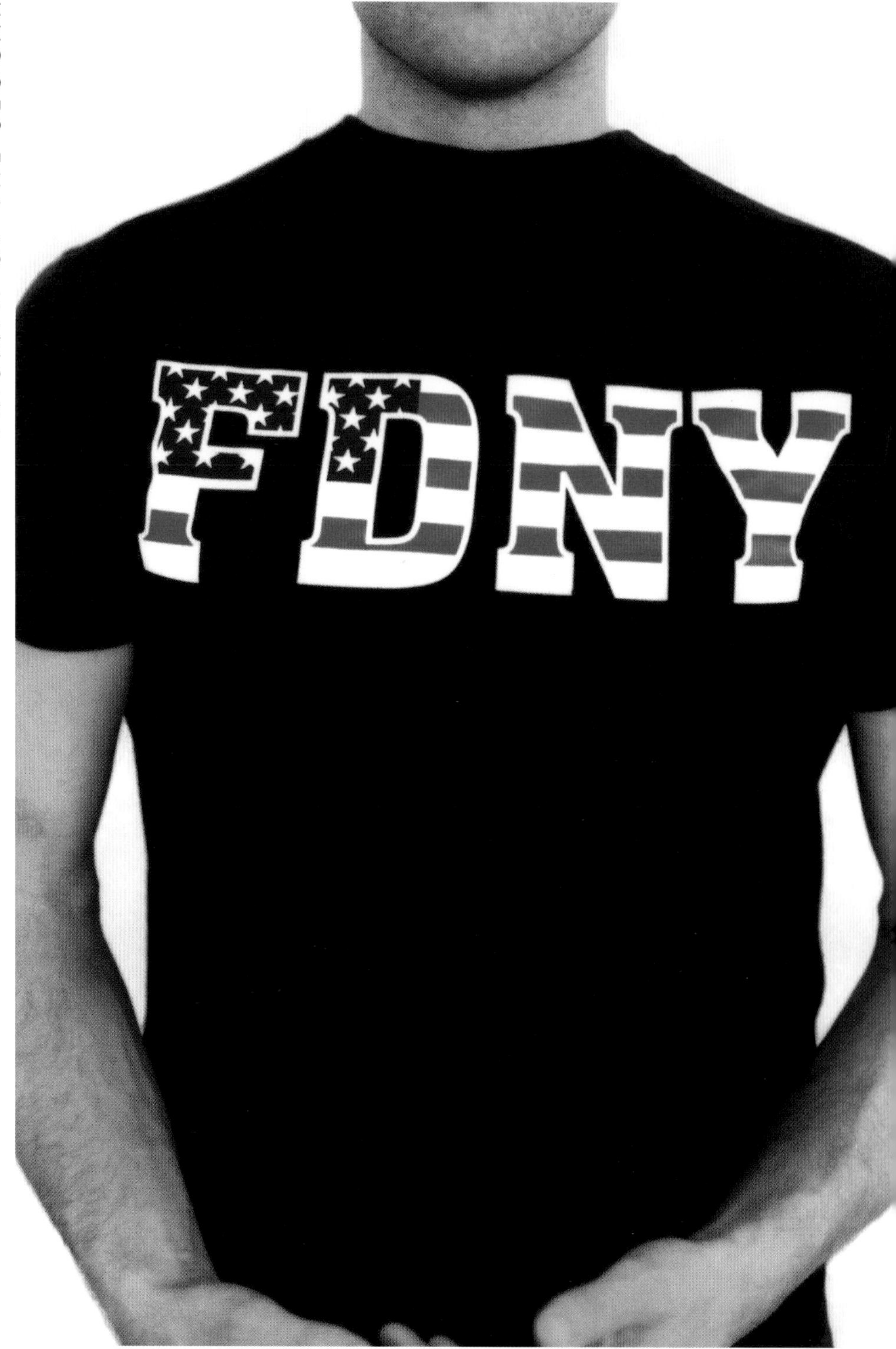
FDNY

Above: The T-shirt is consistent with the latest news, acting as a moving poster. After the attacks of September 11th, 2001, Osama bin Laden has been enemy number one of the United States and the world's most wanted man. Opposite: New York licks its wounds and pays tribute to its heroic firemen with T-shirts bearing the logo of the city's fire department.

Always keen to be at one with their public, stars would also sport "cause"-inspired T-shirts. During a 1971 demonstration against the detention without trial of certain IRA members, John Lennon did not shrink from wearing a T-shirt proclaiming: "Victory to the IRA against British imperialism." Some years later, Clash singer Joe Strummer would show his solidarity with the murderers of Aldo Moro by wearing a T-shirt glorifying the Red Brigades. The impact of the slogan-bearing T-shirt was that of an epidermic piece of clothing which, much like a tattoo, ended up being the ambassador for the whole body.

In the late 1980s, it showed up on the chests of Act Up activists. This organization, founded to protest for the rights of people with HIV and AIDS, opted for the path of civil disobedience and provocation. "We had learned how to get the AIDS message across as if it were show business," explains Didier Lestrade, one of the founders of Act Up France. In Paris the association saucily slipped a gigantic pink condom over the obelisk in Place de la Concorde. T-shirts printed with the upside-down pink triangle and the slogans "Silence = Death," "Action = Life," and "Knowledge is a Weapon" rang out like so many declarations of war. "They're crucial at public demonstrations held in a rush, because they instantly identify the Act Up struggle," the association explains. They are

SAY
NO
TO DRUGS

also a not insignificant means of collecting money for people suffering from AIDS.

In a most unusual, one-off initiative 59 top fashion designers came together—under one T-shirt, as it were—to lend their brand name to help a cause (or was it the other way round?). From Azzedine Alaïa to Yves Saint Laurent by way of Christian Lacroix and Claude Montana, all signed the "Everyone Against AIDS" T-shirt, the profits from which went to the Fondation de France. Less in-your-face, agnès b. urges prevention with her T-shirts that read "Let's Protect Ourselves...," and campaigns for a deprived continent with the extremely simple "Long Live Africa!" model, 6,000 of which have been sold worldwide.

Of all the various weapons employed in political struggles, the T-shirt has at least two huge advantages: a practical advantage in that it is definitely more comfortable to wear than a paper poster, and, once the battle has been won, it can return to its original function. Another advantage is that ultra-fast production techniques mean that the T-shirt can be ready for immediate action, to be deployed the moment there is cause for indignation or protest.

Opposite: The star-spangled banner used as a worldwide symbol of the anti-drug campaign.

Next pages, left: A T-shirt created by Philippe Starck. Health is a cause that is championed on T-shirts worldwide. A pregnant woman reminds us of the ravages of tobacco during pregnancy.
Next pages, right: Top model Christy Turlington invites us to combat smoking, wearing a sexy sequined T-shirt.

After the acquittal of the notorious L.A. cops accused of beating Rodney King, a young black man, nearly to death, it took just a few hours for a T-shirt reacting to that verdict to appear. On the front it bore Rodney King's face with the words "Victim King," and on the back a photo of the cops in the process of trying to beat him to death with the words: "What the fuck is going on?" Just four days after the September 11th attacks on the World Trade Center in New York, the street vendors' stalls in Chinatown were offering $5 T-shirts either preaching vengeance—"Evil Will Be Punished"—or commemorating the event—"Never Forget the WTC." A week later there were others printed with bin Laden's face proclaiming "Islam Is My Blood," that sold like hotcakes in Muslim Indonesia. As for Pakistan, in its tricky position—torn, as it is, between Islam's tight grip and modernity's loose promises—in T-shirt stalls in Lahore, "Pepsi, Pakistan new Generation" T-shirts have been upstaged by pro-bin Laden T-shirts, for the moment, at least.

As a pure product of globalization, the T-shirt has shared its glories as well as its tensions. It's worth remembering that in China T-shirts are manufactured for no more than 20 cents—a basic cost that accounts for just 0.5% of the final selling price, and even less when importers pass off these exotic T-shirts as products "Made in the U.S.A." In the sports

D.A.R.E.®
TO KEEP KIDS
OFF DRUGS

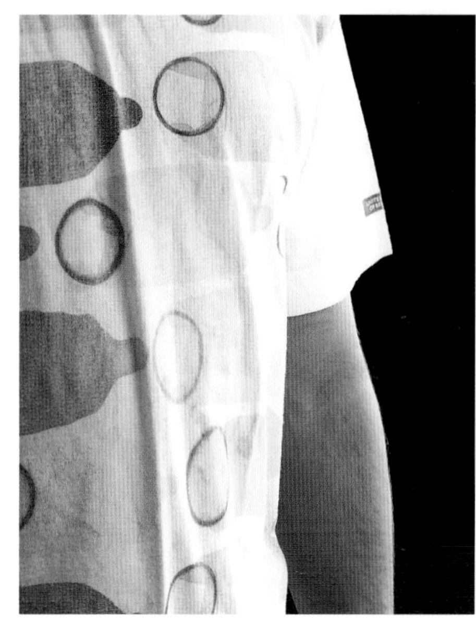

footwear sector, similar juggling operations have set up Nike—and its CEO Phil Knight—as militant students' favorite enemy, outraged as they are by the sweatshops they employ. Yet it is indeed on this global instrument that anti-globalization activists express their complaints. In Genoa, at the 2001 rallies against the G8, many of the 50,000 demonstrators and protesters displayed on their chests: "You G8, Us 600,000,000" and "The world isn't a commodity."

Above: At times, advertising and politics get their wires crossed. The Italian clothing brand, Benetton, is a master of high-impact, sensational messages, and adapts its posters, created by Olivier Toscani, to T-shirts. An AIDS prevention campaign features its united colors in the form of condoms printed on its T-shirts.

Opposite: A New York messenger turns into a standard-bearer for preventing drug use among the young.

Tie-dye

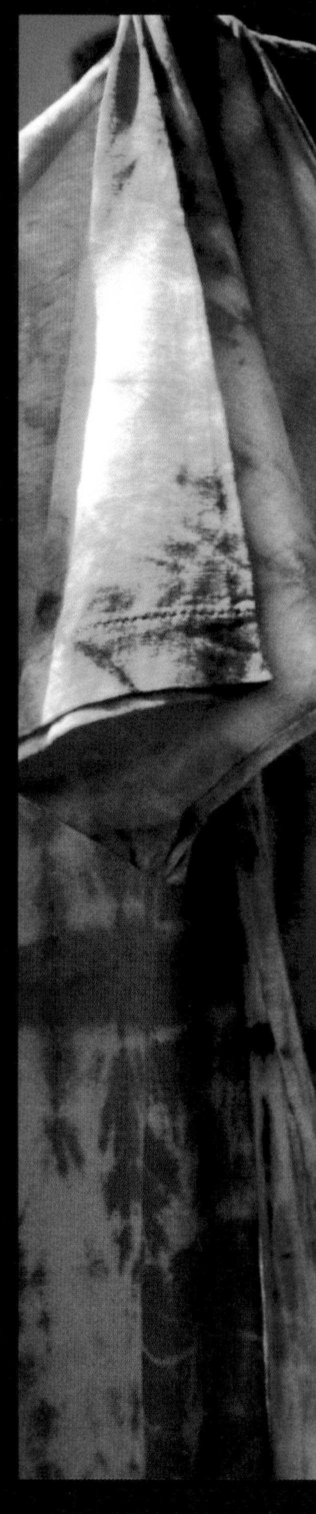

The tie-and-dye, or, as it is more commonly known, tie-dye T-shirt, popular in the years of Flower Power, encapsulated the psychedelic aesthetic of the moment with its sunburst-like blazes of color and its random stripes. This printing process originated in sub-Saharan Africa and involves plunging a piece of fabric that has been knotted, tied, folded and even stitched here and there into a dye bath. This style happened to overlap with the new interest in ethnic fabrics, and the traditional craft techniques of cottage industries. Multicolored marbled and mottled effects, sunburst patterns, and rib designs not unlike nerve systems—with the tie-dye process it is possible to produce endlessly varied patterns and colors which allow the imagination to run riot.

The tie-dye process is quite simple: the parts of the T-shirt that are folded and tied retain their original color, while the other areas become steeped in dye. The tighter the fabric is tied, the greater the contrasts. To make marbled and mottled effects, the dampened T-shirt is rolled into a ball, working from the sides toward the middle. Once this bundle has been squeezed and tied several times (the number of stripes is dictated by the string marks), it is then immersed in the dye bath for about a minute. If this operation is repeated several times over with different colors, it is possible to create interplays of multicolored marbled patterns.

In another version the dyer takes one end of the T-shirt, squeezes it into a tube-like shape, and ties it at one end as tightly as possible. Its entire length is then twisted, as if to wring it out. When the two ends of this cylindrical length of fabric

Petit
Mustique
Canouan
Tobago Cays
Petit St. Vincent
Petit Martinique

have been attached, it is tightly bound from end to end before being plunged for five minutes (more if the knots are very tight) into the dye, from which it will emerge coated with colors.
The T-shirt (just one thickness) can also be pinched in the middle of the chest to make a tip, then, with the other hand, rows of knots are made, radiating out from this tip. After being steeped for ten more minutes in the color, the T-shirt becomes printed with concentric—and hypnotic—circles, which vibrate like ripples in water.
Or instead of being knotted from a single point, the fabric may be pleated lengthwise at intervals, like an accordion, then tied tightly in a bundle. Once dyed, the T-shirt is decorated with a pattern of broken stripes, looking rather like scars.
To dye a T-shirt, all you have to do is boil a couple pints of water and pour in the dye (and its fixative), along with 4 ounces of coarse salt; this mixture is then stirred until the powder has been completely diluted. The still wet T-shirt can then be put into this hot bath and left there until the desired color is obtained. The last stage involves rinsing the T-shirt in cold water until the water is clear and then putting it out to dry.

**Previous pages:
Bequia Islands,
Grenadines,
1992.**

**Opposite:
Joe Cocker at the Isle
of Wight Festival, 1969.**

CHAPTER 7

The T-shirt and advertising

Advertising and subverting

T-shirts are no more left or right wing, capitalist or communist, than televisions and telephones. In the years when hippies and activists raised them as a banner against consumer society, this same society used them to broadcast its own markets. In 1939, Metro-Goldwyn-Mayer caught a glimpse of the huge advertising potential of the T-shirt, and made the most of it to promote one of the first color movies ever made in Hollywood, Victor Fleming's *Wizard of Oz*, the King of cult films. Oddly enough, it was not until 1965 that "trivial" advertising started to leave its stamp on T-shirts, following the example set by Budweiser, the most popular American beer. The following decade did actually adapt the T-shirt to suit all manner of logos—Cinzano, Martini, Xerox... and dozens of others would follow. Their success

BiC

Nestlé
Quik

Dickies

ENTERTAINMENT FOR MEN
SEX ON THE SIDE LINES:
N.F.L.
CHEERLEADERS
BARE ALL!
JOHN TRAVOLTA STEPS OUT:
A VERY CANDID INTERVIEW
FARRAH COMES
BACK—BIG!
MAJOR NEW SERIES
SEX IN AMERICA
PLUS GUNTER GRASS,
GREENBURG, F. LEE BAILEY
THE N.B.A. COACHES'
TEAM, SEX STARS OF '78 AND
ALL, IT'S CHRISTMAS) MUCH, MUCH

was surprising to say the least, in that period when the commercial foundations of American society were being disparaged if not reviled. In the same manner as jeans, the T-shirt took advantage of a personal, private connection with the person wearing it. Emblazoned on the torso—hub of the body's vital functions—the advertising slogan became more human, with a flesh-and-blood quality, as if signing and sealing a pact with the brand. It also enabled people to display their personal likes and dislikes (individualism was in the air in those days), and their loyalty to a particular product.

Like the knights of yesteryear, who sported banners and coats-of-arms in the jousting ring, the clothes of the American throng acted as an arena for the battles waged between brands and makes. Heineken offered its riposte to Budweiser. A Pepsi T-shirt tried to outdo rival Coca-Cola's "Enjoy" T-shirt. And inasmuch as the powerful tobacco promoters in the U.S.A. still had a free rein, we could all see the Marlboro cowboy flexing his pecs, while the pouting Camel mascot covered college campuses with hazy images of the East. In that decade of naive enthusiasm, advertising rarely missed its mark. A survey conducted on American teenagers showed that the targeted markets—kids owning a T-shirt showing a brand of cigarettes, and capable of quoting one of its slogans—were twice as likely to actually start smoking.

As if to increase its flock, every product designed for mass consumption stakes out its territory with images suggesting a certain lifestyle. The *Wall Street Journal* T-shirt doesn't frequent the same places as the *Playboy* T-shirt. One wouldn't mistake the McDonald's model for the Burger King model. Needless to say, these subtle differences go totally unnoticed in the Third World, where multinationals join forces to impose western culture as the sole reference. "Verbal and visual references to sitcoms, film characters, advertising slogans and commercial logos have become the most straightforward communication tools between cultures—an easy, instant 'click,'" writes Naomi Klein in her book *No Logo*.

Previous pages: In the 1960s, the T-shirt acted as a billboard for major brands. Two decades later, Bic used T-shirts to promote their famous ballpoint pens. In no time at all this T-shirt became a fashion phenomenon.

Opposite: With the transfer process, any company can print its brand name on T-shirts.

Well before all this, people had realized that the innocent T-shirt could be an instrument of cultural oppression. And they subverted it. Drugs, the ultimate weapon of the counter-culture—insofar as they put their users outside the mainstream—dynamited marketing constructs by short-circuiting its logos. In the 1970s, a T-shirt borrowing the Coca-Cola logo, displayed the words "Enjoy Cocaine" in those familiar

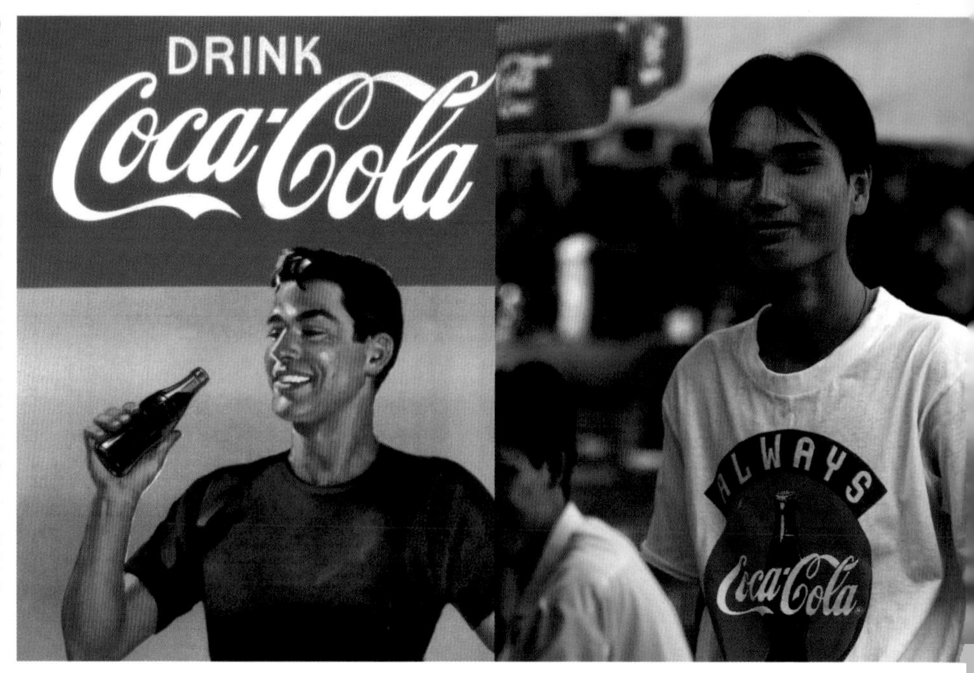

As a symbol of relaxation and youthfulness, the T-shirt is used as a guarantee of cool on early Coca-Cola billboards. A few decades later, the most famous of all American fizzy drinks had colonized the whole planet.

arabesques (with a double punch as the coca leaf was used in Coke's original formula) while Pepsi became "Peyote." Since those days, visual hallucinations have flourished everywhere. By becoming Adihash, the manufacturer Adidas unwittingly promoted getting stoned. More inspired present-day ravers have turned Rice Crispies into "Nice Tripsies," and flaunt on their T-shirts slightly silly characters with very obvious names like Sniff and Crack. In Japan, the Hysteric Glamour brand's graphic artists have changed the Johnson's Baby Powder slogan to "Junkie's Baddy Powder."

Some little-known brands have seized upon this tradition and made a killing by hijacking the logos of institutional products. The California manufacturer of Fuct skateboards, starting with a name ideal for every manner of pun, simply borrowed the Ford logo—a hazardous, high-risk game of appropriation, especially when the owner is not just any old company. In 1996, Robbie Fowler, a British soccer star, pulled off his jersey to reveal a red T-shirt bearing the message: "500 Liverpool doCKers sacked since 1995." But the CK Calvin Klein brand group were bad sports and took the footballer to court, ending with Fowler coughing up a large fine. Personal T-shirt or not, you don't play around with logos, which, thanks to copyright laws, are nowadays as protected as the coats-of-arms of ancient nobility.

Enjoy
Cocaine

ENJOY
COKE

Enjoy
Coca-Cola

Enjoy
Ibiza®
TM

ЦЕНА
McLenin's

Marijuana
OVER 1 BILLION STONED

Above, left: Snoop Doggy Dogg.

Above right and opposite: The logos of major brands have inspired some politically incorrect appropriations. On the right, French writer F. Beigbeder wears a T-shirt urging people to boycott Danone in the wake of a massive layoffs in France.

Previous pages, left: The famous fast-food brand ironically redubbed with the picture of Lenin. right: Rapper Doc Gynéco.

Depoliticization and political fashion

In the 1960s, the messages put forth on T-shirts were real social commentaries which aroused strong feelings. But there was a certain dash or irony about that struggle for a world patrolled by advertising and show business ready to appropriate anything and everything. "The spectacle has become muddled up with all kinds of reality by irradiating it," wrote Guy Debord in his book *Comments on the Society of the Spectacle*. Action was replaced by words. Endlessly repeated images turned out to be mere commodities—merchandise emptied of meaning by mass production. As in Andy Warhol's silkscreen prints, the images of Mao Ze-dong that were printed on T-shirts became effigies that were at once hollow and sacred, just like Mickey Mouse and Coca-Cola. And when, in the 1980s, Perestroika sounded the death knell for the Cold War, fashion took up the communist phenomenon, devoid now of its substance, and printed T-shirts with its repertory of insignia and symbols. USSR, hammer and sickle, and red stars were all the rage, and all the more so because nobody was afraid of them. In spite of everything, in 2001 we saw the romantic myth of the "red hero" come back into circulation. In a Germany struggling with reunification, shock "alternatives" brought back T-shirts

DA NE

Above: In the 1970s, the naughty *Playboy* bunny displayed its long ears and bow-tie on T-shirts. Opposite: Thirty years later, Chloé fashion designer Stella McCartney transformed the Bunny into a skull, after being at loggerheads with the Playboy Co.

depicting Andreas Baader's gun. Baader, a so-called Robin Hood of the 1970s, and head assassin of the Baader-Meinhoff Gang's Red Army Faction, has become a favorite subject of appropriation imagery. "The Red Army Faction is mythical—you can make pop stars out of those terrorists really quickly," explains the fashion photographer Andreas Schiko, who borrows famous scenes of bloodthirsty duo Bonnie and Clyde in a series for the German magazine *Tussi-Deluxe*. In Japan, empire of a rising fashion void of meaning, people are crazy about the Arafat headdress, the *kaffiyeh*—an exotic, now unsettling knick-knack—while the Phantom label is cleaning up with its FBI T-shirts. Better still, thumbing its nose at everyone, the Italian brand Dolce & Gabbana, known for having made a prestigious ornament of its own logo, boldly prints its T-shirts with the title of the most famous anti-globalization tract—Naomi Klein's book *No Logo*.

Right: Soviet imagery recycled as tourist souvenirs in Budapest.

Opposite: In Berlin, after the reunification of Germany, a hawker offers souvenir T-shirts.

Next pages, left: The "neighborhood" T-shirt sells well among tourists. Right: A souvenir store in Sydney, Australia, 2000.

Souvenir T-shirts

More than any other article of clothing, the T-shirt reveals the intimate attributes of its wearer. Like a much-cherished reminder, T-shirts are witnesses to the events that have left a mark on our lives. We bring them back from journeys, either as gifts or to proudly proclaim "I was there." Tourist meccas have all been quick on the uptake. In Egypt, alongside postcards and miniature pyramids, the T-shirt bearing a printed sphinx gets top billing. In the world's major cities, you can find T-shirts embroidered with golden Eiffel Towers, or styles showing such mythical monuments as Big Ben and the Statue of Liberty. Even particular neighborhoods have their own souvenir T-shirts. One printed with the word "Harlem" clearly shows the pride felt by those who live in New York's

9. NOVEMBER '89
ICH WAR DABEI !
3. OKTOBER '90
T-SHIRT
20.

NEW YORK
CITY

No.1 in boxing.
OLYMPIC GAMES
Sydney 2000
AUSTRALIA
OLYMPIC GAMES
Sydney 2000
AUSTRALIA

Above: "Paris" T-shirt by French designer Isabel Marant.

Opposite: The "Harlem" T-shirt.

Next pages: The white T-shirt has become one of the most widespread communications and marketing tools. Relatively inexpensive, it is displayed on billboards and in shop windows on the chests of scantily clad dummies to promote sales.

dominant African-American neighborhood, and has also become a tourist trophy. Old hands at manufacturing spin-off products, the Walt Disney Company sells these textile souvenirs to visitors to their theme parks, who then return home to their local playgrounds with proof positive of a visit to some more exotic part of the world of Disney. Dallas, Beijing, Amman, Bali, Acapulco...T-shirts stamped with the names of every branch of the Hard Rock Café mean that you can travel round the world without so much as a change of scenery. But the T-shirt also immortalizes more cultural outings. People bring them back from the Van Gogh Museum in Amsterdam, adorned with the house logo, or choose the model bearing an excerpt from a letter written by the famous painter's brother Theo. People who have been to Bilbao to visit the futuristic monument of the Guggenheim Museum can come away with a sketch of the building made by its architect, Frank Gehry. At the British Museum in London, the star mummy—Seshepenmehit—stares out from many a T-shirt, along with the famous Rosetta Stone. Sometimes, though, when memories become less vivid or fond, this undershirt finds other uses—it may even end up stuffing a pillow, before being committed to the rag bag.

Harlem

TAXIS
Rue de La Pompe
I ♥ BOUVARD
PARIS
16:30/LES GROSSES
TÊTES DEPUIS 25 ANS
RTL
VIVRE
ENSEMBLE

STOP
STOP
MECHANTS SOLDES
STOP
MECHANTS SOLDES
STOP
MECHANTS SOLDES
2ème DÉMARQUE*

I love New York

The "I love NY" T-shirt logo was invented in 1976 by the graphic artist Milton Glaser, to promote the image of the Big Apple. Since then, it has become nothing less than a symbol of the United States. It is now imprinted so deeply in the collective psyche that it sometimes verges on becoming a hackneyed cliché. With its big red heart and long black letters, this T-shirt has often acted as New York City's ambassador. In 1979, Fidel Castro was given one when he made a visit to the United Nations headquarters. In California, there was a move to counter this East Coast adulation in an outburst of jealousy with an "I hate New York." This simple, punchy logo has become one of the most popular and copied in the history of the T-shirt. Souvenir vendors the world over have adapted it to all the world's capital cities. From "I love Paris" to "I love Sydney," the famous heart now knows no boundaries. After the destruction of the World Trade Center on September 11th, 2001, New Yorkers rediscovered their symbolic T-shirt, and flocked to tourist vendors to buy it. Like a banner of heroism and hope, it has been fluttering for several months in the city streets, alongside its big brother, the Stars and Stripes. Certain rotten eggs may admittedly have taken advantage of the situation by turning the slogan into "I loved NY," but its inventor nevertheless managed to adapt it to the circumstances by bedecking the heart with the colors of mourning, and affixing to the original slogan the words "...more than ever." This sentence "was an important realization—in the same way that when somebody you love is injured, the intensity of your love for them increases," explained Milton Glaser to the *Los Angeles Times*. A-buzz with ideas, the artist and draughtsman is already concocting his next work: a logo depicting the Twin Towers in the shape of a T.

I
NY®

D&G
Danza
I ♥ NY
Nuova formula!
LINEA FORMA su fianchi sformati
Danza

2

Previous pages:
T-shirts with Milton Glaser's original design from 1976.
1: Dolce & Gabbana's spring/summer 2002 collection.
2: After the September 11th attacks, Milton Glaser's design is revised: "I Love NY more than ever."
3: Mourning in Washington Square Park, NYC, after the World Trade Center attacks.

3

CHAPTER 8

The T-shirt and art

In the 1980s, against a backdrop of soaring prices, New York artists invoked the name of Jean-Michel Basquiat and the graffiti artists to forge links with figurative art forms, given its style this time around by various forms of street culture. Following in the footsteps of Keith Haring's trademark dancing figures, Kenny Scharf and one or two other artists popularized the graffiti-style movement in New York, whose inspiration came from street artists in marginal neighborhoods—but their initial success eventually fell victim to the art market crash. Their works, bursting with life and deliberately disorderly, had a homemade look about them, pointing to the democratization of a particular discipline—Art with a capital A—which many saw as being elitist. T-shirts had more vitality than posters, and thus came across as the natural medium for getting their works out to the turned-on throng. For the T-shirt is something that offers freedom by flowing with the body's movements rather than restricting and confining them. In the privacy of their studios, many artists turned the T-shirt into their ordinary working garb. Just as Picasso painted in striped jerseys in the 1930s, Jackson Pollock, tortured genius of Action Painting, was certainly one of the first artists—along with Willem de Kooning—to work in a T-shirt, back in the immediate postwar years. A three-piece suit would probably have suffered considerably from his flying squirts of paint.

The high priest of pop art, Roy Lichtenstein, who managed to raise the comic strip to the rank of high art, presents his self-portrait. This work shows the painter's body in the form of a white T-shirt, symbol of mass consumerism. For his head, a mirror essentially making of his face an "every man."

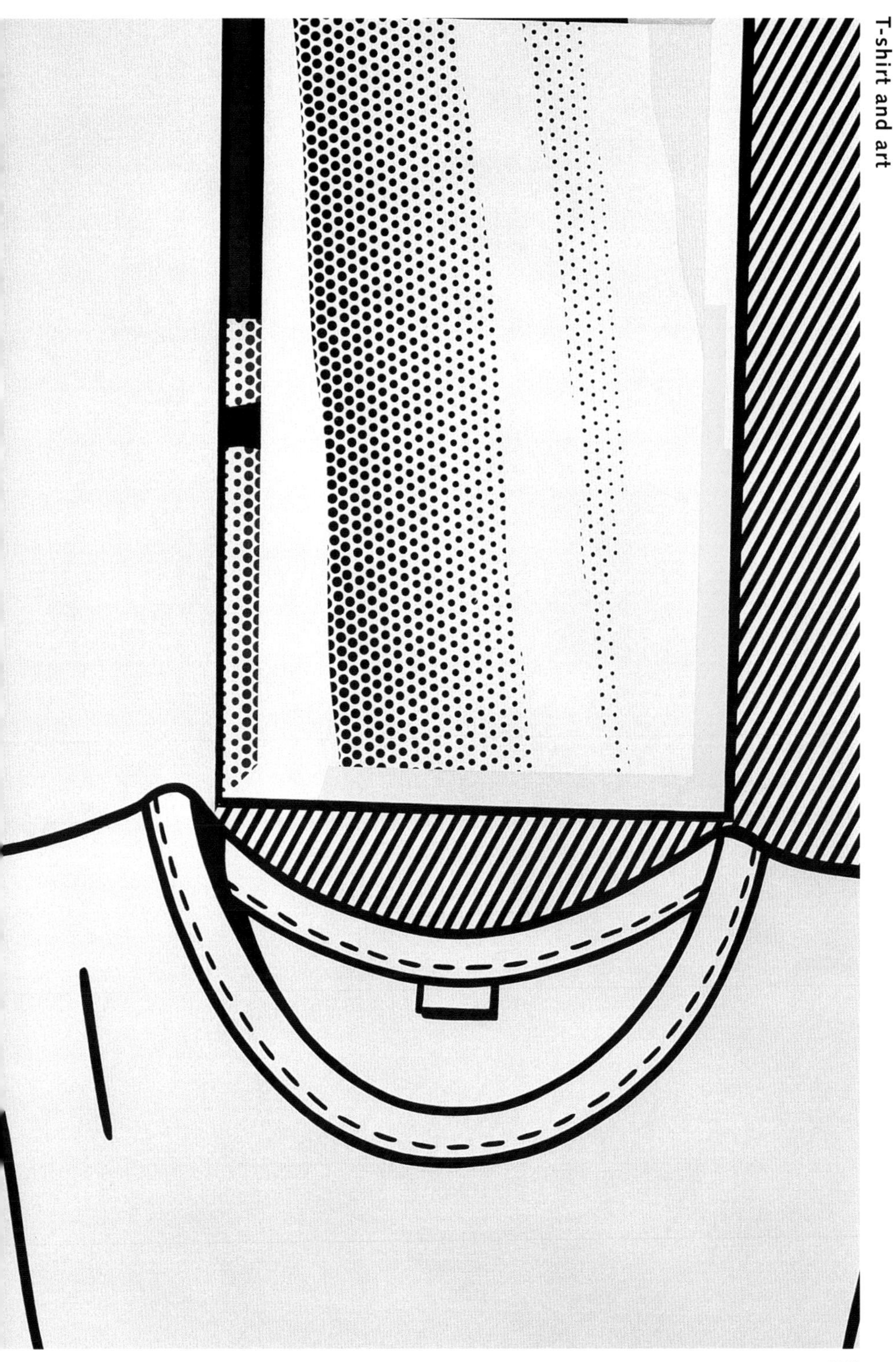

Popular T-shirt art

In the 1980s, the king of New York graffiti, Keith Haring, opened his Pop Shop, a store that offered everyone access to his works—which until then could only be found spray-painted on city walls. Now even art had become democratized through the T-shirt.

While the 1980s ushered fashion into museums—at the same time rejoicing over the demise of haute couture—the lowliest of clothing items was being promoted by artists as a by-product, well-suited to offering their works to the private needs of the public. Several things helped the T-shirt to permeate the boundary between high and low. The hippies' favorite cartoonist, Robert Crumb, had already featured his long-haired layabouts on T-shirts, just as other comic strip authors—Walt Disney first and foremost—had done with their characters. The issue of uniqueness, combined with the work-of-art status, now seemed nothing if not obsolete, ever since the photograph, lending itself quintessentially to reproduction, had been elevated to the ranks of the "serious" arts. By making Pop Art an outrider of mass production, Andy Warhol's silkscreened portraits gave the T-shirt free rein.

Elsewhere, as early as 1978, Roy Lichtenstein, one of the most famous practitioners of this art movement, readily featured this piece of clothing in a self-portrait. In a pictorial style borrowed from the comic strip, the painter depicted himself in a simple white T-shirt surmounted by a mirror.

Ceci n'est pas une pipe

In the early 1980s, Laurie Mallet, a U.S.-based, French businesswoman, commissioned 20 artists to make an original painting to be reproduced on a T-shirt. For the very first time, the sketches of Keith Haring, Di Rosa and Speedy Graphito were assigned the task of undulating over pectorals. A few years later, Keith Haring got seriously involved in the business world by opening his own Pop Shop offering bags and T-shirts, where you could not only appreciate but purchase his works too—including the famous crawling baby. This is how Haring explained it: "The Pop Shop makes my work accessible. It's about participation on a big level, the point was that we didn't want to produce things that would cheapen the art. In other words, this was still art as statement."

Media and surfaces suitable for artistic expression, whose production costs have consistently dropped with industrialization, also enable "amateur" artists (thanks to the transfer technique) to put their works on view for large audiences. Henceforth, anyone and everyone can be a creative artist.

Opposite: The famous work by surrealist painter René Magritte, *Ceci n'est pas une pipe*, 1929.

Next pages, left: The crocodile of tennis-player René Lacoste on one of the earliest models of the brand's athletic shirts.
Right: This kind of polo shirt has been used, among others, by the designer Barnabé, the photographer Nicole Tran Ba Vang, and the urban artist André.

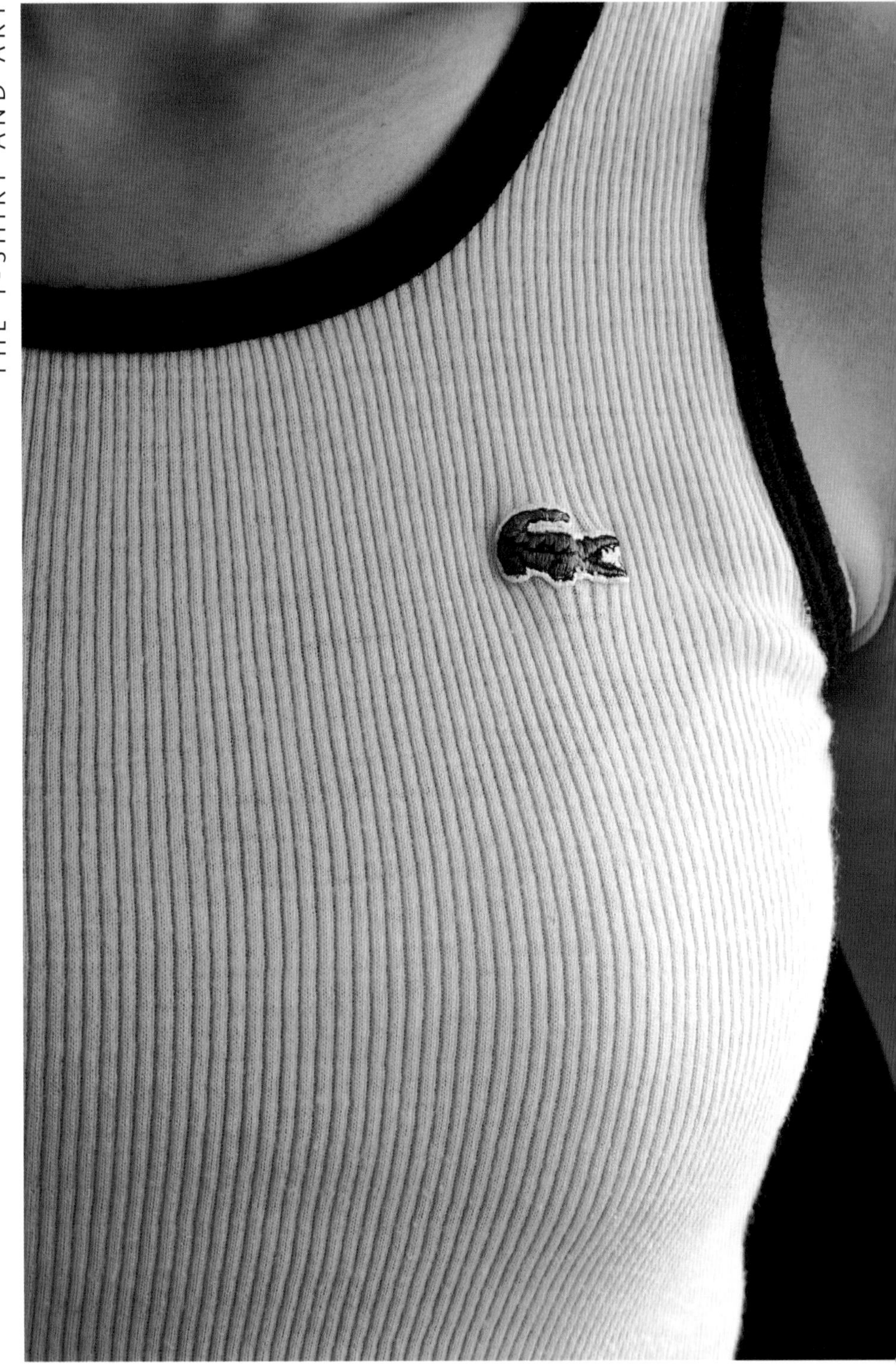

1212

ATD
ATD

Japanese cartoons

Takashi Murakami, billed as an heir of Pop Art, took as his subject matter the icons of the *otaku* subculture—i.e., Japanese cartoons and comic strips. His powerful and much-respected art even goes so far as to stress to an almost nonsensical degree the grotesque aspects and hypertrophied eroticism of comic strips—for instance his half-naked girls with huge inflated breasts. The tone is fiercely ironical, yet tinged with affection. In 1992 Murakami created Mr. Dob, a kind of energetic and insipid huge-eared Mickey Mouse, who soon became his preferred logo. The artist reproduced Mr. Dob in the form of large inflatable sculptures—exhibited in 2001 at the Cartier Foundation in France—as well as on T-shirts, computer mouse-pads and other spin-off products, all marketed through the Hiropon Factory, which was both a workshop/studio and a sales office. In the same cultural arena, the Thai painter Navin Rawanchaikul, a major creator of spin-offs and peripherals, frequently uses the T-shirt as a promotional medium. So much so that each series of his works spawns another line of T-shirts. After bringing several colleagues together to mount a traveling show in a taxi, the artist brought out a commemorative T-shirt with the caption "I love taxi," using the famous heart symbol from the "I love NY" slogan.

Japanese Takashi Murakami exhibits at the Emmanuel Perrotin Gallery, in Paris, 2001.

T-shirts in museums

Opposite: A witty view of the family, signed by the French artist Alain Sechas in 1997. The generation gap is expressed on T-shirts. The parents sport peace-loving slogans from their hippy days, while their children display desperate and aggressive messages.

Next pages, left: A Japanese cartoon T-shirt by agnès b. entitled *Futura 2000*.
Next pages, right, from top to bottom: T-shirts signed by artists Gaston Chaissac, Ben and Arman.

Hailing from the Fluxus movement, the Nice-based artist Ben—aka Ben Vautier—finds expression through sentences written with white acrylic paint on black surfaces. This art form, with its clearly subversive intent, invited all manner of commercial reproduction: posters, postcards, and ordinary objects, and, before long, T-shirts. In 1982 the shop at the Pompidou Center in Paris put on something akin to a preview, offering two works by Ben (including a "j'emmerde l'art" = "Fuck Art" slogan) printed on T-shirts. No sooner had this Paris museum opened its doors, in 1977, than it started giving priority to its merchandising operations by selling books, posters and postcards, often imported from the United States, where this kind of business—officially introduced to "democratize art"—was generously swelling the coffers of MoMA and the Guggenheim in New York. In 1985, show-offs and poseurs sported snippets of literature on Proust-inspired T-shirts (bearing the much-quoted opening lines: "For a long time I used to go to bed early" when they weren't flaunting a Calligramme by Apollinaire. This was all tantamount to saying that the actual interest of the work often counted for less than its impact. Selection was readily focused on cultural symbols and hackneyed, commonplace works that were worshiped out of habit, and instantly identifiable. Because of their graphic simplicity, drawings often stole the show from paintings. Seen from this angle, the T-shirt owed allegiance to the applied arts.
When commissioning artists to design a T-shirt, it goes without saying that the artists are free to do whatever they will. In 1998, the Pompidou Center suggested to the artists Gilbert & George that they reproduce some of their works on T-shirts: for instance "Coloured Friends," "Street," "Day Man." Bertrand Niaudet, who is in charge of the Flammarion 4 T-shirts—Flammarion being an erstwhile supplier of the Pompidou Center—explains: "In the spirit of provocation, Gilbert & George have brought out works with a scatological tendency, but, at the end of the day, I opted for softer works... It's never been possible to do that with Andy Warhol, because his works appropriate brand labels (Heinz, Coca-Cola, Campbell's) which determine their image." The fact remains that museums are much happier ordering original works for their T-shirts than reproducing existing pieces. The problem, which goes way beyond the mere T-shirt issue, is to find contemporary

PEACE
LOVE
SUICIDE
BITCH

取扱注意
aerosol attack
Use with adequate ventilation

CHAISSAS

Je suis
unique
au monde
Ben

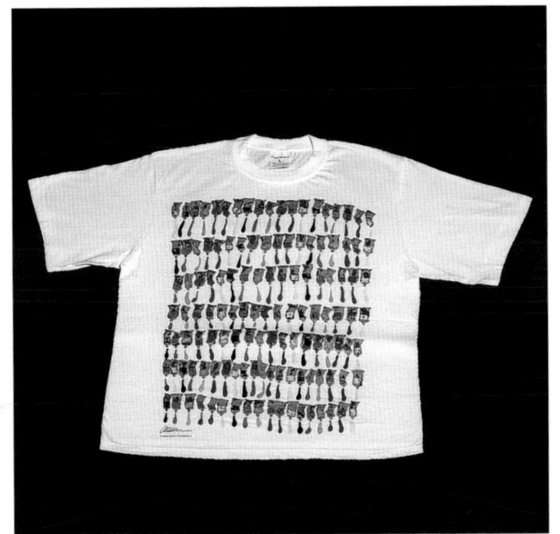

artists of sufficient stature willing to participate. This was nevertheless done with the Arman T-shirts (depicting multi-colored paint tubes), the Tinguely T-shirts (exclusive multicolored cogwheels produced for his 1988 Retrospective at the Pompidou Center), and T-shirts made by several other artists such as Robert Combas, Daniel Buren, Richard Serra, Anne-Marie Jugnet, etc., all exhibited since 1986 at the CAPC contemporary art center in Bordeaux. In her day, Nikki de Saint-Phalle was also honored by Pompidou Center T-shirts. "For her, it's above all a way of offering a cheap work to a public that she doesn't manage to connect with in galleries. She doesn't believe that this contradicts or compromises her work," Bertrand Niaudet remarks. "Hasn't she set up a Foundation in Italy around a sculpture garden, complete with a store to fund it?"

Opposite: *Fame, No. 4* in an indivisible series of four photographs by Jean-Pierre Khazem, exhibited in 1998 at the Emmanuel Perrotin Gallery in Paris.

Below: A T-shirt by Gilbert & George.

Art with guts

American artist Jenny Holzer has made a career out of using media techniques to get her messages across as a commentary on this very medium. In 1977-1979, she affixed her messages, called "Truisms," on the streets of Manhattan and the billboards around Times Square. So for her T-shirts were a natural. Some of her T-shirts proclaim in large letters: "Protect me from/what I want," and: "Lack of charisma can be fatal." And in 1992, for the Venice Biennale: "Abuse of Power cause I'm not surprised."

The same year, the Nice-based publisher GDL, in cahoots with Les Ateliers du Paradis, brought out a line of T-shirts titled "variable multiple," signed by three French artists—Pierre Joseph, Philippe Perrin and Philippe Parreno. At the Air de Paris gallery, which represents Philippe Parreno in Paris, they offer the following explanation: "The artists wanted to play with the idea of communication. Aware that the everyday vocabulary used by an adult rarely exceeds 500 words, they grouped these words together through the association of ideas. The word selection worked a bit like a game of consequences." The T-shirt

Opposite: The artist Nicole Tran Ba Vang challenges fashion and capsizes the concept of clothing. The latex T-shirt becomes like skin and exposes the body to another kind of disconcerting nudity.

Next pages, left: Conny & Vence, the characters created by Swiss artist René Walker for the 2001 Lyons Biennale, are like extra-terrestrial beings out of a box of Cornflakes. "They wear T-shirts because I wear them. Everyone should wear them like a standard." Next pages, right: An agnès b. T-shirt by Jo One 56.

qualified for artwork status as a communicating object, and as such, was worth being immortalized on the cover of Philippe Parreno's book *Snow Dancing*. He also chose an image showing five people all inside one gigantic T-shirt, shadowing the performance that reproduced the scene, this time according it artwork status.

In August 2001, Marcel Wallace—Simon Boudvin and Seul Gi-Lee founders of the Paris Project Room Gallery—organized an exhibition around what artists' thought about T-shirts. Noteworthy was the semen-stained T-shirt of video artist Ange Leccia, the T-shirt produced by Eleana Gonzalez for her final exams, and a model by Cyril Dietrich buried under tea leaves. Once given cachet as art, the T-shirt is redeemed in the eyes of fashion, like a prodigal son.

In the same twilight zone between fashion and art, former fashion designer Nicole Tran Ba Vang—now a photographer and computer-imagery technician—capsizes the idea of clothing. As a second skin, the T-shirt is invited to become the first skin, through trompe l'oeil effects, by adopting the texture—and even the hairiness—of the epidermis. In a photograph showing a modern couple sitting scantily clad on a sofa, the boy wears a T-shirt and socks embellished with hair. Another shows a man in the process of pulling a see-through latex T-shirt off his female partner, as if to un- and discover her breasts.

CONNI
NENCE

The basic white T-shirt, either as "art" or museum promotion piece, is one of the best-selling spin-off products in museum stores.

Next pages: In choreographer Jérôme Bel's work, *Shirtologie*, dancers wearing several T-shirts on top of each other strip off their layers, one by one revealing all the different signs and logos written on them.

In the manner of art

The latest cross-disciplinary canons encourage clothing designers, on the one hand, to flirt with art, that great arbiter of culture, while also keeping ahead of fashion—an industry where profits are often very lucrative. In pioneering times, "artists'" T-shirts were often mediocre products sold in cardboard boxes. As fashioned by art-smitten designers, they are nowadays becoming the most profitable of all types of advertising. In the year 2000, Jean-Charles de Castelbajac caused a minor riot by offering a T-shirt with the exhortation "Kill All Artists" ["Tuez tous les artistes"], signed—ironically—by an artist, the American sculptor Tom Sachs. A fine move for Castelbajac who, since the 1980s, has been producing T-shirts created by Keith Haring, and who has always injected his fashion concepts—the Snoopy sweater in his collection is from the 1970s—with the colorful graphics of childhood. On a fleeting visit to the world of couture, for his autumn-winter 2001-2002 collection Castelbajac introduced speech bubbles and

onomatopoeia by putting Barbarella and Pravda the Survivor, those fantastic heroines of the 1960s, on his T-shirts.
Another Parisian designer, agnès b., has always been a patron of the arts, accommodating painters, photographers and visual artists in her Rue du Jour Gallery. Here, artists' T-shirts are par for the course; like the model signed by Felix Gonzalez-Torres in 1995, with "Nobody" written on the front and "Owns me" on the back, in an edition of 5,000. As a famous conceptual artist of the 1980s, now deceased, agnès b. would commission exclusive works from Gonzalez-Torres, earmarked as ammo for her T-shirts.

Deliberate organized shortage

In 2001, a T-shirt bearing a very simple slogan: "J'adore Dior" was successfully sold for about $175. This price made it considerably cheaper than other Dior items, but a whole lot pricier than an ordinary T-shirt. Because it is not easy for artists and designers to compete with the main fashion houses in terms of prestige, they are instilling the T-shirt with the semblance of rarity bequeathed by haute couture. By working against the "democratic" calling of vulgar undershirts and athletic shirts, they are elevating the T-shirt into something rare, a collector's item for those in the know. And they are doing this by limiting production runs to just a few hundred articles. In 1998, once urban artist André—author of the childlike fellow with top hat and stick legs—had finished taking his courses with Xüly Bet, Ungaro and Balmain, he began selling T-shirts with cursive captions, under the brand known as Rare by André, in limited editions of 100. Artists Brian Reed and Mike Dawson have also come up with the idea of selling a T-shirt twosome, one proclaiming "Lavish," the other "Conviction," with both items packaged and sealed together. This was a by no means gratuitous allusion: "You have to break the seal to open them, and in so doing you're destroying the artist's work," say Brian Reed and Mike Dawson.

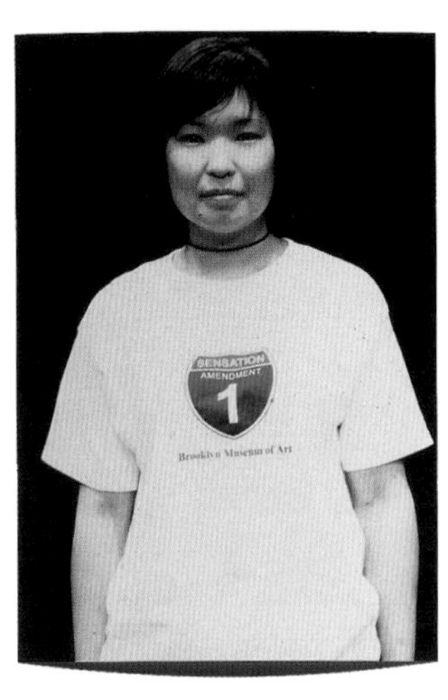
SENSATION
AMENDMENT
1
Brooklyn Museum of Art

DANCE 2
ACID

KINGS
3

ELEVEN
7-ELEVEN STORES

8
VANHEULE

9

11

11

12

Go-Girls

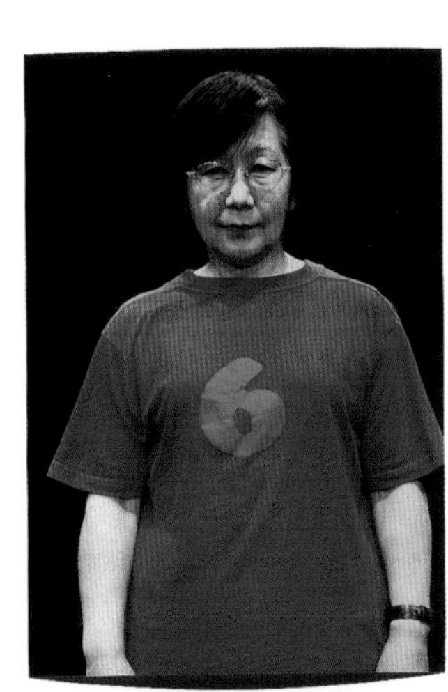
6

10

TEN

X

向陽
13

14

take
me

Fruit of the Loom

With its five ounces of spotless cotton, round neck, abbreviated sleeves, and fruity logo, the Fruit of the Loom T-shirt has everything required for myth status. It came into being at the beginning of the 20th century and, as a basic article beyond the vagaries of fashion, it has managed to make its way through the decades without ageing. In 1851, the daughter of one Rufas Skeel, an American fabric merchant, started to apply her gifts as a painter to her father's materials: plump apples and sparkling bunches of grapes made their appearance. In 1871, this autumnal still life became the official logo of the Fruit of the Loom brand. Almost 40 years later, Jacob Goldfarb started marketing Fruit of the Loom underwear on a grand scale, and the T-shirt embarked on its path toward fame, first of all with sailors in the U.S. Navy, and later on at universities, covering the muscled torsos of sports teams. Time has certainly not worked against the mythical T-shirt, probably due to its being a quality product, and its "historical legitimacy." As well as managing its own cotton fields, the Fruit of the Loom company loom-weaves its yarn itself. Before the T-shirts are packaged in lots of three, they undergo no less than sixty checks and inspections. As the fetish garment of nascent rebels of the 1950s and preppie young people of the 1980s, all eager to wear it under a suit or twinset complete with pearl necklace, and adopted, too, by Sesame Street characters and multicolored Pokemons, Fruit of the Loom has managed to adapt to all trends and all age groups. But the myth very nearly toppled. This huge company, which was number one in the world T-shirt business until the 1990s, has just been rescued from bankruptcy.

HOW TH

) APPEARS ON A LIGHT BACKGROUND

DO NOT USE AS ARTWORK

MYTHOLOGY

POLLY

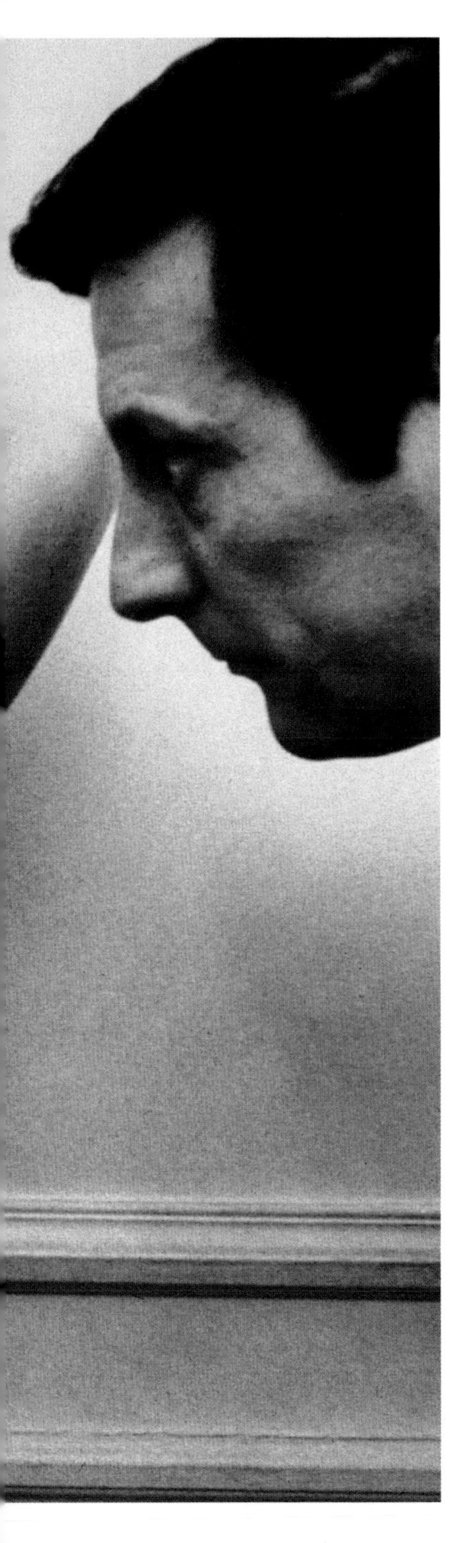

CHAPTER 9

The T-shirt and fashion

The T-shirt goes fashionable

It took less than a century for the T-shirt to be admitted to the pantheon of basics, pigeonholed somewhere between jeans and the little black number. Designers and manufacturers have been forever improving its proportions, bettering the quality of its materials and dressing it up with messages. We have seen this modest cotton tube playing lead roles in the realm of luxury, slipped on beneath a smart suit or surmounting a frilly skirt. Even the world of haute couture could no longer shy away from turning the uniform of the proletariat into a unique article with a pricetag sometimes running into the tens of thousands of dollars. For the spring/summer haute couture of 2001 at Christian Dior, John Galliano had this garment re-embroidered with pearls by the makers of costume jewelry in the Lesage workshops. For men, monochrome basics, as seen on reality TV shows, were being sold in threes, immortalizing the trendy, boyish look of the late 1980s. At a time when Friday wear is shaking up dress codes in the workplace, the well-cut T-shirt in cashmere or silk is tending to replace the shirt. Invaded by brand logos, it has also become an outward sign of wealth, and as such has also spawned a whole industry busily making fakes.

T-shirts come into fashion

Previous pages: One of the heroines of *Who Are You, Polly Magoo?* wears a printed T-shirt. This cult movie, made in 1966 by the photographer William Klein, poked satiric fun at the worlds of fashion and media.

In the United States in 1945, the T-shirt was controlled by two powerful brands: Hanes, established in 1800, and Union Underwear, which had just patented the name Fruit of the Loom. When the T-shirt landed in France in those GI kitbags, it would have an immediate effect on children's fashion too. The Petit Bateau brand fitted the T-shirt with its broad cut neck, known in French as the "American fit," designed so that large infant heads could be slipped easily into their babywear. Where grown-ups were concerned, it was not until the summer of 1957 that people saw St.Tropez starlets borrowing their boyfriends' white Fruit of the Loom T-shirts, sparking the mass appropriation of T-shirts and jeans in the teenage world. These articles were then being sold in packs of three in American surplus stores. A year later, Mrs. Vachon, the budding seaside resort's official fashion designer and purveyor of clothes to such young stars as Brigitte Bardot, was selling athletic shirts, tank-tops and undershirts, all made of striped cotton jersey, like hot cakes. This was the very model that the pioneering Chanel was wearing as a sweater on the French Riviera as far back as the 1930s.

In the 1960s, street fashion snatched ready-to-wear clothes away from now outmoded dreams of elegance. Youth was vaunted as the supreme yardstick, with androgyny and slenderness the order of the day, as if declaring—in the guise of a revolt against "the system"—a refusal to

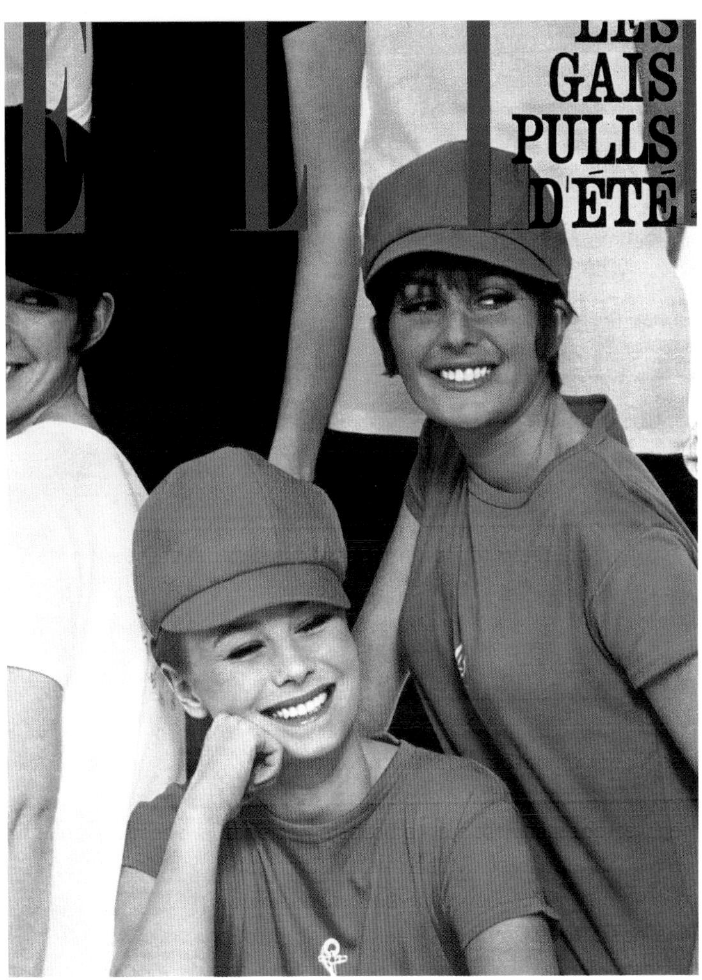

Right: In 1963, *Elle* magazine gave the T-shirt another name—the "summer sweater."

Opposite: A disco T-shirt titled "Mr. Freedom." In the 1970s, the fashion designer for Tommy Roberts, the famous London boutique, featured Mickey Mouse and Goofy on very Pop Art T-shirts for the Walt Disney Co.

grow old. And this, of course, is still very much part and parcel of our early 21st century society. So it was in the 1960s, too, that haute couture took over the fetish T-shirt that came from the United States. The first "couture" T-shirt was probably a striped velvet model, shown by Christian Dior for the summer of 1962. Two years later, Nina Ricci's workshops were producing an evening T-shirt made of crepe and embroidered with pearls, while Jacques Heim was dressing his models in lamé T-shirts, foreshadowing the advent of Lurex. Among more run-of-the-mill manufacturers, the T-shirt had embarked on its great odyssey by way of varied colors and designs: flounces, floral patterns, differing degrees of fading and bleaching, varsity initials and psychedelic prints.

The 1970s

In 1972, Jackie O could be seen strolling round the streets of New York looking gorgeous in a navy-blue T-shirt. This was as good a way as any for this arbiter of elegance to put her imprimatur on the humble T-shirt. From the peace-and-love movement, which peaked with the hippies of the early 1970s, to the punk culture marking the end of the decade, we find a street phenomenon that wanted to edge out fashion and set the body free. The T-shirt was a pivotal player in this revolution of lifestyles and attitudes, and would be used by the various anti-fashion trends. In France, couturier Yves Saint Laurent, who had just launched ready-to-wear in his Rive Gauche boutique, produced a long-sleeved blue T-shirt bearing his name in white lettering, and declared that "all a 20-year-old girl needs is a T-shirt and a pair of jeans." He even made a T-shirt of silk

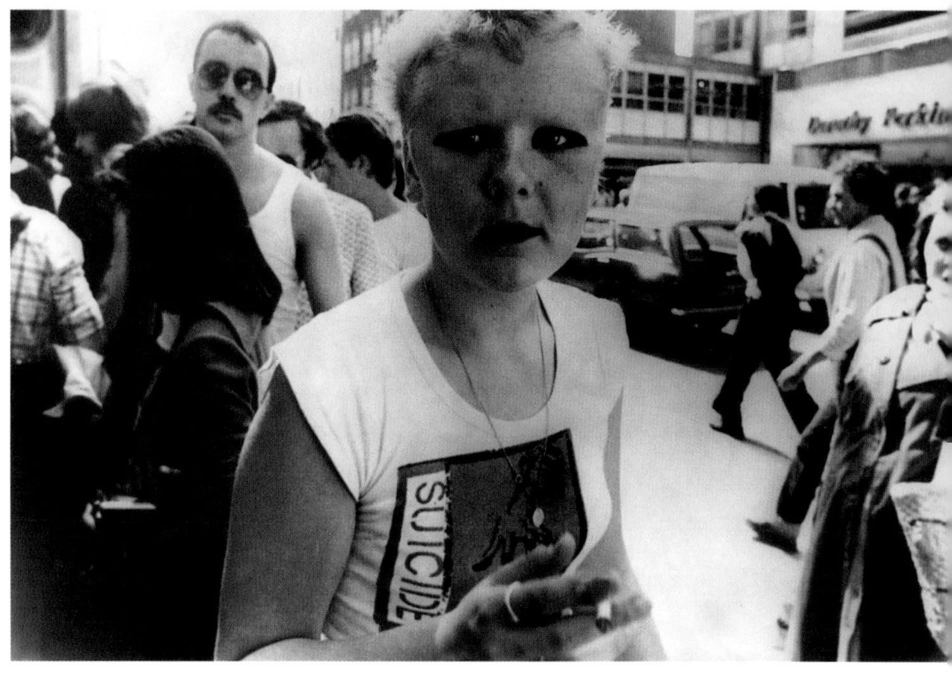

Previous pages, left: Sonny and Cher.
Previous pages, right: Fans at a Rolling Stones concert in Hyde Park, London, 1969.

Above: Young Punk in Paris at the end of the 1970s.

Opposite: Vivienne Westwood and friends at the store Let It Rock, 1970.

jersey for elegant ladies. In less than 15 years, the T-shirt had become an essential article in any woman's wardrobe.

It was in the 1970s that the portals of the fashion world really opened up to the T-shirt. The English model Jean Shrimpton wore it in white, embellished with her own portrait, and signed with her own name. In April 1975, *Elle* magazine wagered that the T-shirt would become a basic item of clothing that would never go out of fashion, rather like the trench coat. Designers, couturiers and consumers all discovered at the same time that this form, which hugs the shape of the body, is the most natural and simple, and, at the end of the day, the one best suited to all manner of variation. All it takes is a bright material to turn a maxi T-shirt into an evening gown. And with a slightly fuller cut, it will trim down a body that's become a little rounded. Made in an unusual color it can bring out the best in a skirt. It was at this time that Sonia Rykiel affixed catchy messages to her T-shirts: "Artists," "Champion," "Love." In Italy, there was a preference for the taunting kitsch of Elio Fiorucci, who had established his anti-fashion in Milan back in 1967 under the banner of ironical protest. Before printing his T-shirts with his two daydreaming cherubs, the maestro had sold a signature line of red-and-white striped models.

RIUMPH

The 1980s

After the punk interlude was turned into a fashion genre by Vivienne Westwood—who came up with asymmetrical T-shirts for neo-romantics—the 1980s ushered in the come-back of the shirt proper, along with suits and dresses, in a word, smart clothes. The T-shirt covered with imitation jewelry, may have hallmarked the golden age of Disco, but it was the black T-shirt that offered a patent of trendiness to young gallery owners in the hip neighborhoods of New York, Paris and London, one or two fashion designers, and to "working-class" singer-songwriters like Bruce Springsteen. The T-shirt also brought into vogue an innovative fabric that would help revolutionize it: Lycra. Developed by Dupont de Nemours chemists, this versatile fiber made it possible for the garment to cling to the body without constricting it. Fashion, in this decade, switched to sport, and many brands would gradually launch second lines, focusing more on sportswear. Henceforth, T-shirts, sweatshirts and boxer shorts all became part of trendy wardrobes. Giorgio

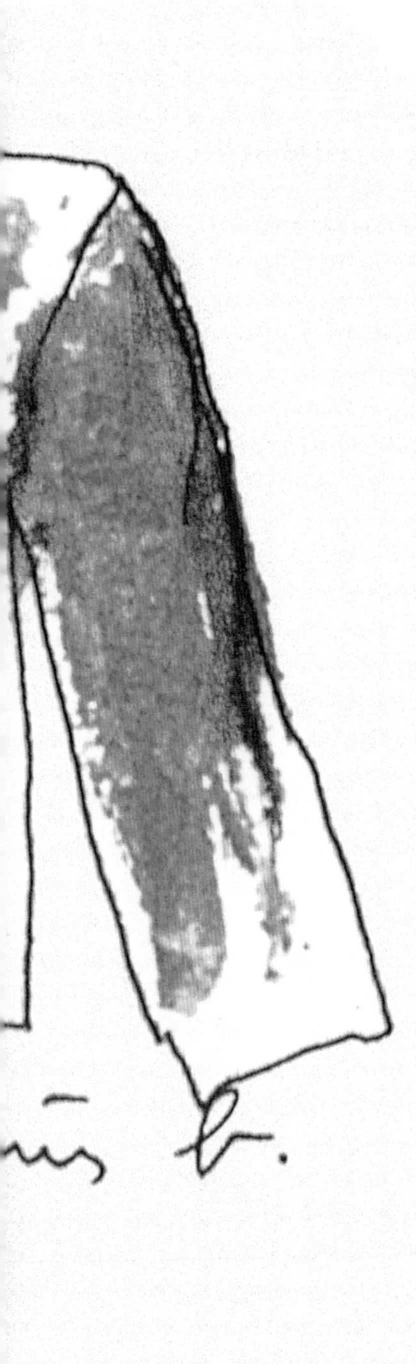

In the 1980s, I designed a cardigan for myself. I wanted to have a sweatshirt that was open in front, with lots of snap fasteners so that it would look like a Renaissance garment—children's clothing for grown-ups, or the other way round.

agnès b.

Previous pages: Whether layered, knotted or just plain casual, the T-shirt made the look of the 1980s.

Above: A T-shirt for Alan Parker's musical, *Fame*, in 1980.

Opposite: Combined for the very first time with a Chanel haute couture jacket, the T-shirt, worn here by model Inès de la Fressange, shook up many a haute taboo.

Armani created the Emporio Giorgio Armani line and launched a very beautiful T-shirt collection, while Thierry Mugler appropriated the graffiti fashion for his T-shirts. Among all those using the T-shirt, the Italian-born Franco Moschino, who formerly worked in advertising, injected a touch of irony by setting it up like a canvas on a wooden frame at a fashion show called "To Be or Not To Be."

At the height of the Falklands War, British designer Katharine Hamnett walked up to Mrs. Thatcher (whose war it very much was) in clothes that were nothing if not shocking—an oversized T-shirt flaunting the slogan: "98% of people don't want Pershings" (these being missiles fitted with nuclear warheads which had been sold to the British by the Reagan government, to the great satisfaction of the Iron Lady). In producing these clothes, her company was taking quite a risk: "When we made those T-shirts, it wasn't for the publicity, but because I felt genuinely concerned," said Hamnett in her book *London Fashion*.

Above the perennial merry-go-round of fashion, the 1980s were to lay the foundations for the decade to come by honoring a handful of Japanese designers in Paris, their intent being nothing less than to revolutionize the entire structure of the clothing industry.

STOP
ACID
RAIN

Christian Di
MONSIEUR
P. Assouline
prie M.
de lui faire le plaisir d'assister à la présentation de
la collection Printemps-Été 1988
le Vendredi 4 Septembre 1987 à 14 h 30
Palais des Études
École Nationale Supérieure des Beaux-Ar
14, rue Bonaparte, 75006 Paris
NINA RICCI
Défilé Printemps-été 2002
Ecole Nationale Supérieure des Beaux Arts
14, rue Bonaparte 75006 Paris
Mercredi 10 octobre 2001 à 19h00
Chloé
Collection Printemps /
Musée du petit pal
Défilé
Mercredi 11/10

The T-shirt invitation

The 1980s saw a revival of fashion. Once again, fashion was in fashion. Designers tried to outdo one another in imagination when presenting their collections, cat-walks and runways grew ever larger, and fashion shows turned into nothing less than major productions. In this setting of on-going creativity, the T-shirt would play a new role. As a surface for every manner of message, even the most fleeting, it would act as a playful invitation-card for ready-to-wear collections. This "wearable invitation-card" had the dual advantage of fitting nicely in any wardrobe and being impossible to leave behind the day of the event. This type of T-shirt is still much sought-after by collectors, who rank early invitation-card T-shirts among their "vin-tage" items.

Previous pages: In 1984, Peter Lindbergh launched an advertising campaign for London fashion designer Katharine Hamnet, famous for her oversized white T-shirts embellished with environmental and pacifist messages such as: "98% don't want Pershings" and "Stop Acid Rain."

Opposite: T-shirt invitations for haute couture shows.

Ricordo Di Firenze
éfilé 30-6-'95
DRIES VAN NOTEN
SUMMER
1996

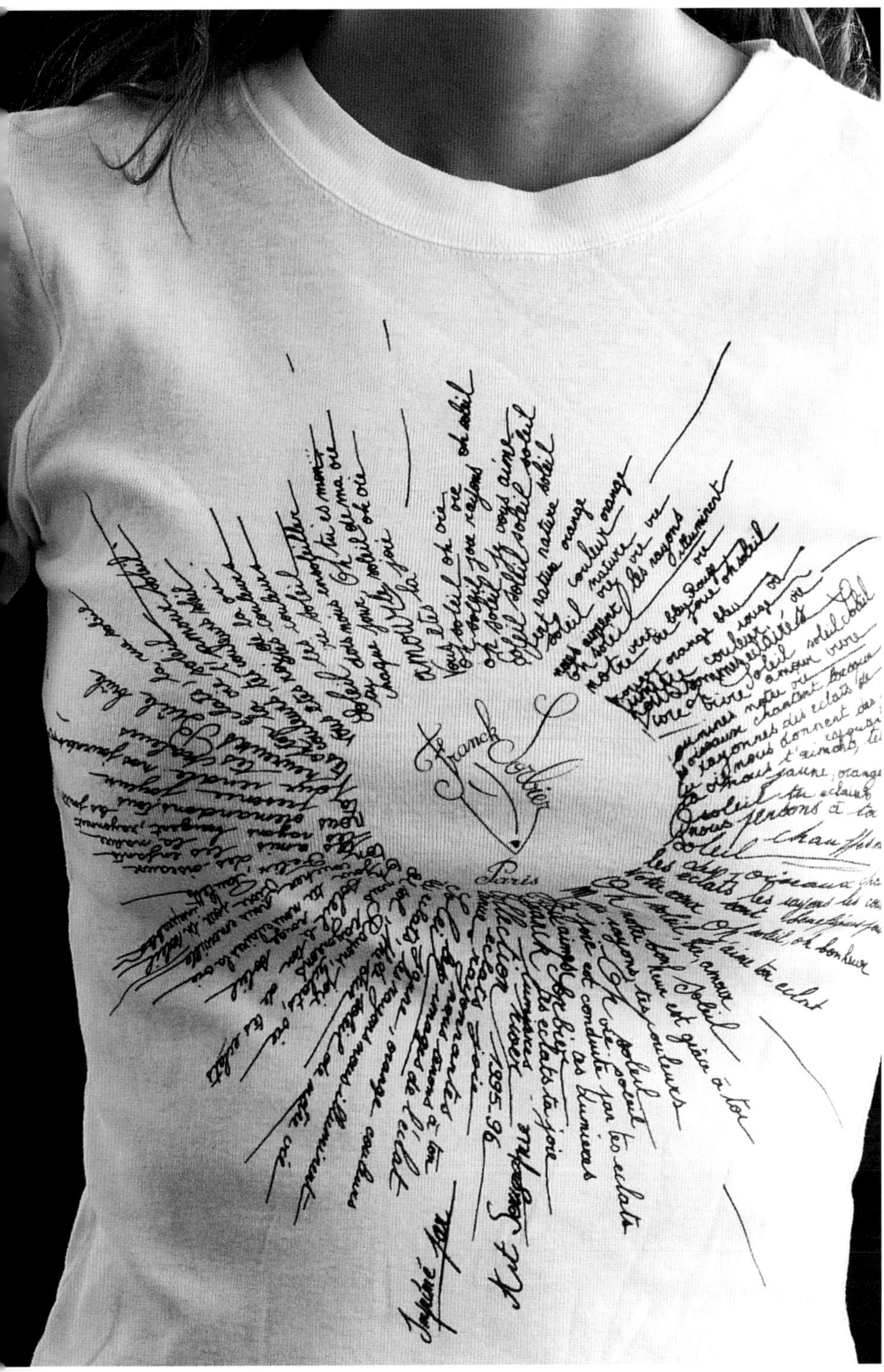

The 1990s

Previous pages, left: In 1996, Belgian fashion designer Dries van Noten used a T-shirt to announce his men's fashion show, staged outdoors at the Pitti Imagine Uomo in Milan. Previous pages, right:T-shirt invitation of French designer Franck Sorbier.

Opposite: Comme des Garçons, *Marie-Claire*, June 1994. Photograph by Jacques Olivar.

In order to have construction there must first be destruction. So it was that black—not the dinner-jacket black of high society evenings, or the grim, depressing black of the Punk and Gothic movements, but rather the absolute non-color black, with all its cerebral overtones—reemerged in those oddly stitched-together pieces putting in a bid for the status of clothing. The first among the Japanese designers to deconstruct the T-shirt was Yohji Yamamoto, who turned his T-shirt into his own personal uniform, while he gave his male customers a chance to wear white T-shirts with dark suits, thus inventing a new chic that would be a huge success. In the 1982-1983 autumn-winter season, for her Comme des Garçons brand, the most avant-garde of the Japanese designers, Rei Kawakubo, presented woolen sweaters full of holes over an asymmetrical T-shirt. The collection was deemed revolutionary, and rightly so. There was even talk of a "post-Hiroshima" look. Ten years later, Kawakubo would play around with asymmetry with T-shirts inspired by constructivism. Black, green and fuzzy orange then jockeyed for position in abstract geometric designs. For the "bosses" collection (spring/summer 1997), Comme des Garçons did away with hackneyed criteria of female beauty by rebuilding the body on new shapes and volumes. Did these tops with their padding filling out the neck still come under the category of T-shirts? Not far away, the T-shirt was enjoying a more classical career under the keen, observant eye of agnès b., who wore hers in the 1970s under a leather vest or waistcoat with black tights and pumps. Since then, her lighter sailor shirts have sported

seasonal shades: pastel pink and white, brick-red and grey, rasta red, yellow and green. The 1990s saw a serious financial crash, an upsurge of HIV/AIDS, the rack and ruin of many an 1980s master of the universe, the triumph of Puritan America over an Old World bogged down in recession and mere weariness. It was a decade that encouraged the individual to hunker down in clothes reduced to their essentials. From this moment on, all things functional topped the value chart, abbreviating the range of expression in fashion by several octaves. At times this development went hand in hand with a certain degree of violence, tinged with a philosophical brand of pessimism. At the beginning of this new age, Martin Margiela, one of the Belgian designers who was a source of inspiration for the vogue of black, was first to come up with punkoid T-shirts. For the summer of 1990 he presented T-shirts made with plastic supermarket bags—this recycling spirit would become his trademark. Eight years later, he produced oversized tank-tops worn like a shirtfront, with a simple elastic fastener behind.

In this period, Belgium did indeed shine forth in the fashion world, but the dictates of the most blindly followed designers now hailed from New York and from Milan, where Giorgio Armani—a slightly older designer focusing on younger people—posed for all the world's photographers in a black or navy blue T-shirt, revealing bulging biceps. In his men's fashion shows, the Great Deconstructor promoted the style of the T-shirt worn under a suit with neither padding nor lining. Fashion minimalism was born: "Like anything, the most important element for me is the choice of fabrics and materials. They can range from simple pure cottons to precious cashmere and technical rayons. I tend to choose colors that I have based on nature, so tones normally range from white, blue, sand, stone and ruby, to green and earth." Ecology and recycling were hot topics and found their way to the showrooms. The organic cotton T-shirt also made its appearance. For his summer 2001 Armani Jeans collection, Giorgio Armani would even push his aesthetic sense to the point of making T-shirts in organic materials like cotton, hemp and flax with biodegradable buttons, labels and stitching.

In this mad dash for spareness, the T-shirt reverted to its original calling—a simple undergarment that highlighted the body beneath—as originally established in the land of its birth. For the designer Calvin Klein, who built his empire on a line of jeans and underpants, single-handedly put the erotic back into the plain white undergarments. In

Opposite: Calvin Klein Jeans, an epitome of chic & sexy leisure wear. Spring-Summer 2001 T-shirt, photographed by Inez Lamsweerde and Vinoodh Matadin.

Next pages: Marithé et François Girbaud spring/summer 1996 show.

the early 1980s, he successfully sold a variety of undershirts, crew- and V-neck, and simple athletic shirts and tank tops. As illustrated by photographer Bruce Weber, tanned demi-gods with their painstakingly sculpted muscles enhanced the spotless white of signed athletic shirts—which would soon be adapted to female bodies. The designer declared: "I think there's something incredibly sexy about a woman wearing her boyfriend's T-shirt and underwear." As underwear, the CK T-shirt would become one of the major icons of minimalism. The third founding father of this new trend, the Austrian Helmut Lang, had not yet emigrated to New York. When he did, he created the clingy undershirt and the stretch T-shirt which the whole world would then copy. Mr. Lang, who was way ahead of his time, had actually focused on the white T-shirt in his very first collection, because, as he says, "it's the only piece of clothing that adapts to your desires. It is at certain times an undergarment, at others an outer garment, and it changes with habits and seasons."

At the other end of the spectrum from grim minimalism, the Italians were playing the sexy high-tech card. For men, Gianni Versace came up with the synthetic, glittering football shirts. In 2001, following Gianni's murder in Florida, his sister Donatella would take up the torch by presenting a close-fitting T-shirt made of "scotchgard."

At the beginning of the decade, Dolce & Gabbana, who hailed respectively from Lombardy and Sicily, flooded the whole world with glamorous T-shirts, first shown on

Page 228: Clockwise from top right: Paco Rabanne, ready-to-wear spring/summer 2000. Helmut Lang, spring/summer 1999. Anne Demeulemeester ready-to-wear spring/summer 2001. Moschino printemps-été 2001.

Page 229 : Jean Colonna, spring/summer 2001.

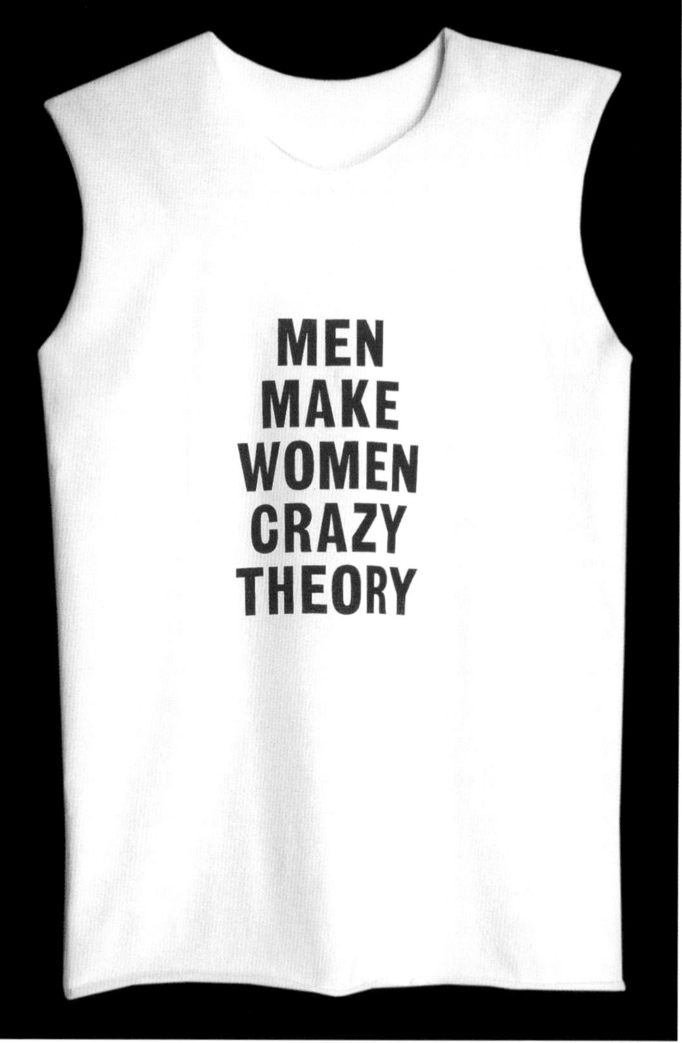

Opposite: APC has come up with many different links between fashion, music, and even film. Here, a summer 2001 sleeveless T-shirt bearing the title of Zoe Cassavetes' first film *Men Make Women Crazy Theory*.

Right: Thierry Mugler, spring/summer 2000 show.

runways in macho versions worn under a classic striped suit. A sexy look, yes, but one with a sense of humor. In 1995, a long-sleeved white version for men flaunted the striped wording: "The Rock Sex Symbol." The designer explained it thus: "For us, the T-shirt is a democratic item of clothing. The simple cut means that we can play with designs and decorations and materials to create a garment that's both comfortable and elegant, functional and glamorous. The main thing is for the proportions to stay balanced." For their women's 2001 spring-summer collection, they produced a T-shirt bearing the image of Madonna (so

SONIA RYKIEL
Celebrity
PARIS 15.10.98

Chic or scruffy.
Too tight or too big.
Graphic or theatrical
Written on, covered with imitation jewelry, full of holes, covered with sequins and glitter, flock printed or hip BoBo*.
Pop Emotion or decorated, embroidered, striped.
Red lips, gold Beetle, or green apples.
Like jeans, T-shirts are objects of desire for teenagers, BoBos, snobs, Men, Women, Everybody.

Sonia Rykiel

* Bourgeois Bohemian

Sonia Rykiel has been making T-shirts with a message since the 1970s. Adorned with words like "Champion" and "Artist," the "queen of knitwear" was still playing around with words for her summer 1998 collection with very VIP long-sleeve T-shirts.

Above: Castelbajac, men's ready-to-wear, summer 2002.

Opposite: Gabriel Martinez and Malin Person for Dolce & Gabbana. Fall/winter 2001-2002.

sought after that there are still 300 names on the waiting-list), as well as deconstructed versions, cut and then put back together again using safety pins, or else made with mesh, gauze or stretch cotton.

Paris had been upstaged by Milan, but the Parisians still didn't give up on their T-shirts. In 1992, Karl Lagerfeld signed his Chanel athletic shirt with two interlocking "C"s. Two years later, in 1994, the designer combined his ladies' suits with long-sleeved Petit Bateau T-shirts. From that moment on, lingerie embarked on its great comeback and underwear was worn as outerwear. The underlying retro trends propelled Petit Bateau-wear to the rank of fashion icon. That same year, sales of long-sleeved T-shirts increased a thousandfold. It was Sharon Stone who offered an example of the new elegance the following year when she sported a basic Gap stretch T-shirt over a Valentino skirt for the Oscars ceremony in Hollywood.

Henceforth, completely liberated from the narrow category of sportswear, the T-shirt was also paired with a dinner jacket or tuxedo, and with a skirt as an evening gown. As the designer for Chloé from 1997 to 2001, Stella McCartney—daughter of that most gifted of Beatles—gave the T-shirt a glamorous, off-beat image. Every season it is her latest take on the T-shirt that is the most eagerly awaited item. Just a month after delivery of their orders, retailers consistently find themselves out of stock. (It's true, of course, that Chloé restricted production runs to around 4,500 items.) Although the designer failed to obtain authorization from *Playboy* for a sequined T-shirt bearing the famous Bunny, her 2000-2001 spring collection nevertheless managed to turn a rejection into a tremendously acclaimed and successful image: the famous bunny transmogrified into a skull.

Debbie
Debbie
Debbie
D&G
DOLCE & GABBANA

For the Dolce & Gabbana spring/summer 2001 women's collection, we produced T-shirts emblazoned with the image of Madonna, and these turned out to be nothing less than a cultural phenomenon. Madonna is actually one of the most important icons of the last few decades, and our tribute to her image instantly aroused the interest of the press all over the world. From all the versions presented at fashion shows, and drawing our inspiration from the rock star herself, we chose just two for production and distribution—the T-shirt with the *Ray of Light* cover, and the one with the *Music* cover. We made a particularly elaborate version of this latter T-shirt with embroidery and Swarowski crystals, which was only produced to order in an edition of about 200.

Domenico Dolce
Stefano Gabbana

MISS
KISS

LIKE
A
VIRGIN

HOLIDAY

GIRL

Above: Penelope Cruz wearing Ralph Lauren's "Pink Pony" T-shirt.

Opposite: Dolce & Gabbana greet Naomi Klein's book *No Logo* with mockery.

Next pages, left: Donatella Versace and Naomi Campbell.
Next pages, right: Mary J. Blige in 1999.

Logomania

Up until the early 1970s, brand logos were hidden away on labels inside the shirt. By the end of that decade, however, first the Lacoste crocodile and then the Ralph Lauren polo player began to make their appearance on the front of sports shirts. Calvin Klein came hot on their heels in the mid-1980s, putting his label on the back pocket of his signature jeans and then on the elastic band of his famous underpants. This was an instant success. By the end of the 1980s, acronyms, initials and logos besieged T-shirts. This logomania was a major cause of the explosion of a worldwide industry based on pirating and fakes (it currently accounts for a staggering 7% of the world's multitrillion-dollar GDP). "At the root of plagiarism lies admiration and love," remarked Gabrielle Chanel in philosophical mode, presaging the flood of fake Chanel T-shirts that has flourished since the 1980s. The T-shirt is the cheapest article of clothing there is. In southeast Asia, T-shirts cost a mere 25¢, while brand originals are sold for no less than $75. Pirating techniques are extremely straightforward: all you need to do is flock-print the brand name or initials on a basic white T-shirt. Fashion is highly coded, and has also undergone its share of witty (mis)appropriations and send-ups. Fashion victims sacrifice their idols by wearing shirts emblazoned with "Claude Monotone," "Fairy Mugler," "Jean-Paul Goat Yeah," "Martine Shitbon," and "Has been Alaïa." And in the early 1990s, Yves Saint Laurent and Gucci, each in their turn, fell victim to their own success. Their signatures were pirated loud and clear on T-shirts, like so many fake trophies, along with sports logos such as Nike, Adidas and Reebok.

D&G
NO LOGO

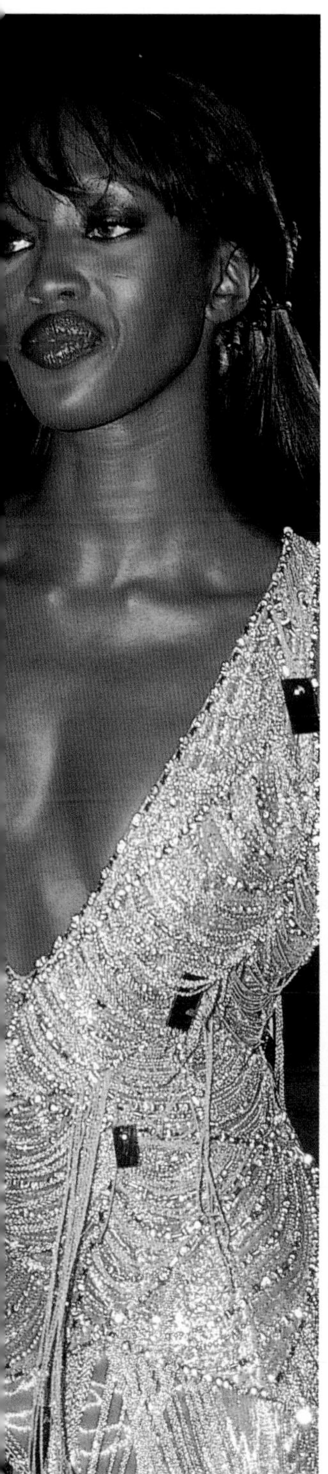

Today's T-shirt is a standard, a banner and a manifesto, a subtitle and a visiting card—almost an ID card. It proclaims loud and clear what people are thinking deep down. It's like an extremely private skin; it is cut and scratched, tattooed and painted, all to become customized. Whatever else they may do, people never put on a T-shirt just like that—thoughtlessly. Form is every bit as important as content. Everyone wants it to have ideal proportions, as well as an ideal cut and texture, because the T-shirt extends, rebalances and magnifies our shapes and sizes. But I don't recognize any fetishes in them, even if I usually wear those that are overdyed and printed with a red cross from a certain surplus store in London, and even if I've been fond of designing for causes like Act Up and AIDS.

Christian Lacroix

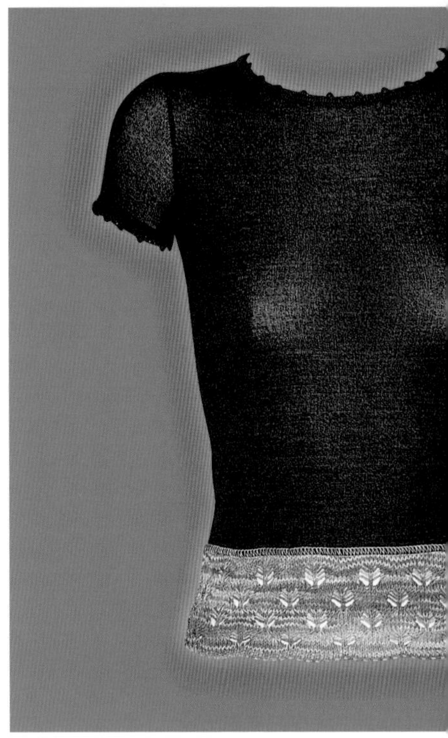

The designer T-shirt

After establishing itself as a classic clothing item among most fashion designers, the T-shirt has crossed over into luxury land. The undershirt has managed to win over the most traditional of houses: in the Hermès men's wear, it crops up in a version made of a light-colored reindeer skin, while Cerruti has produced one made of silver mink. The most respectable of fashion houses have now taken over this mundane piece of clothing and invested it with the spirit of their collections. Basking in the glow of prestige and the glamour of designer labels, the T-shirt has become a universally desired object, an ambassador for name brands. Customers will readily spend more than $150 to purchase this most desirable of trends. All the more so because, in luxury ready-to-wear collections, the T-shirt is still the most affordable item; and it often gets the most media coverage. Nowadays, when worn of an evening under a dinner jacket or tuxedo, or over a long skirt, the luxury T-shirt deals a blow to seasonal schedules. At Christian Dior, one of the house must-haves is suitable for summer and winter wear. But the T-shirt has also managed to invade haute couture runways as a one-off item. For summer 2001, John Galliano called on the services of Parisian manufacturers of costume jewelry and accessories when creating, for Dior, a T-shirt adorned with Coca-Cola bottles, hearts and crosses, entirely embroidered over with beads from the Lesage workshops. What's more, the couturier has adopted the habit of taking styles from the haute couture line, simplifying them and making them available for the ready-to-wear collections. Jean Paul Gaultier was admitted to this inner sanctum of design in 1997, but this didn't mean that he turned his back on his own fetish item. On the contrary—and more than anyone else—he managed to lend it the dream-like dimensions of finery. For summer 2002, this designer produced an embroidered model in flesh-colored tulle, embroidered with a constellation of imitation jewelry and black jade beads. For the same season, the eccentric Russian twosome, Seredin and Vassiliev, introduced the T-shirt in a surrealist vision—huge iridescent beetles seemingly devouring a white T-shirt.

Above: Pierre Balmain, ready-to-wear, spring/summer 2000.

Opposite: Chanel, spring/summer 1992.

Next pages, from left to right: Yohji Yamamoto spring/summer 2002; Comme des Garçons ; Gianfranco Ferré; John Galliano for Dior.

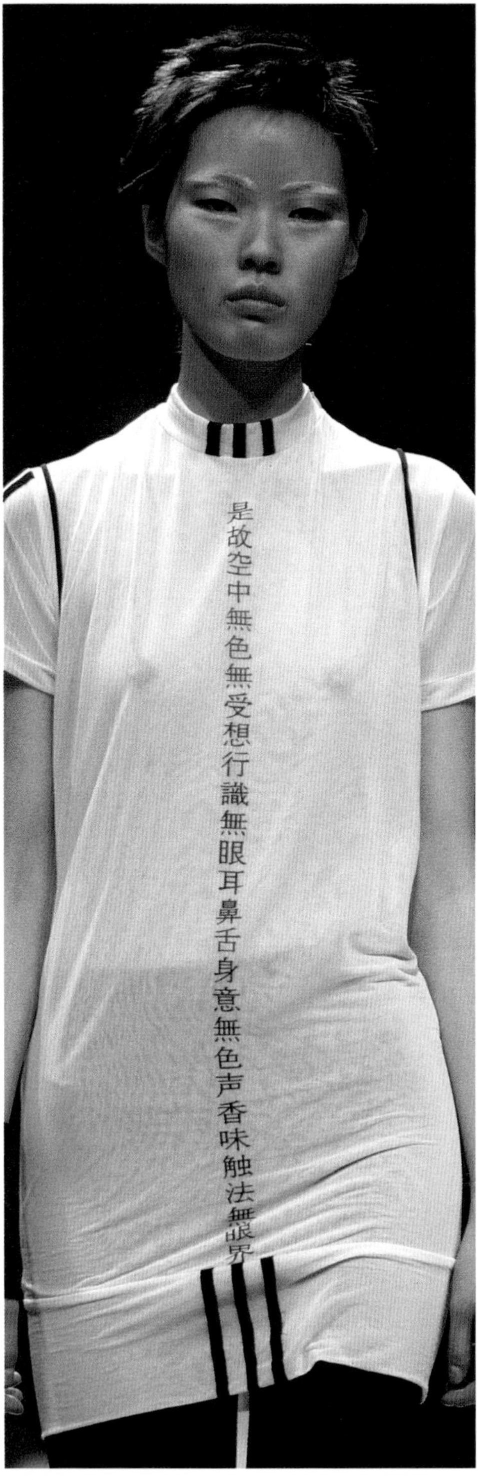

KUSAMA
YAYOI
KUSAMA

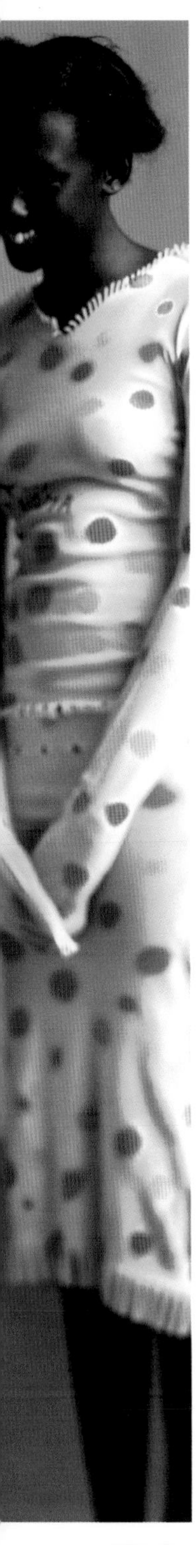

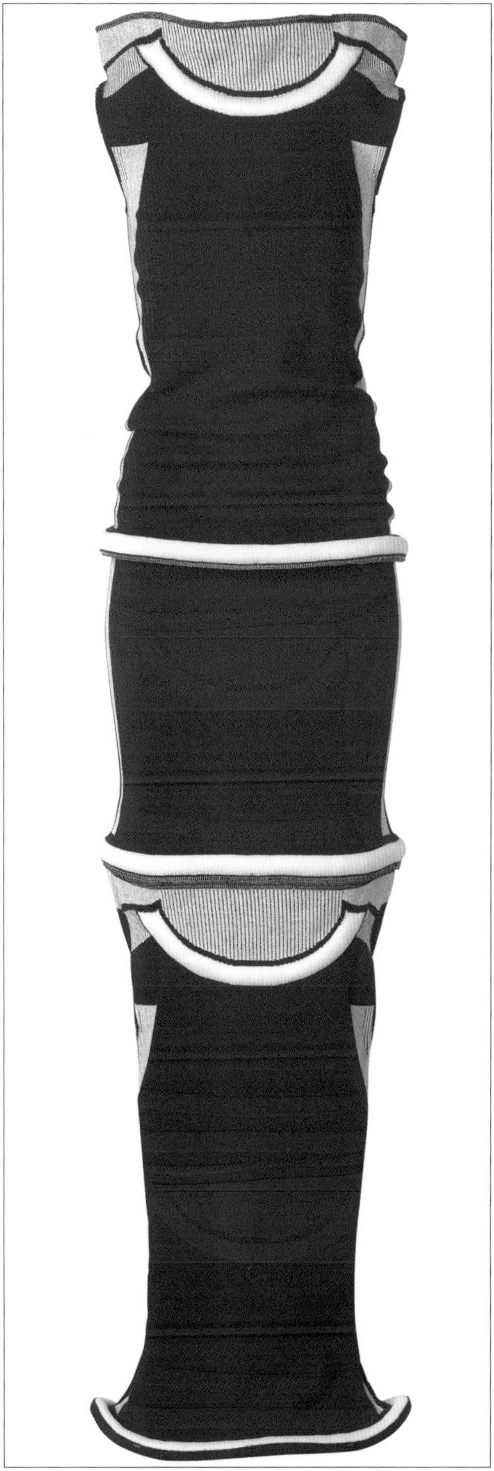

Left: Creations by Japanese artist Yayoi Kusama.

Right: Issey Miyake and Dai Fujiwara came up with the A-POC (A Piece of Cloth) concept in 1999, enabling them to produce an item of clothing from a single piece of fabric. Its computer-generated shape is made directly in the fabric without any stitching and can be altered at will.

Opposite: A Céline athletic shirt, worn by the top model Gisele Bundchen. Spring 2001 ready-to-wear collection.

Basic

Once adopted by fashion, the T-shirt saw its shape, form, color and decoration change, depending on the season. Yet, from as far back as the 1930s, the classic white T-shirt—then an undergarment—has remained a must. It has survived decade after decade without becoming dated, and it has established itself as the essential garment in any wardrobe. To emphasize its timeless nature, Americans call it "basic." "The white T-shirt is like the basic shape of everything above the waistline. It is the only piece that accomplishes whatever purpose you want it for, as an underwear or outerwear piece, according to season and use," explained designer Helmut Lang in 1998 to the *Daily News Record*. Besides white, the spectrum of this classic item also encompasses grey, back and navy blue. It owes its fame—and fortune—to two mythical brands: Hanes and Fruit of the Loom, whose T-shirts come in vacuum-packed sets of three. In the 1970s, the mood was more for a wide range of colors and shapes, but the following decade rediscovered the white T-shirt of the 1950s. At the same time as the bomber jacket and Levi 501s, it was thus admitted to the very exclusive club of basics. At an early stage, the Gap did its utmost to make this garment something indispensable, elevating it to the quintessence of the relaxed American style. Launched in 1984, the pocket-T, a symbol of simplicity, is still one of the brand's cult styles. In Europe, Benetton established itself as one of the kings of basics. In the early

Above: A Braille Benetton T-shirt.

Opposite: Design by Xavier Ricolfi and Stéphanie Moisan. In the dark, this T-shirt displays "on," "off," or both at once, and through a system of small stainless steel pieces shows off signs of femininity, masculinity or both.

1990s, against a background of economic recession, fashion went back to the values of simplicity and authenticity. The classic T-shirt really came into its own in the minimalist climate, vying in terms of spare lines and neutral shades. Calvin Klein, Donna Karan and Giorgio Armani were the apostles of this at once luxurious and casual style which would take over even in the world of work, with the introduction of Friday wear. From then on, it was okay to wear a basic T-shirt to the office—it could just as well be a Gap or a Ralph Lauren—under a jacket with khaki trousers. In 1998, sales of white T-shirts went through the roof in the United States—Hanes alone recorded double-digit growth. But if it is still the symbol of democratic clothing, not all white T-shirts are created equal. Among designers, the cotton has to be of the highest quality, the neckline more elegant, and the sleeves more anatomically designed. And all of this helps to explain price differences—$50 for an Armani T-shirt, $2.50 for a Fruit of the Loom.

the practice
you like
the sex
you want
ON
ON OFF
T.U
one
size
coton
100%
cotton
XAVIER RICOLFI
by
STEPHANIE MOISAN
ON

The striped T-shirt

As the fetish garment of designers Jean Paul Gautier and agnès b., and the uniform of upper-middle-class types, the striped T-shirt has become a classic item in the unisex wardrobe. In 1858, the French navy adopted it as the official clothing for its sailors and sea dogs. Fifty years later, it embarked on its civilian career, clothing Breton fishermen, who would slip one underneath their navy-blue jerseys when the weather turned a tad too cold. In the roaring 20s, it was the hallmark of the new elegance in sportswear, embodied by Coco Chanel. Soon, artists vacationing on the French Riviera, like Picasso and Dalí, adopted the seafaring style before it became a fashion phenomenon in St.Tropez in the 1950s. While Parisian students in T-shirts protested against the established order in May 1968, slinging cobblestones at riot police, the T-shirt cropped up in China, worn beneath the Maoist jacket. Ten years later, you could find it neatly arrayed on shelves in the chain of boutiques owned by designer Agnès b., who offered it in a whole palette of new colors (every season, the line is given between 15 and 18 new shades). Jean Paul Gaultier, who has made the striped T-shirt the symbol of his ready-to-wear line, for boys or girls, men or women, he even produced it in a furry version for his very first haute couture collection in 1997, before turning it into a box for his mens' perfume, aptly named "Le Mâle."

Opposite: The artist Maurizio Cattelan's art work of Picasso wearing his famous striped T-shirt, Emmanuel Perrotin gallery, 1999.

MYTHOLOGY

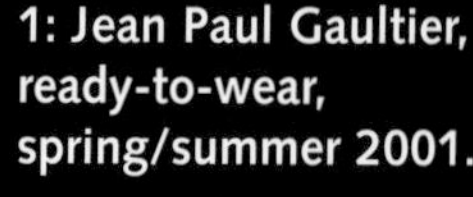

1: Jean Paul Gaultier, ready-to-wear, spring/summer 2001.

2: Gondoliere in Venice.

3: Emporio Armani Woman, spring/summer 2002.

4: An ad for Jean Paul Gaultier's cologne for men, Le Mâle.

CHAPTER 10

The ego's representative

The triumphant minimalism of the 1990s veiled people's personalities in beige, grey and black basics. As the third millennium dawned, the T-shirt found its tongue again, and became the reflection of the person wearing it. Basic white for Bruce Springsteen, striped for Jean Paul Gaultier. T-shirts were promoted to fetish status by celebrities, identifying particular personalities, and putting their signature to styles and looks. Well removed from political messages, advertising slogans and anonymous logomania, the T-shirt is still the ideal mouthpiece of a contemporary mood. Since the 1980s, it has allowed a new generation of men to give a different kind of expression to their professional image. Nowadays, one often comes across people wearing suits and T-shirts in the worlds of fashion, communications and new technologies. The T-shirt is replacing the traditional shirt with a more casual, sexier, yet still elegant version. The T-shirt has become everyone's personal (and custom-made) medium. Because it is universal and adaptable, it straightforwardly expresses moods, commemorates events in people's private lives, and fuels the "me" cult. The film of our life now files past in a T-shirt. Once a symbol of mass consumerism, this item of clothing is associated nowadays with things exceptional and unique. T-shirt fans scour stores in search of an old classic at the ends of the earth—that is, when they're not putting in bids at online auctions in the hope of buying some rare gem. Now produced in limited editions, sometimes even numbered like

Tom Ford, creative director for Gucci and Yves Saint Laurent Rive Gauche.

works of art, the T-shirt tends at times to forget its democratic origins to satisfy the whims of a handful of people forever seeking out something to give them a special cachet. At a time when the craze for vintage things has the ghosts of bygone fashion parading past us, for better or for worse, T-shirts are exhuming the dozing figures of kitsch and pop culture and elevating them to iconic status. Whether tattered and torn, bedecked with zippers and imitation jewelry, or scribbled on with graffiti and slogans, the customized T-shirt now mixes ancient and modern, old and new, transforming it into that special, one-off article, sanctioned by fashion. Hot on the heels of this trend, the major brands are striving to give their products a human touch. Far from flaunting impersonal logos, T-shirts are now being covered with graffiti and adorned with drawings and designs, imitating the old, traditional crafted look, the better to portray a kind of heart and soul. As a reminder of the past and a snapshot of the present, the 21st century T-shirt has something spiritual about it.

Opposite: Japanese designer Yohji Yamamoto, 1992.

Below: Milanese designer Giorgio Armani.

T-shirt looks

In the worlds of fashion and music, the T-shirt has managed to find high-profile ambassadors who have helped earn it its fame and fortune. The fashion designer Giorgio Armani has beautifully illustrated the elegance of this garment by turning it into his official attire. "A dark blue or white T-shirt has long become part of my working uniform...I literally live in T-shirts, because I appreciate the comfort, enjoy the luxurious materials they are made of, and feel confident wearing them in any situation, whether it be for work, sport, relaxation, or an evening out," explains the maestro of Milan. His French counterpart, Jean Paul Gaultier, has also turned the striped sailor's T-shirt into his signature look. On one famous occasion when the two of them met, both designers played on this image by symbolically swapping their

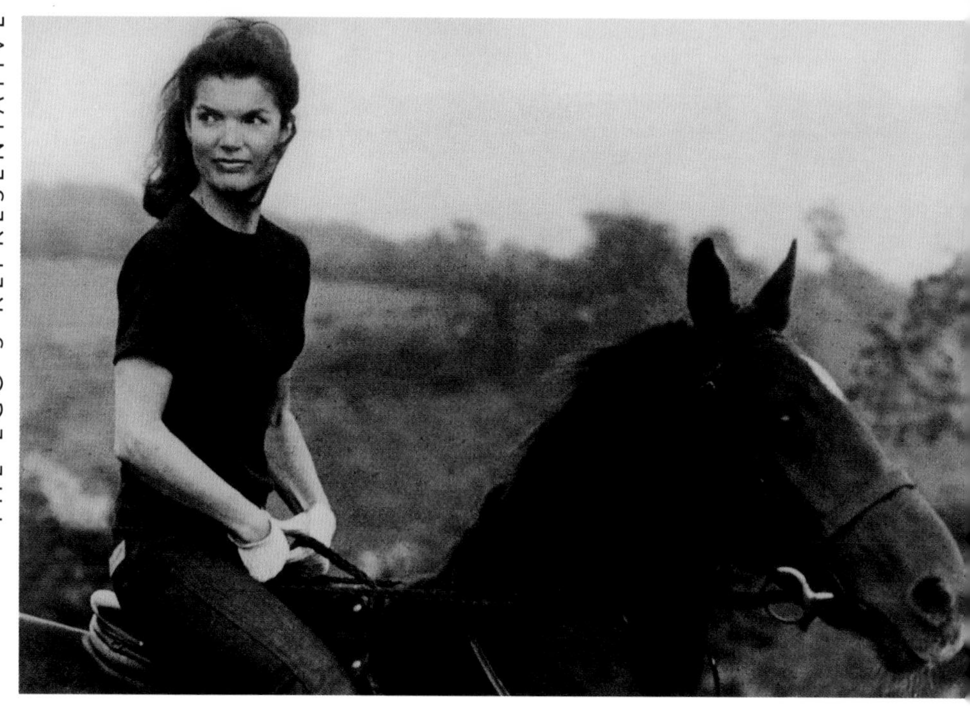

Above: Jackie Kennedy Onassis in 1968.

Opposite: Jane Birkin in Cannes, she has remained faithful to this look since the 1970s.

Next pages, left: John Galliano wearing his "Who's afraid John Galliano" T-shirt, with Naomi Campbell in 1994.

Next pages, right: Jean Paul Gaultier and his signature striped T-shirt, 1994.

fetishistic T-shirts in front of a horde of camera lenses. Wearing a T-shirt and dark jacket, Gucci and Yves Saint Laurent Rive Gauche artistic director Tom Ford plays the role of the *éminence grise* of fashion, and embodies the graphic aesthetics of both houses with an all-black look. This style is diametrically opposed to that of the eccentric John Galliano, who doesn't have any qualms about swapping his pirate shirts, plunging, as they do, way down the chest, for more colorful T-shirts. Declaring "Jimi Hendrix" and "Who's afraid of John Galliano?," switching from icon to self-parody, the T-shirt can be tailored to every kind of wisecrack. In music, likewise, it has immortalized certain looks. In the pared-down vein, Bruce Springsteen has immortalized the T-shirt in the "working-class hero" style. On the cover of his *Born in the USA* LP, the singer poses with his back toward us, wearing a white T-shirt, jeans and biker boots with a red bandanna in his pocket. More recently, Madonna has swapped Jean Paul Gaultier's sharp-breasted bustiers for a new kind of sartorial barb: the T-shirt bearing a sexual message. Most strikingly of all, though, the provocative singer has managed to personalize the T-shirt by having her son's name—"Rocco"— written on it, and asking Dolce & Gabbana to customize especially for her a Britney Spears fan-club T-shirt with safety pins.

WHO'S
AFRAID O
N GALLIA

A personal medium

"The personalization process has championed a crucial yardstick—the criterion of personal achievement. [...] However, something else is at stake: the desire for self-expression, whatever the nature of the 'message' might be, and the narcissistic right and pleasure to express oneself for no particular reason, but relayed and magnified by a medium" (Gilles Lipovetsky, *The Age of Emptiness: Essays on Contemporary Individualism*). The T-shirt is probably the ideal medium for giving public vent to one's ego. In 2001, in order to personalize their messages, the English team behind Company C+P even decorated their basic T-shirt with a piece of Velcro complete with a set of letters, making it possible for the wearer to display his or her thoughts and feelings. As we are reminded by fashion designer Sonia Rykiel: "...printed words stir our imagination and tickle our curiosity, they're a gesture made toward the other, a cry that says 'me.' The message-bearing T-shirt is a way of revealing or expressing yourself, an anecdote, a way of not being altogether like other people." These days, fashion is reverting to its nonconformist, subversive origins in the 1960s and 1970s but with a twist, using messages that are more in the vein of glamorous irony. The American brand E-vil brought the Sex Pistols' famous "God Save the Queen" slogan back into vogue, and has since been exploring fashion's potential for wittiness—and bad taste—using actual

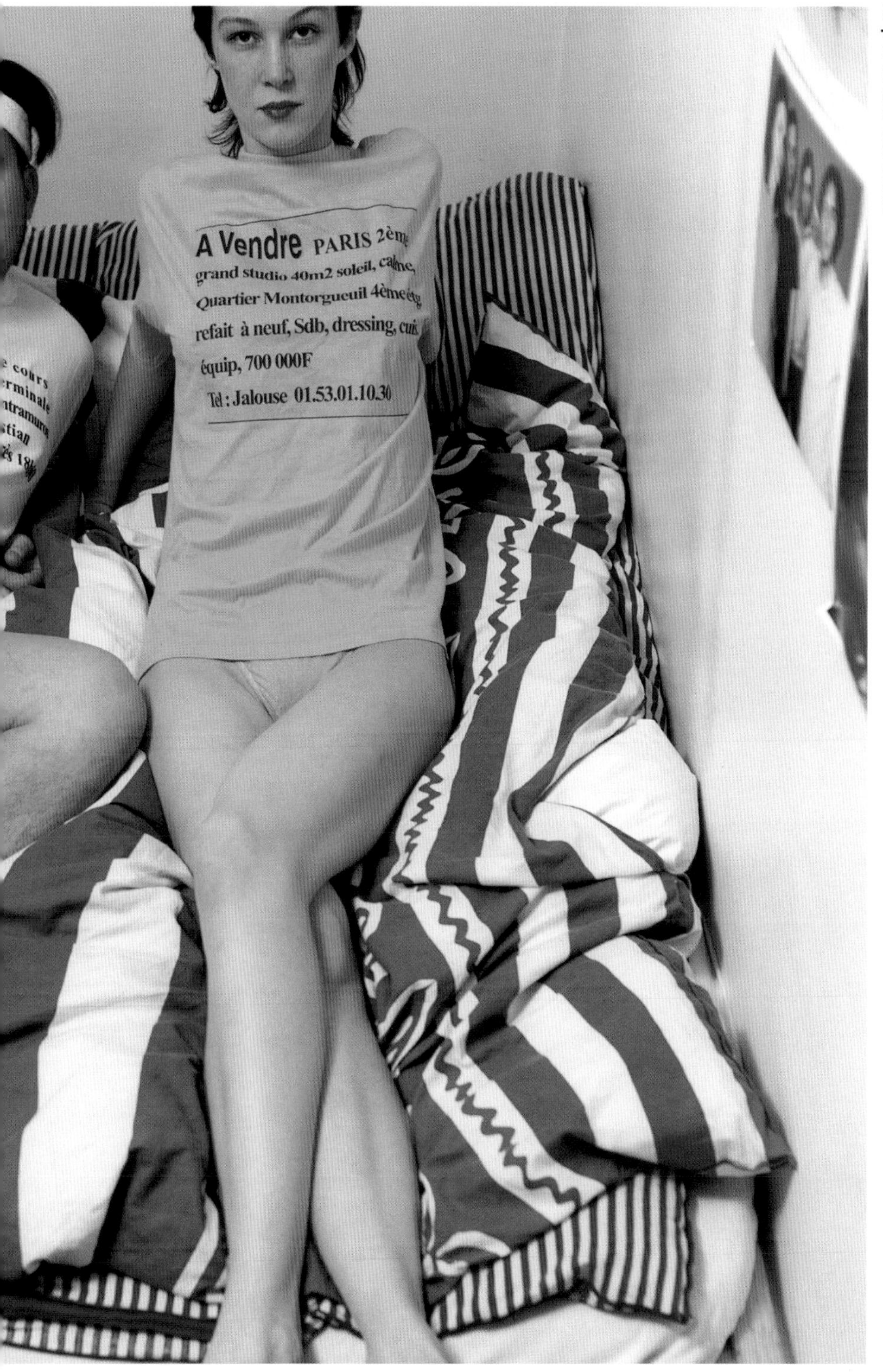
A Vendre PARIS 2èm
grand studio 40m2 soleil,
Quartier Montorgueuil 4ème
refait à neuf, Sdb, dressing,
équip, 700 000F
Tel : Jalouse 01.53.01.10.30

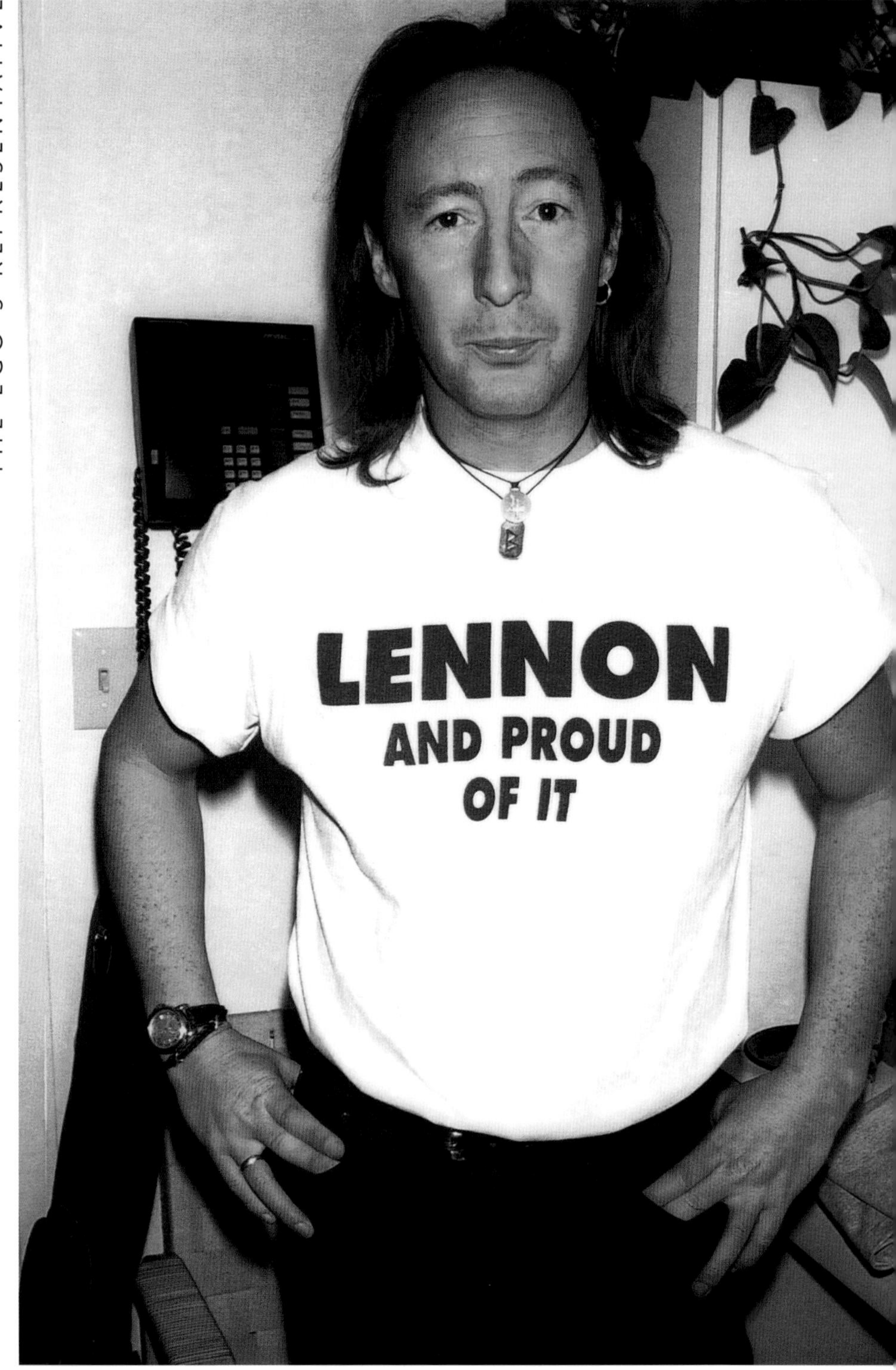
LENNON
AND PROUD
OF IT

ROCCO

À 28 ANS,
IL HABITE
TOUJOURS
CHEZ SES
PARENTS

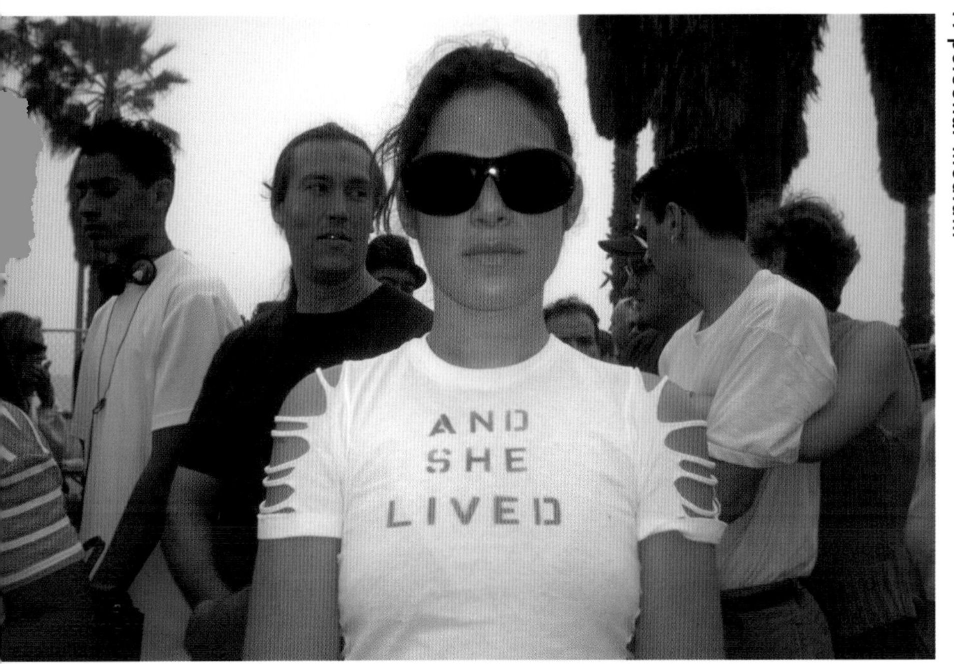

Pages 266 and 267: In 2001, Orélie and Miguel printed their classified ads on their T-shirts.

Previous pages, left: Julian Lennon, in 1999. Previous pages, right: Madonna wears a T-shirt with her son's name at a concert in London.

Above: Example of a custom-made T-shirt.

Opposite: At 28, he still lives with his parents.

fashion clichés. So, depending on your mood, you can wear a "This is a Drag" T-shirt, or one declaring "This is a Monster," or you can display across your chest, "I love chaos" and on your back "I hate confusion," or alternatively you can sport a string of stereotypes like: "Paparazzi, pornography, superman, heavy metal, rock 'n' roll, superstar." The icons of international pop culture are also being sacked for a new remix. The Kulte brand is looking for an alternative to Zara uniforms and coming up with T-shirts which borrow, and at the same time update, imagery from generation X cult films and series. For example, a Starsky & Hutch T-shirt or, in the spirit of the Hell's Angels, a skull wearing a hat.

I am the
BOSS

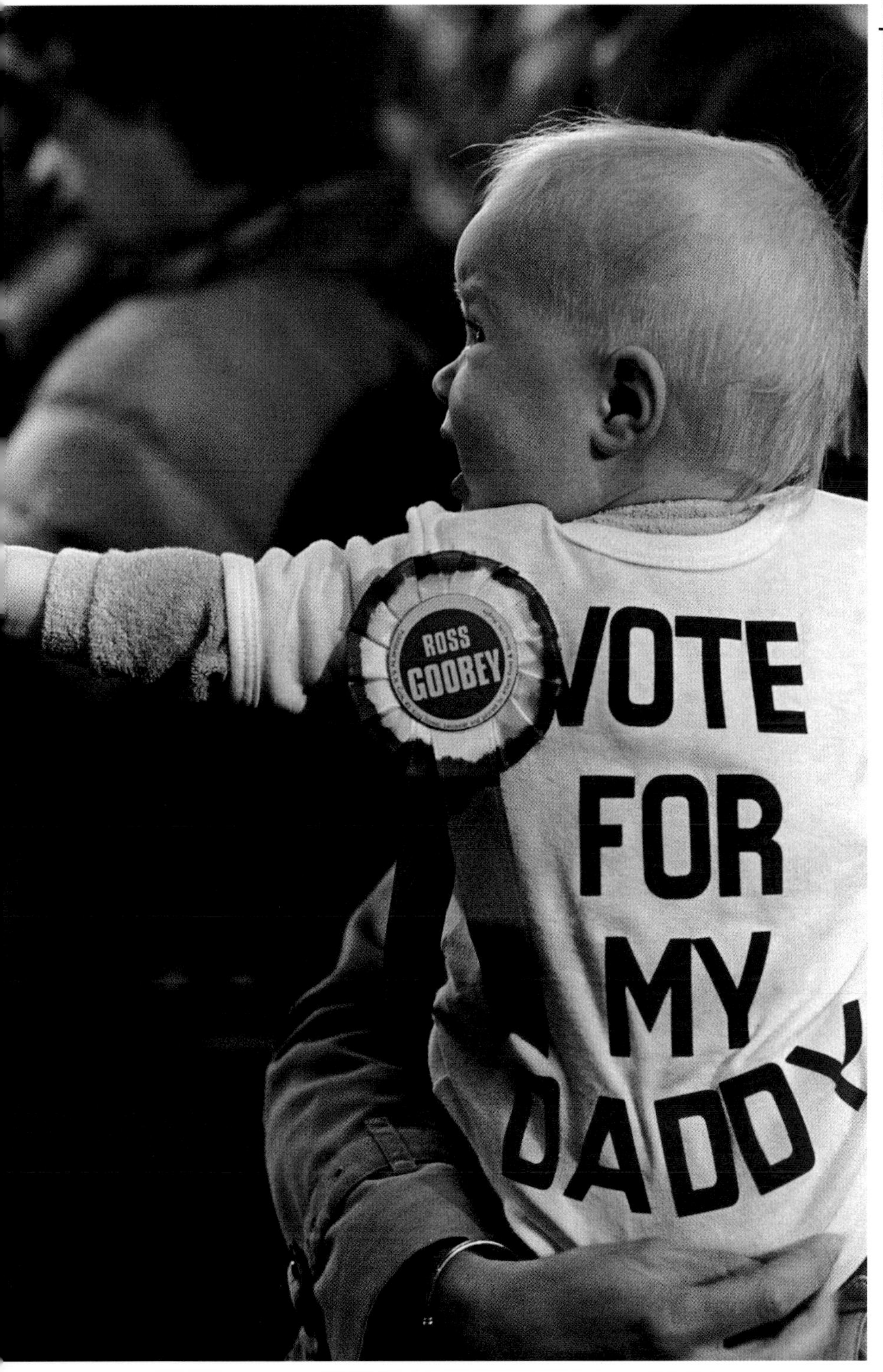
ROSS
GOOBEY
VOTE
FOR
MY
DADDY

ANARCHY
IN THE U.K.
SEX PISTOLS

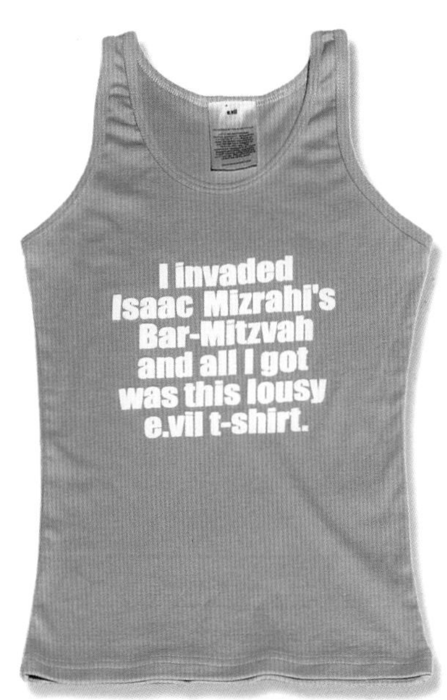

Previous pages, left: A Somali soldier in 1993. Previous pages, right: A young English boy urging people to vote for his dad, in 1979.

Above: E-vil T-shirt.

Left: A "Sex Pistols" collector.

Vintage and collector's items

When produced in limited editions, the T-shirt strives to transcend its image as a mass-consumer product. Unlike the Gap model which crops up all over the world, the limited-edition T-shirt is intent on becoming a collector's item, a rare article satisfying the desires of a clientele looking for something unusual and one-of-a-kind. The T-shirt is consequently borrowing from art codes, focusing its production on the manufacture of limited lines. Creative fashion design is becoming more particular and specific, and the idea of luxury is coming full-circle, back to its original calling—to remain aloof from the mainstream. At APC, French Touch sweatshirts, adorned with original silkscreened designs by graphic artists Alexandre Courtès and Abäke, target a handful of members of the "happy few" club. No more than 250 fans of Air, Daftpunk and Phoenix managed to purchase these collector's items. Based on the example of gallery shows, T-shirts from 20 fashion designers, including Vivienne Westwood, Paul Smith, Roberto Cavalli and Michael Kors for Céline, were shown in September 2001 at the Concept Store gallery run by Jean-Charles de Castelbajac. *Dealer de Luxe* magazine, the mastermind behind this project, had given the gallery a free hand. Just as The Little Prince asked: "draw me a sheep," *Dealer* asked certain designers: "Make me a T-shirt."

overdose.

sunshine
makes me
high.

Previous pages: Customized T-shirt, front and back.

Opposite: Designer Jeremy Scott's T-shirt.

Below: Customized T-shirt.

Next pages: T-shirt for the "Fuck me I'm Famous" party at the Bains Douches club in Ibiza, 2001.

Junko Shimada has incorporated a bra in his T-shirts, while Christian Lacroix has turned them into a kind of readymade. The vintage T-shirt also emphasizes the wish for authenticity and personalization. In the United States, Lara Flynn Boyle's appearance at the 2000 Golden Globe Awards ceremony in a vintage Bob Seger T-shirt, bedecked with 3,000 strass studs, under a black tuxedo made quite an impression on the assembled gathering. For winter 2000, the comeback of punk and the trash rock 'n' roll spirit brought old Led Zeppelin, Kiss and Guns 'n' Roses T-shirts back into style. A lot of clothing designers have bought up these concert souvenirs to re-cut and decorate them. While Louis Vuitton offers bags that have been pre-graffitied by Stephen Sprouse, the customized sector has become all the rage. Well removed from standardized clothes, fashion is looking for a new human quality in graffiti, things deleted and erased, and punk-like slogans. The designers Fabrice Lorrain and Vava Dudu have turned the T-shirt into one of their favorite items of clothing. For their summer 2001 collection, they designed tops with a zipper at one breast with the words "Peace and Love" scribbled on them, all enhanced by a skull, and a sleeveless black T-shirt covered with zippers opening to reveal the skin, rather like scars. The softer Fille Unique [Only Daughter] brand decorates T-shirts picked up for bargain prices in the flea markets of London and Paris with transfers (and matching badges) bearing the names of the seven deadly sins. Alternatively, it transforms a baseball shirt into evening wear by adding a woven braid to one of its sleeves. The Bargain Hunters Club buys up whole stocks of university and sports shirts and customizes them with imitation jewelry, turning them into one-of-a-kind items which can sell for as much as $225. For summer 2001, Jean Colonna also tried to rethink the message image in a craftsmanlike vein. He has been working with the artist Paul Ritter to convey, by graphic means, his loathing of middle-class conformity with slogans such as "Dirty Word" and "Bourgeois vous

VIVA

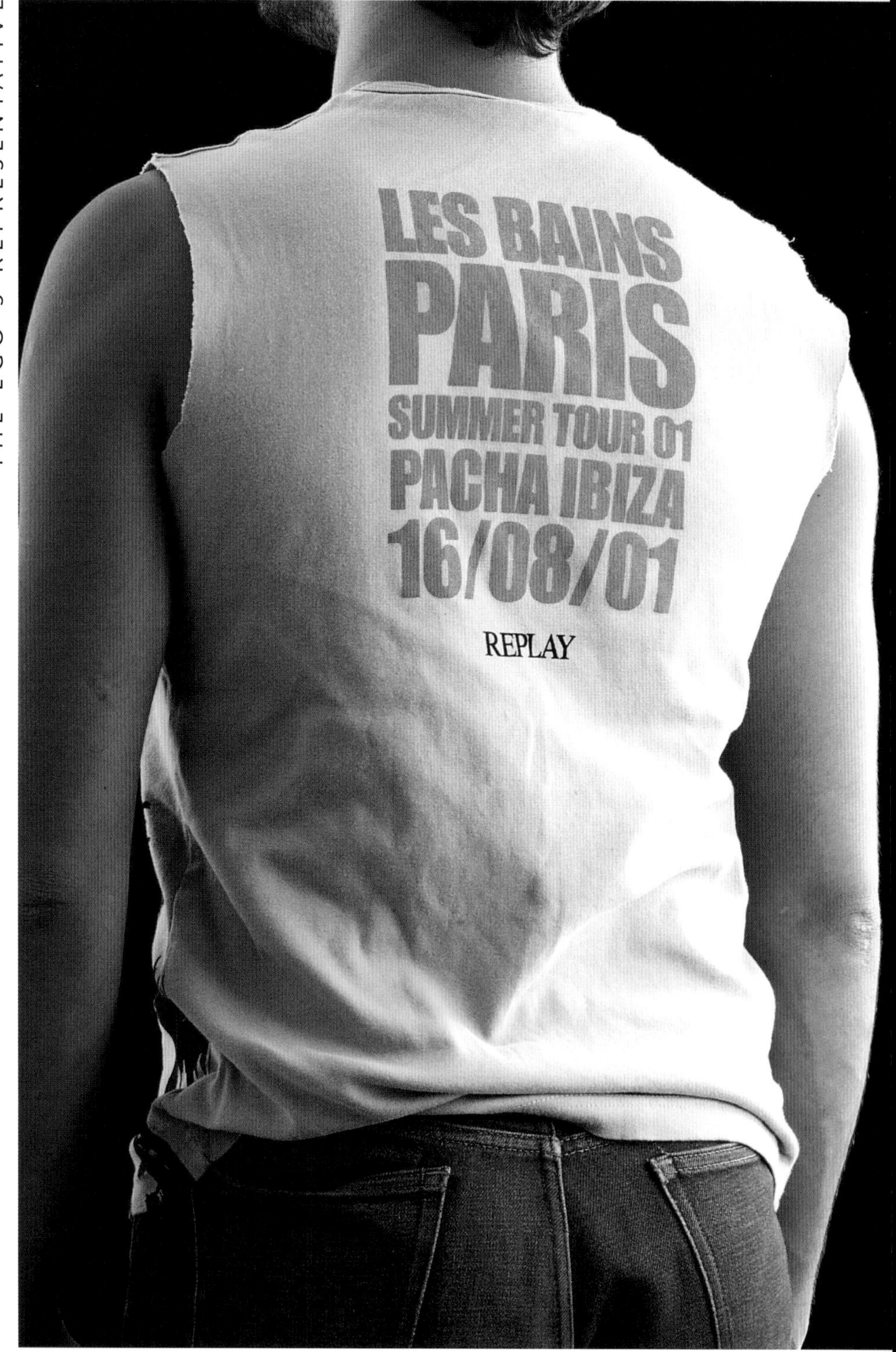
LES BAINS
PARIS
SUMMER TOUR 01
PACHA IBIZA
16/08/01
REPLAY

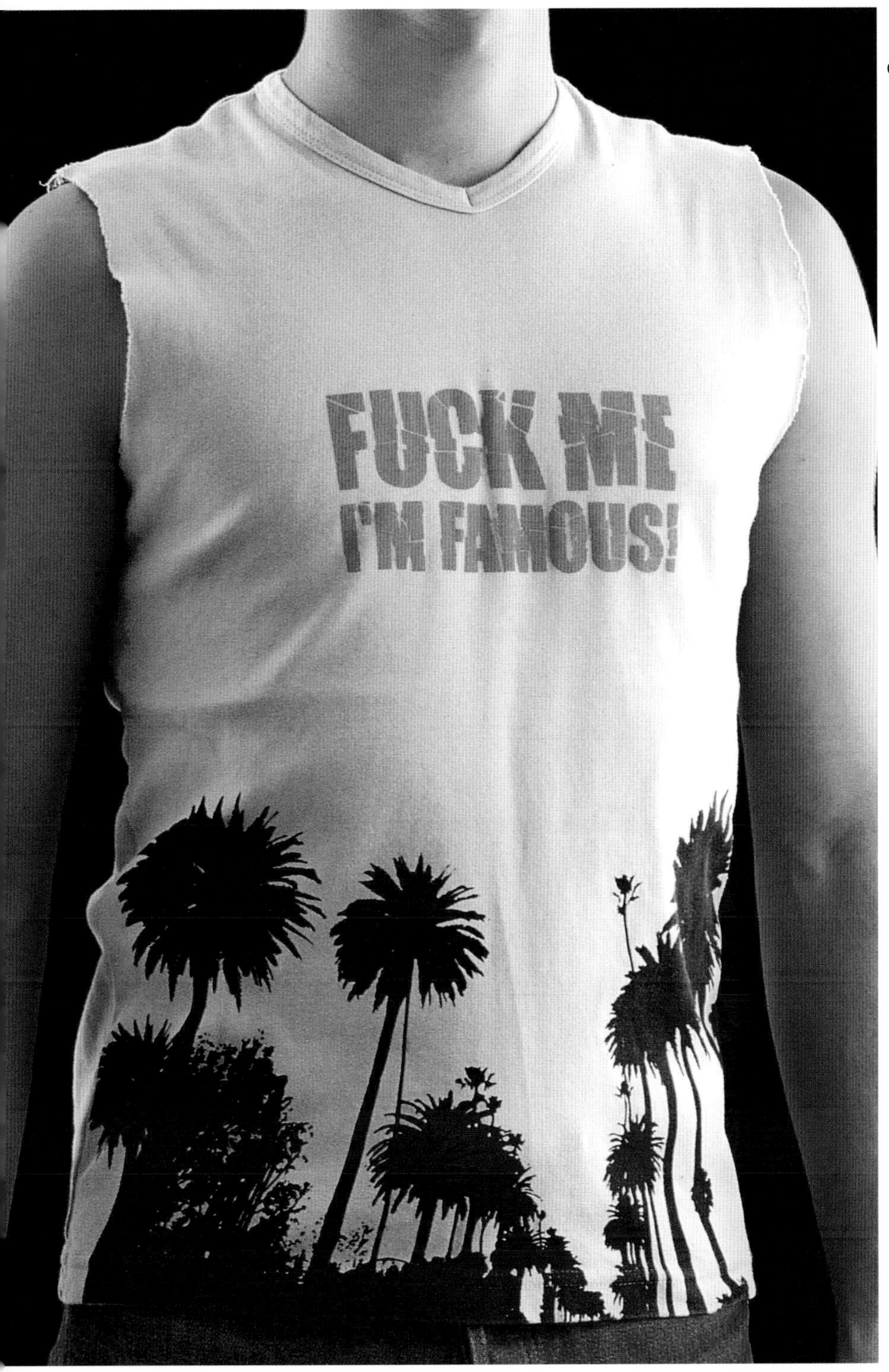
FUCK ME
I'M FAMOUS!

SUPER
XXII
BOWL
19
87
DENVER BRONCOS
AFC CHAMPIONS

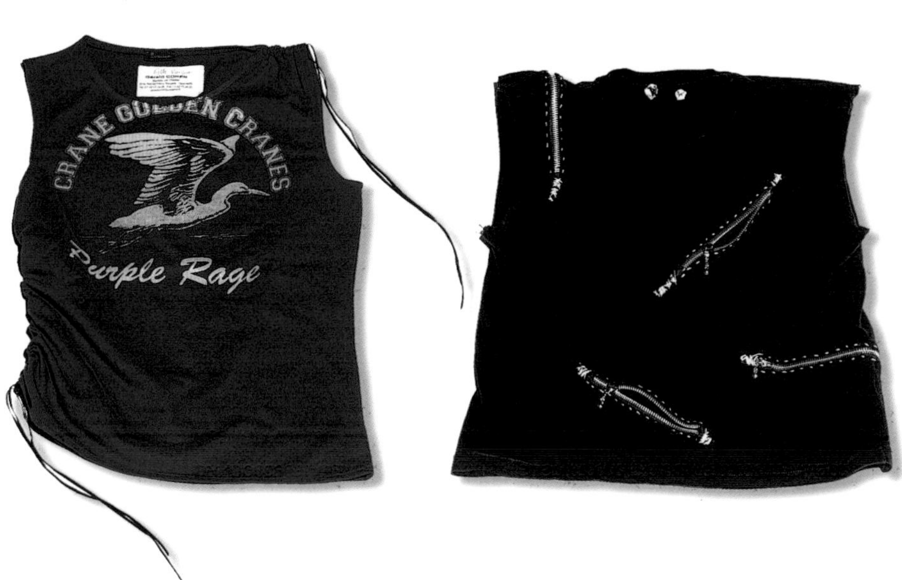

pposite and
ove left: Fille
nique brand
shirts twist the
llege spirit.

bove right: Vava
udu and Fabrice
rrain revive the
nk trash style.

ext pages:
T-shirt brought
t for the meet-
g of London
ghtclub DJs
shca and Trade
Ibiza in 1998.

ge 287: "Avant
emière"
istomization kit
r french
partment store
leries Lafayette.

n'avez rien compris" [The middle classes just don't get it]. Like so many spare parts, the message has been cut up and then put back together again like a remix. These couture items, either made of cotton or printed on pieces of polyester chiffon, are washed five or six times to create an aged look, and a sense of the item's history.

Following in the footsteps of these creative outbursts and assaults, mass consumption brands like Morgan are joining the bandwagon. Whether decorated with sequins in the red, white and blue of the Union Jack, or printed with trompe-l'oeil anarchist badges, the T-shirt gives the impression of having been worked in a slightly rough-and-ready, traditional way, even though it's been mass-produced. Issey Miyake's new concept, called A-Poc (meaning A Piece of Cloth) enables customers to alter their clothes as the spirit moves them. This machine, created in 1999 with Miyake's associate Dai Fujiwara, helps the designers to devise and manufacture a piece of clothing using just a single length of fabric that can be used in different ways. Its shape is controlled by a computer and made directly in the fabric, thus avoiding any need for cutting, sewing or stitching. So you, the purchaser, decide how long your T-shirt is to be, whether to shorten the sleeves, and so on. All you have to do is trace your design along the dotted lines.

PUSHCA MEET
VERY SEXY
VERY LO
VERY PUSHCA

RADE
OON
TRADE
IBIZA 98

The made-to-measure T-shirt

Even if brands have a self-appointed mission to satisfy passing yearnings for rebellion and protest, and even if they are usually one step ahead of the desires of the most trendy crowd not only by anticipating those desires but by creating them, the T-shirt is quite capable of escaping the well-worn track trodden by marketing strategies. "The fact is that a kind of production that's rationalized, streamlined, expansionist, centralized, spectacular and rowdy, is having to cope with a production of a quite different type, described as consumerist, which is hallmarked by its tricks-of-the-trade, by the way it can crumble and fragment as particular occasions require, by the things it poaches, and by its underhand secretiveness..." explains Michel de Certeau, who dedicated his book *Invention of the Humdrum: Ways of Going About It* to the man in the street. For in this day and age, when consumers are rising up against the globalization of taste, personalization and customization help everyone express their individual desires.

In spring 2001, the chain Galeries Lafayette offered T-shirts customized to order by students at Duperré school. *Elle* magazine, for its part, plunged headlong into the graffiti revival trend by offering its readers a graffiti course with the urban artist André. The customization concept certainly isn't new—after all, hippies and punks alike had turned the DIY culture into a creed—but the means and methods are. Since the early 1990s, the techno world with its rave parties brought a whole new generation of graphic artists and

VIVIENNE
WESTWOOD

Pages 266 to 271 and 273: T-shirts are exhibited in galleries like art works. Jean-Charles de Castelbajac's Concept Store Gallery showed unique pieces made by 20 designers, produced for *Dealer de Luxe* magazine.

Page 272: The "More Beautiful" T-shirt by Martine Camillieri, decorated with false hair.

designers into being. These designs, which were often one-of-a-kind intended for just one party and usually printed on T-shirts—or flyers—represented a creative boost. Since that time, graphics software systems and the Internet have made this imagery available to all. These days it's child's play to make unique and personalized T-shirts in a professional way.

In 1998, Nova Development came up with a kit—including a Fruit of the Loom T-shirt—for designing T-shirts yourself using a PC. Armed with 3,000 ready-made designs, 20,000 pictures not subject to copyright laws, and transfer paper, budding designers can swiftly turn themselves into professional T-shirt-makers, creating their own designs and messages exactly the way their imagination dictates. You can cover your T-shirt with a photo of your kids, you can create a unique model to celebrate a birthday or a friendly sporting event. The customized thing is all the rage on the Internet, too. The www.fashion.fr website offers a range of personalized T-shirts. Net surfers can not only choose from various colors and patterns, but also from a variety of fabrics and materials that can be mixed, sleeve options (long or short), and neck options (V or round); the back and front of the T-shirt can also be selected independently. The whole thing will be delivered to your doorstep within ten days. Then there are all the shops and stores with their busy workshops

SONIA RYKIEL

ROBERTO
CAVALLI

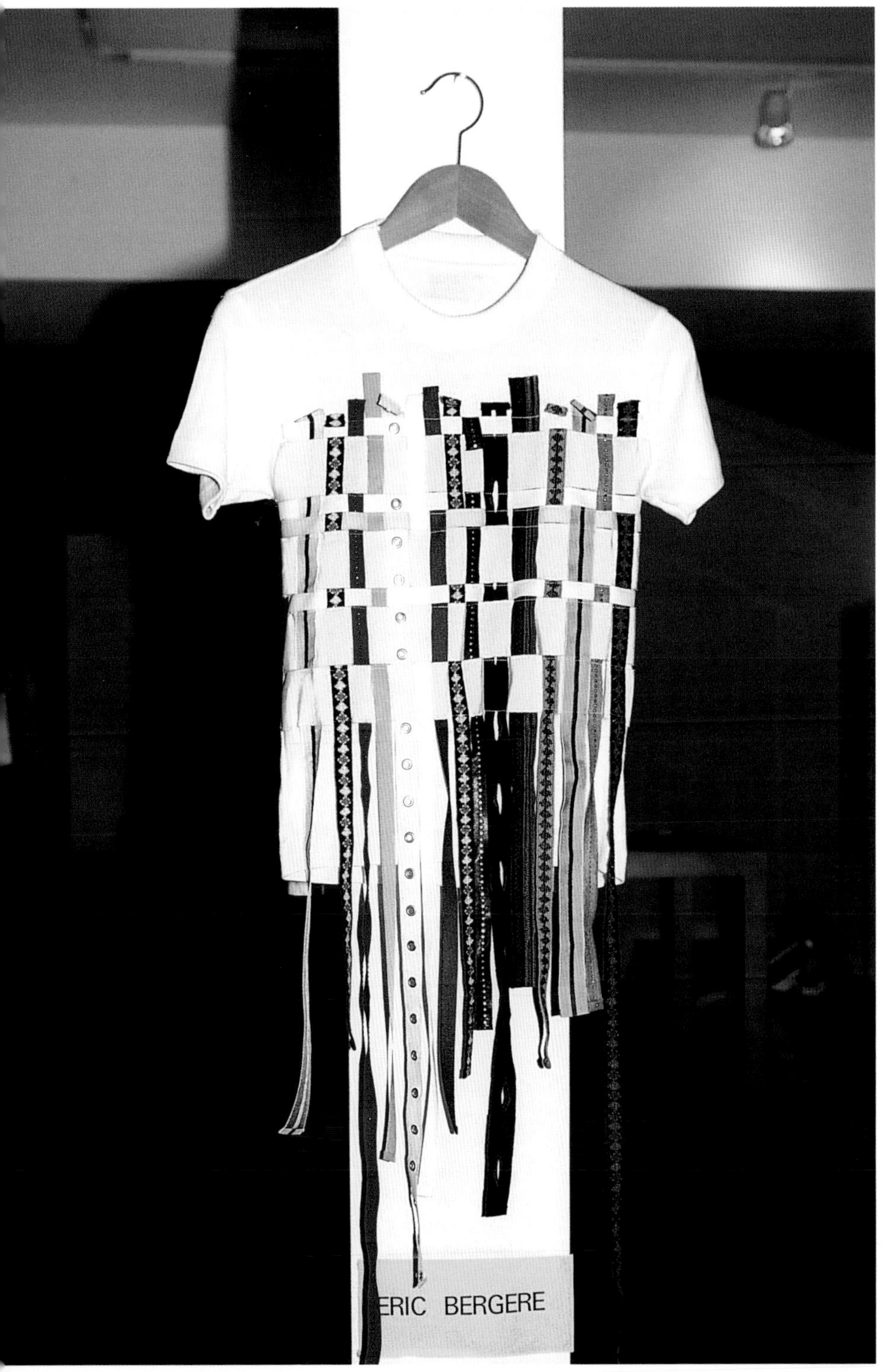
ERIC BERGERE

RIBEIR
POUR CACH

EMANUEL
UNGARO

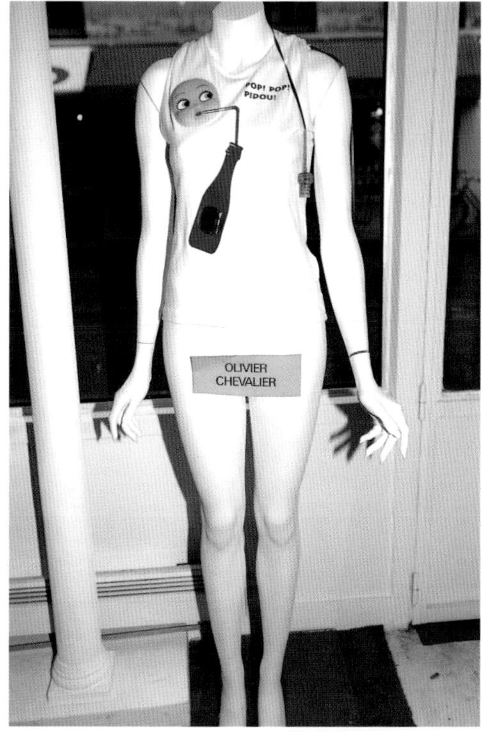
POP! POP!
PIDOU!
OLIVIER
CHEVALIER

offering to silkscreen print T-shirts and make personal transfers to order for customers, private individuals, music groups and labels. The fact is that there can be an original T-shirt made to record for posterity any event or happening you care to mention. As a public mouthpiece, the T-shirt has managed to bear witness to our private lives, just like photographs. "Math lessons, apartment to let, collector seeks, lost cat, indecent proposals—anything and everything goes on the front of a T-shirt," to borrow the caption that appears beneath a photo of two T-shirted models in the magazine *Jalouse*. "Serious young man gives math lessons..." and: "For sale, New York, Soho." Be it as travel souvenir, reminder of some fabulous party, cult object or bauble, the T-shirt has its very own aficionados—collectors who put real passion in their pursuit. Bruno Collin is the editor in chief of the streetwear magazine *Wad*. He's been collecting T-shirts for some 20 years, and now has a collection numbering at least 800 items. He buys two or three T-shirts a week, but he also gets a whole lot free of charge. One of his favorites is a T-shirt-cum-invitation to the Dries van Noten fashion show that took place in 1996 during the Pitti Imagine Uomo show. He always washes this T-shirt with a pair of jeans to give it a faded blue hue. He is also the proud owner of a Manu Mission T-shirt, souvenir of a party on Ibiza attended by no less than 14,000 revelers.

A creation produced by Bless group designers No 9 in a "merchandising" series: T-shirt with the image of the designers.

The smile T-shirt

A yellow circle, embellished with black eyes and a smile stretching from ear to ear, Mr. Smile is a paragon of optimism and good humor. Before this little fellow became the fetish of house music fans, he was first of all an advertising logo. Going hand-in-hand with the slogan "Have a nice day," he was first displayed in the U.S. in the 1960s on a yellow button handed out to people insured with the State Mutual insurance company. In 1972, Marc Bolan, singer with T. Rex, sported Mr. Smile emblazoned on a T-shirt on the cover of *Superhebdo Pop Music* magazine. His fans could order the singer's T-shirt by mail, unless they preferred the transfer version with Mr. Smile chewing a marijuana leaf. Twelve years later, his blissed-out smile was taken over by ravers. Being round, just like ecstasy tabs, it wasn't unusual to see the symbol etched on these pills alongside Disney and Japanese cartoon characters. More recently, this symbol was taken up by the Internet, where it's used like a linguistic hieroglyph, constructed with brackets and semicolons. When the eyes are shut, this means something is funny; when the smile is upside-down, it means something's gone wrong, or the person using it is upset or in a bad mood. Fashion has also appropriated this little icon. In the late 1980s, Franco Moschino printed it on his T-shirts.

***Arsfutura*, a performance piece by Olaf Breuning.**

1: Christian Dior, 2001.

2: A John Galliano T-shirt for Dior, 1988.

3: Rave party in 1988.

4: Antoni & Alison's T-shirt.

3

4

CHAPTER 11

Tribes

The various music trends that jockeyed for position in the first half of the 20th century were often no more than an excuse to introduce new dances. In the repressive atmosphere of the 1940s, some forms of music were akin to manifestos, spawning their very own uniforms. Jazz-loving hipsters during the German Occupation in their too-short trousers, and zoot-suited Latinos decked out with baubles and trinkets foreshadowed the parkas of black-clad Existentialists hoping to find the "Blue Note" in the basements of Paris's Latin Quarter. After the shiny short-sleeved shirts and the rockabilly neckties of the heirs of rhythm and blues headed by Elvis Presley, the T-shirt, as a sexy symbol of the abolition of patterns, was printed in a wide variety of riffs and wording, and became the banner of a "classless" society, where the only thing that mattered was being young. But although mainstream pop may have retained its hold until the end of the 1970s, the punk bomb would

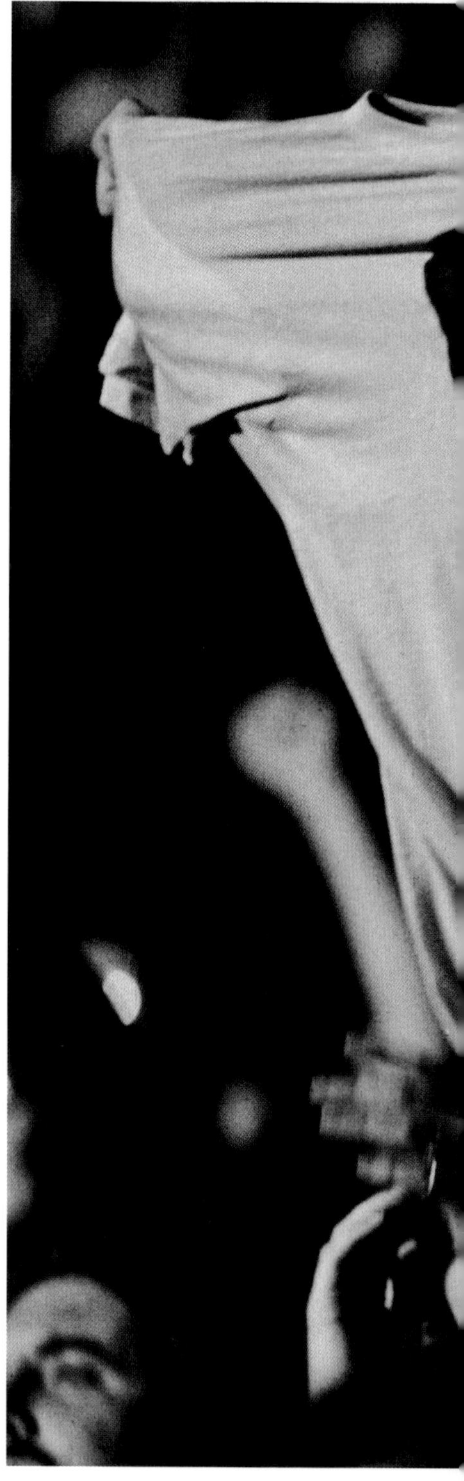

The who

Previous pages: A Who concert.

Above: The T-shirt is the banner of the West Coast biker outcasts in Richard Rush's film *Hell's Angels on Wheels*.

Opposite: T-shirt designed for a bikers' meeting.

Next pages, left: The mouth designed by John Pash. Next pages, right, from top to bottom: Mick Jagger, Jennifer Blanc and Polson, Victoire de Castellane.

soon smash onto the music scene, and its getups into trends that were as many and varied as they were fleeting. No sooner did they appear than everyone had forgotten all about them and moved on. In this split-second realm, the T-shirt would once again carve out the lion's share for itself. New trends in music gave rise to their own gangs, where outfits—in distinctly anti-fashion mode—cast the T-shirt in a major role.

Rock 'n' roll

In the late 1950s, Elvis Presley took off his jacket and gyrated about in a short-sleeved shirt, thus breaking with the correct attire hitherto required of musicians and singers. His fondness for all things kitsch and the roundness of his waistline made the King ideally suited to ruffles and frills and garish leather with studs. Other rebels, like Gene Vincent, who pounded out his version of *Be-bop-a-lula, She's My Baby* in jeans and leather jacket, sported the T-shirt of the working-class hero, but in a black version—the black of rebellion. And the fans followed their example. Fueled by the purest rock 'n' roll, the bikers of the 1950s and their kid brothers—the Hell's Angels—who threw their weight around for all to see in the 1960s, caused panic among nice, respectable folk with refined lifestyles, and were considerably more sophisticated than Marlon

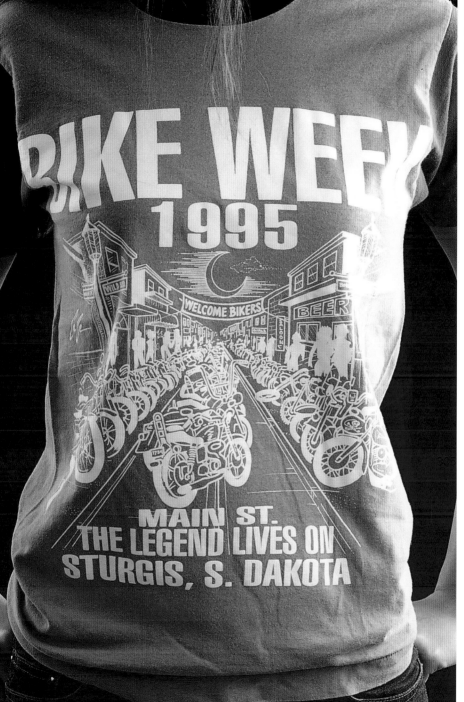

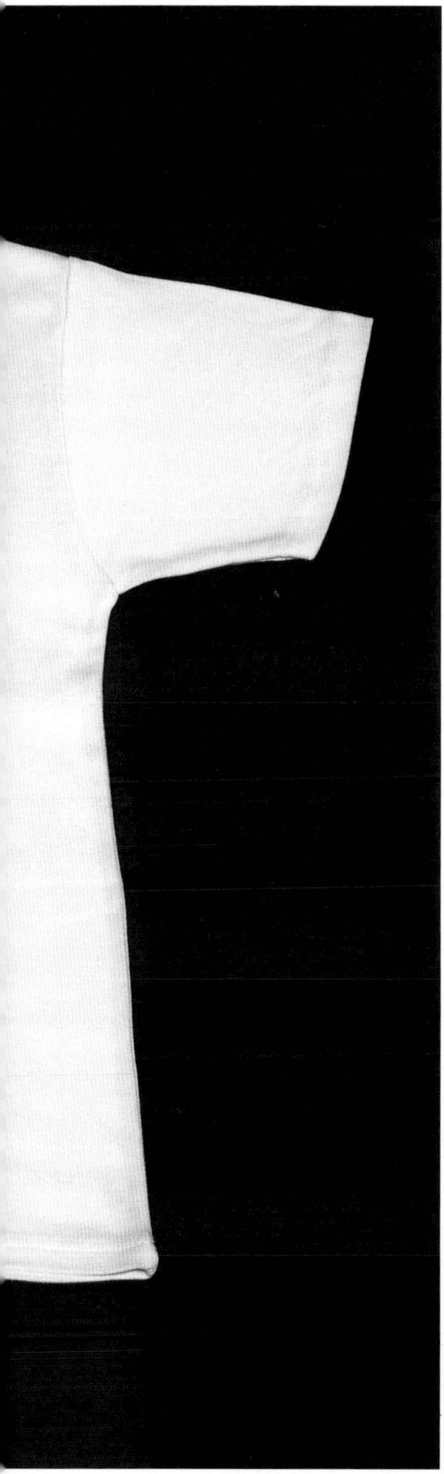

GRAPEFRUIT
YOKO ONO
GRAPEFRUIT
YOKO ONO

Brando's fellow gang members in *The Wild Ones* (1954). It was not that wearing a body-hugging T-shirt, leather jacket, chains and jeans was challenged, but rather that the functional had given way to the baroque and thereby turned all this garb into nothing less than war trimmings—their fashions varying from tribe to tribe. Henceforth, leather clothes were tasselled, studded and tattooed with Confederate flags. Self-glorifying insignia like the numeral 1 in the colors of the American flag, or the make of their bike. They also delighted in insignia designed to scare people, skulls and crossbones and even Nazi swastikas, turned their T-shirts into the uniforms of exterminating angels. The more poetic among them wrote "Night Rider" on one side, beneath the grinning face of a devil, keeping the back to promote a bar or club attesting to their genuine credentials.

Before donning the sober uniform of "groups in suits"—as updated for the modern day and age by Pierre Cardin—and achieving fame and fortune, the Beatles had also performed in black leather and T-shirts in Liverpool's clubs. But in the British Isles of the early 1960s, a typically English movement competed with the rockers and bikers, and clashed with them in street fights. Hailing from the middle class, the Mods were always dressed to the nines, swearing by round-collared shirts and John Stephen suits. Yet even among The Who (the Mods' cult group), Keith Moon saw fit, as the group's drummer, to sport T-shirts with Op Art patterns—hearts, targets and arrows. The personalized music-lover's T-shirt was born. It just had to be industrially produced. Before the end of

Previous pages: John Lennon promoting *Grapefruit*, the book published by his wife, underground artist Yoko Ono.

Above and opposite: Hard rock gave rise to a thriving T-shirt industry. Black, adorned with skulls and crossbones and other morbid imagery, the shirts of cult groups like Motörhead, Kiss and Iron Maiden have become nothing less than icons.

the decade it had found its way across the Atlantic to the United States, where Californians flocked to join the fan club of Jerry Garcia's famed group, the Grateful Dead. Before long, impresario Bill Graham's company was promoting all the music coming out of the West Coast. His T-shirts could be identified by their dark background because, as he himself said, "Black is the color of rock, we were the first to use it."

Hard rock

The energetic musicians of the group Steppenwolf claim that they coined the term "heavy metal," a lyric from their 1968 song *Born to be Wild*, that would go on to become a cult favorite, explains Ted Polhemus in his book *Streetstyle: From Sidewalk to Catwalk*. In the explosive mixture of psychedelic lyricism from the likes of Jimi Hendrix and The Doors, and the warlike rhythms of Led Zeppelin, were the beginnings of a new genre, whose followers proclaimed their angst-ridden teenage world-weariness in the form of long, faded T-shirts topped by dishevelled, unwashed locks. In their zeal to become ever more provocative, rockers soon appropriated the leather gear dear to bikers, along with the associated sado-masochistic paraphernalia, which would now and then veer toward fascist references. Whether leather or not, hard-rock

motörhead

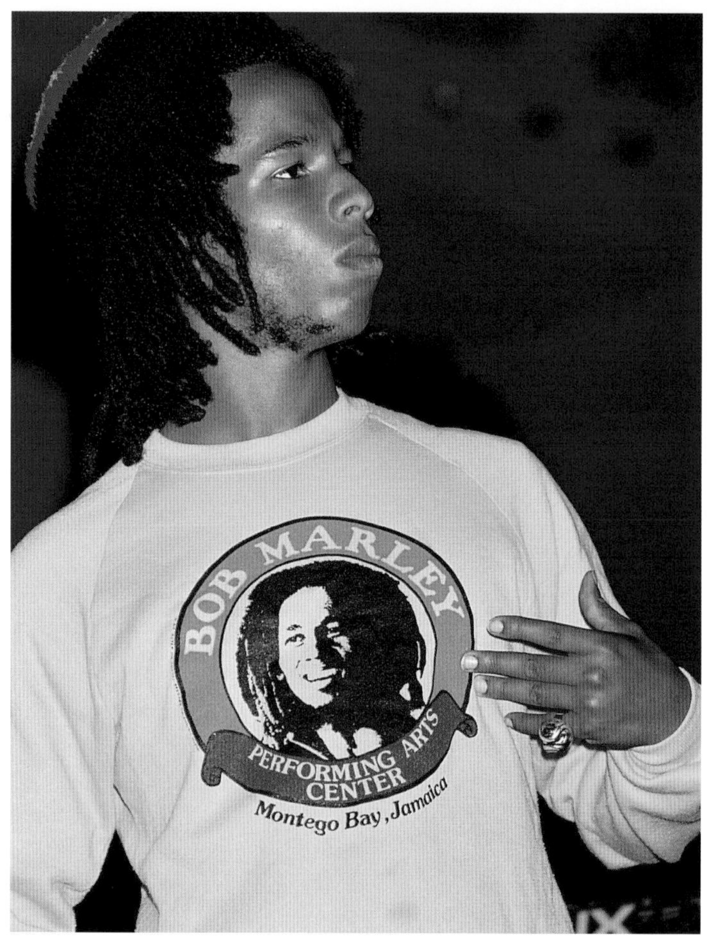

Opposite: In a medallion, Ziggy Marley sports the face of his father, reggae star Bob Marley.

Right: Bob Marley poses wearing an athletic shirt in the Rastafarian colors, green, yellow and red—which are the colors of the Ethiopian flag.

Next pages, left: French singer Tonton David, 1990.
Next pages, right: Jimmy Cliff.

clothing cast the T-shirt in a pivotal role. A mail-order catalogue from the mid-1970s offered more than ten different models, one more heavy-metal than the next. "Rock on your Chest," was how the ads summed it up. These T-shirts were almost all black, and you could only tell them apart by the names of the groups printed on them: Black Sabbath, Deep Purple, Motorhead, Def Leppard, Scorpions, AC/DC, Iron Maiden, etc.

The black wave

Of all musical trends, hard rock has produced the most T-shirts. With their dreadlocks kept in check under copious woolen hats, rastas sport the red, yellow and green of the Ethiopian flag on their T-shirts. Rastafarianism came into being in Jamaica back in the

AFRIKA
must
unite !

Above: The actor Gary Oldman playing Sex Pistols guitarist Sid Vicious in the movie *Sid and Nancy*, directed by Alex Cox.

Opposite: Jordan and Paul Betty, salespersons at Malcolm McLaren and Vivienne Westwood's store Sex, 430 King's Road in London.

1930s, and in due course produced reggae music, complete with its undisputed star, the late Bob Marley. From Kingston to Goa, his charismatic face graces the chests of ganja smokers, akin to a message of peace and love.

In England in the late 1970s, Prime Minister Margaret Thatcher applied the Reaganomics of her American neighbor with a vigor worthy of her nickname "the Iron lady," busting the power of the trade unions in the name of the free market, closing down foundering mines, privatizing the public sector, and throwing millions of working people out of jobs and on to the dole. While the middle class whooped for joy, a wind of despair chilled the hopes of young people, blasting icy gusts through working-class towns. This was the loam in which the punk phenomenon sprouted, flaunting its vague but all-embracing rejection not only of the cruel world of politics, but also of blissed-out, colorfully dressed hippies, as well as the insipid broth of pop music that had been simmering on the back burner too long. Throughout the 1970s, the mood of rebellion bequeathed by Andy Warhol in his early days had fairly and squarely blazed a trail in the U.S. music business. With the Stooges (from whom the contortionist Iggy Pop would emerge), the New York Dolls (aptly dolled-up in subversive, aggressive drag) and,

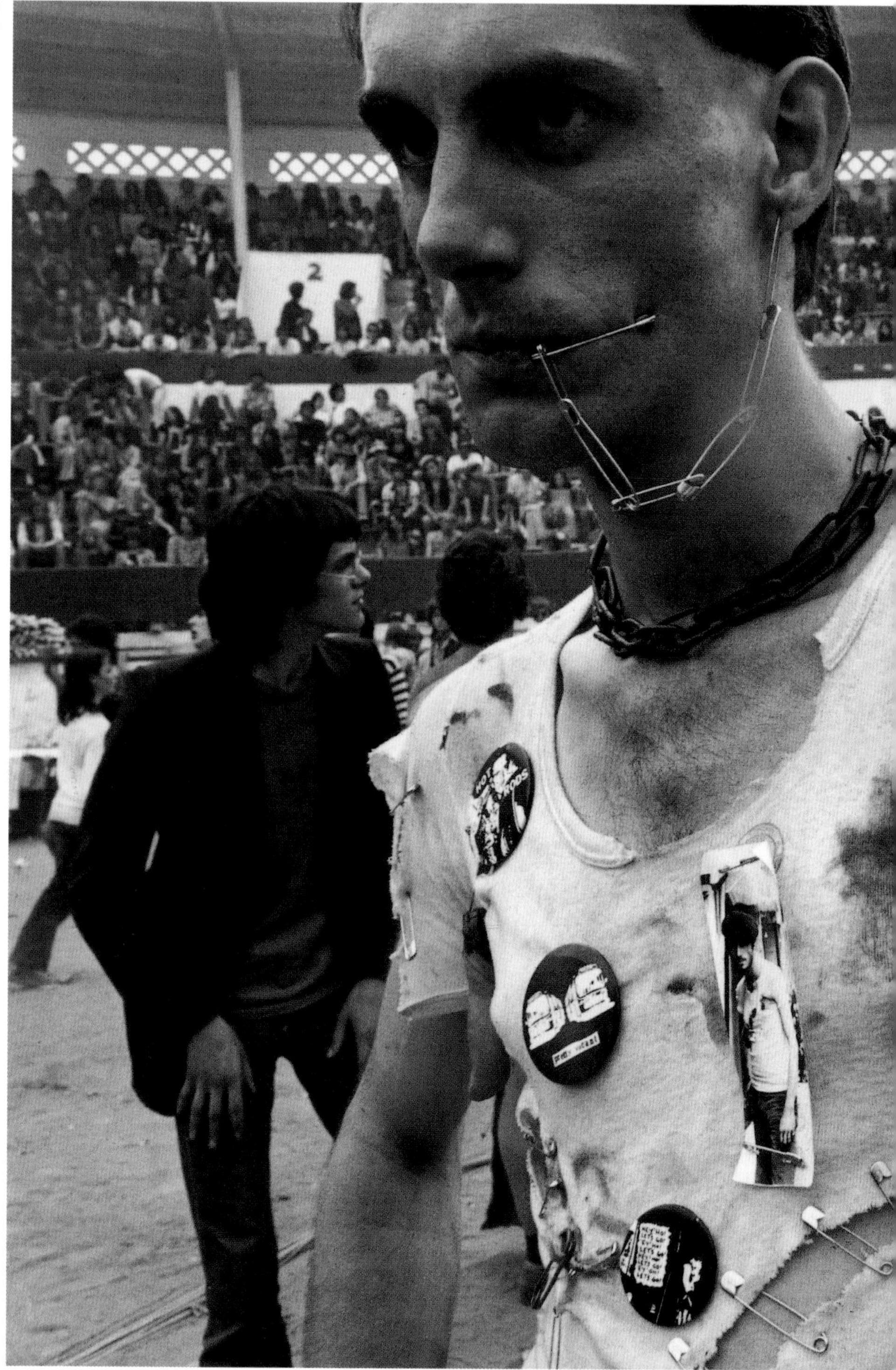
HOT RODS

CULT

above all, the Velvet Underground, whose singer/guitarist Lou Reed was rarely seen without his black T-shirt—*de rigueur* in the world of the blues. At the outset, punk was a typically English movement, and there's still no telling if the driving force behind it was musical or sartorial. It was probably the latter, if we're to go along with the pedigree of the person who put it into orbit. As the manager—or rather the "inventor"—of the Sex Pistols, Malcolm McLaren was first and foremost a clothing designer.

The store called Sex, opened by McLaren and his partner Vivienne Westwood in 1974, became headquarters for the earliest punks in the Bromley Contingent, who had a soft spot for bondage paraphernalia, T-shirts full of holes and chains. Their T-shirts were decorated—"adorned"— with images of Stalin and swastikas, and had slogans like "Only Anarchists are Pretty" scrawled on the sleeves. At an early stage McLaren summed things up thus: "We made clothes that looked like ruins—creating something new by destroying the old stock. I loved making T-shirts, for instance, that I would dye different colors, tread upon, trample, and generally mess up as much as possible. I wanted them to look as if they were just some old rags left underneath a car in a garage. I would adorn them with slogans: "It's Forbidden to Forbid," "Demand the Impossible," "Keep the Dialectic Open" (*The New Yorker*, 1997). Such sayings had flourished many years earlier in Paris on the walls of the Sorbonne, then engaged in "the struggle." What these tawdry, tattered clothes, proclaiming failure and destruction for all to hear, didn't have was an anthem. So they opted for the Sex Pistols' "God Save the Queen," taken from their ground-breaking album *Anarchy in the U.K.*

Just as Andy Warhol put the Velvet Underground together, so Malcolm McLaren molded a bunch of (almost talentless) young guys into a famous group. First he found them a name, the explosive Sex Pistols, then he gave them a style. He described it all very succinctly: "A deadly, sexy chaos." While Sex Pistols concerts brought anarchy into the very heart of the United Kingdom, Malcolm McLaren and Vivienne Westwood opened a new store in 1976 called Seditionaries. McLaren had realized that "Fashion and music, music and fashion—they were the expression of the same needs—and, in retrospect, it now seems natural and right that a

Previous pages and opposite: The punks' favorite piece of clothing was the sleeveless T-shirt, which they often reduced to tatters, and covered with anarchist badges. In London's Hyde Park, in 1985, survivors from that movement pose in Doc Martens and studded leather jackets—proud in their wasted, torn and dirty look.

shop producing a street fashion of boredom should be the venue for its music." In 2001, the "historic" T-shirt worn by the Sex Pistols bass player Sid Vicious (who died at the age of 21 in New York City) bearing the caption "Anarchy," was snapped up for $6,000 at Sotheby's.

In 1977, the Sex Pistols' *God Save the Queen* hit went straight to the top of the British charts. To provide a picture of this heretical version of the national anthem, the artist Jamie Reid produced a work that was every bit as scandalous and just as punk, which soon appeared printed on T-shirts for sale at Seditionaries in London. With her lips pierced by a safety pin and her face set in a halo formed by the words of the song typeset in more or less anonymous lettering: "God Save the Queen, She Ain't No Human Being..." the official portrait of the Queen, signed by Cecil Beaton, turned into a punk icon. On one shoulder of the T-shirt you can also read: "...And the fascist regime." At the time, the group's fans who didn't live in London could buy the Infamous Sex Pistols T-shirt by mail order for about £ 3.50.

Appropriated by the fashion world, this emblem gradually shed its subversive aspect. With the arrival of the 2000 autumn-winter season, the designer Laurent Mercier—who had dressed Lenny Kravitz and the queen of German punk, Nina Hagen—borrowed the famous T-shirt and wrote on it: "Carrier Girl." The following season, it was Dolce & Gabbana, those remix experts, who came up with their particular interpretation of the Sex Pistols T-shirt in a softer, more naïve style. Like a retouched photograph, the Queen's face sported bright colors, and surmounted the graffiti caption "God Save the Queen" with, it goes without saying, the symbolic anarchist "A" ousting the "a" of Save.

Opposite: Bruce Springsteen.

Next pages: Members of the the group Devo.

DEVO
DEVO

DEVO

Above:
Michael Jackson fans, 1984.

Opposite:
French rapper Joey Starr of NTM in 1991.

Next pages:
Public Enemy on the Smokin' Groove Tour, 1998.

The merry-go-round of the 1980s

In the 1980s, the music scene broke up into several different genres: robots, ska, new romantics, and so on. Like some stroboscopic upsurge, one fashion followed hot on the heels of the next—often dovetailing with it—at supersonic speed. Gay communities, all caught up in coming out, had the wind in their sails. Frankie Goes to Hollywood, their cult group, espoused the oversized spirit and bold typography of English fashion designer Katharine Hamnett, and, when their single "Relax" came out, gave their listeners the order: "Frankie says relax." In just a few weeks, nearly every torso in London was sporting "Relax" on it. As back-up for the *Two Tribes* album, a new T-shirt proclaimed: "Frankie Says Peace Not War." Sales of these T-shirts would almost exceed the sales of the group's albums. Little by little, what was previously just a cottage industry, dominated by tie-dyers, protesters and promoters of small rock concerts, turned into a mighty business involving corporations like Sony, Time Warner, Nike, Sarah Lee, and Fruit of the Loom. It's a fact that big stars can earn more than $10 million a year from T-shirt sales. During the Rolling Stones' 1995 tour, which pulled in more than 4.5 million fans, sales of peripheral spin-off products totaled $70 million, 75% of which was accounted for by T-shirts.

NY
REMEMBER...

Above: T-shirt of Com8 created by Joey Starr.

Opposite: Sean "Puffy" Combs.

Next pages: Young American rappers, 1984.

Hip-hop shirt

In 1986, the Run DMC rappers burst on to the charts with their hit *My Adidas*. Complete with gold sneaker pendants, tracksuits boasting the Adidas clover-leaf and three-striped sneakers, this group—just like young, nattily-dressed Africans—gave vent to its brand of fetishism. From this point on, T-shirts would announce their pedigrees in large lettering: Tommy Hilfiger, Calvin Klein, Nike, etc. In the 1990s, worn in XXL models over baggy pants that seemed to lower the buttocks to knee-level, the T-shirt authenticated the rapper look. But it was not until the mid-1990s that the music world launched its own brands. The young designer Karl Kani managed to build a whole empire by dressing the singer Snoop Doggy Dogg, before the latter, in his turn, launched his own line of T-shirts, illustrated with graffiti characters and people from an imaginary hip hop scene—like his modern Al Capone in striped suit, fur coat and

107

chunky gold rings. And there was no shortage of competitors. While Fubu used characters from the Jackson Five cartoon on XXL T-shirts, the French brand Beatum went for nude pin-up photos, and Serial Killer merrily plundered hip hop's cult movies: *Scarface*, *Pulp Fiction*, and anything Bruce Lee. In France, there was an abundance of brands originating from rap, such as Bullrot, Cumpaz, Triad, Royal Wear and Come8, brainchild of Joey Starr, NTM singer. In this chummy atmosphere, brands did not have to be begged to sponsor rappers, so you got Reebok paired up with Passi, and Helli Hansen with NTM.

The colors of music

In the mid-1980s, the Ibiza beat on the Amnesia dance floor captivated neohippies and turned on ecstasy-poppers with the novel vibrations of house music. In London, people wore the sunny colors and psychedelic explosions of the diminutive Balearic isle—Smile T-shirt, tie-dye and those day-glo bridal bouquets worthy of the Grateful Dead in their prime, ideal for getting behind grunge, travelers, techno, and other variations of the hippie revival. Before long, the 1990s broadened the range of synthetic materials and decked out the T-shirt in iridescent patterns and acid orange and green—typical of hallucinogenic trips—thus hallmarking the techno look. T-shirts were now rather short and close-fitting, revealing pierced navels for all to see. The Procapitalist brand took things a step further and fitted their T-shirts with two hidden armpit pockets for hiding ecstasy pills. The new drug with its feel-good effects made people want to be together in a spirit of peace and love. "We are one family," proclaimed the official T-shirt of the 1996 Love Parade in Berlin. On T-shirts, the green alien with the oblong head has become the frightening mascot of the cyber-generation, enthralled by the new technologies. To the punks' "No Future," electronic music fans reply confidently, "Kiss the Future." A maxim which sums up the outlook of W&M.T (Wild and Metal Trash), the brand name of Belgian designer Walter van Beirendonck, whose trademark logo, the extra-terrestrial Puk Puk, is forever displaying his optimism on T-shirts.

Previous pages: Coolio makes his own promotion wearing a T-shirt with his face, 1996.

Opposite: Techno party in 1998.

Next pages: DJ Mecca team.

Page 340: DJ Josh Wink at Exil Festival in Cherbourg, France, 1998.

Page 341, top right: French DJ Laurent Garnier in 1998. Bottom left: Goldie in concert with Madonna.

sonic

me

usa

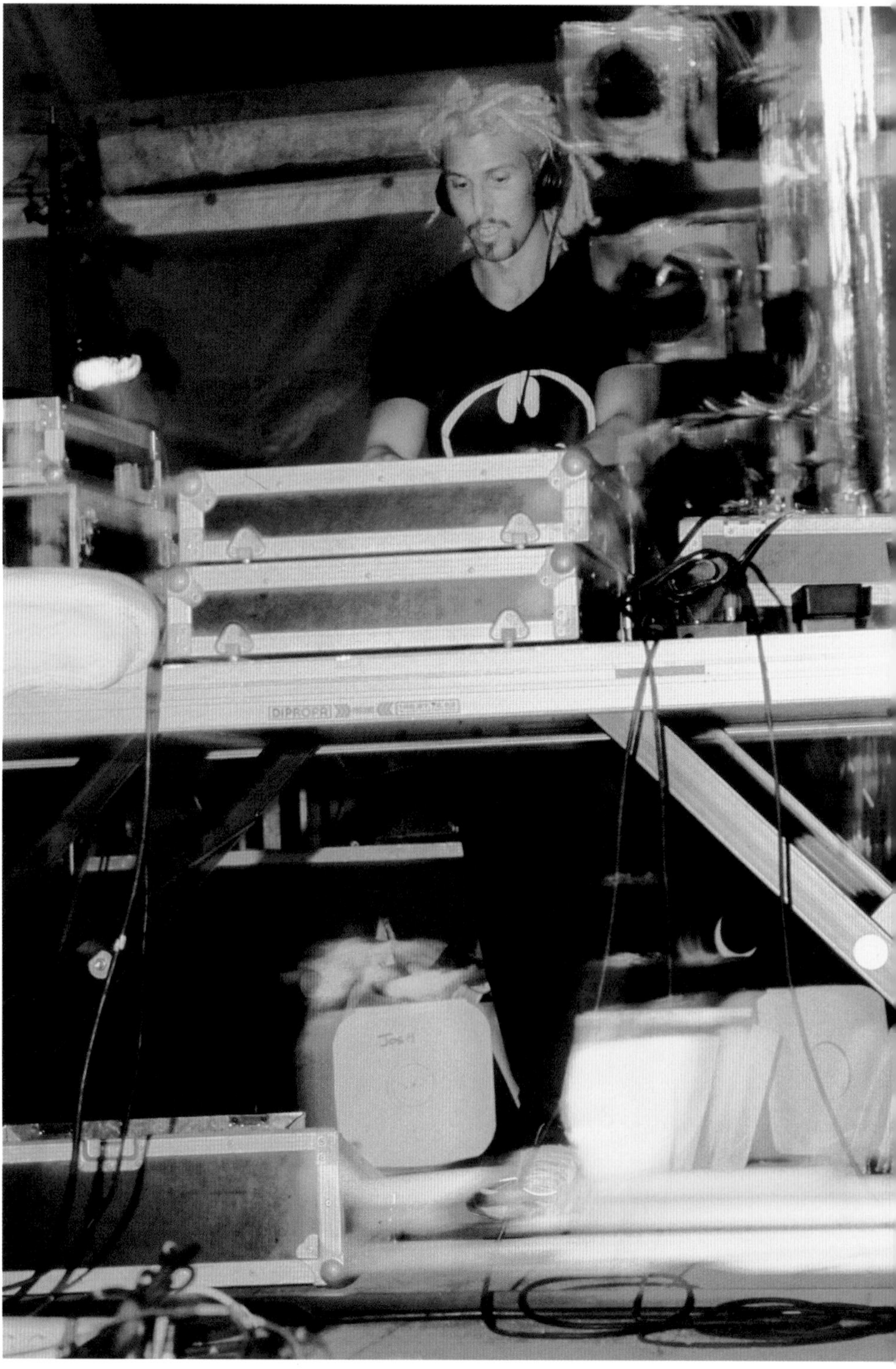

Fubu
05

broke
BROKE
BEAT STREET
RECORDS

THRASHER
WINDANSEA
SURF
CLUB
1962-1999

Above: Actresses Camilla Belle, Stacie Hess, Meleana White and Kanoa Chung on a Hawaiian beach in the movie *Rip Girls*.

Opposite and next pages: Skateboarders' baggy pants and XXL T-shirts adorned with twisted logos and anti-establishment messages hallmark the style of this urban sport which has made its mark on streetwear.

Surf and turf cowboys

In the early 1950s, surfing was no longer just a sport; it was a whole lifestyle, its meccas—Honolulu and Malibu. Alongside those short-sleeved Hawaiian shirts immortalized by the Beach Boys, the T-shirt was already making its presence felt on the noblest of waves, where surfer gangs in their king-size boardshorts vied for supremacy, often in the form of fisticuffs. In the 1970s, boards—smaller versions, needless to say—were fitted with wheels and, in the form of the skateboard, offered an urban counterpart to the ocean surf. In no time at all, this new invention turned the cityscape into a playground. Skateboarding was quickly banned in public places—those early fans didn't have the same dazzle and verve as today's acrobats—and ended up relegated to the city outskirts, in whose neglected wasteland places tribes and clans and gangs were spawned. To start with, skateboarders borrowed the surfing fraternity's highly graphic T-shirts signed Quiksilver and Offshore, as well as their mythical checkerboard vans. After a brief punk interlude—mesh T-shirts, tattered and torn and made of vinyl—skateboarders then went in for the provocative styles on offer from Californian newcomers, Pervert, Jive, Fuct, in a slightly cleaner and very graphic style; their musical counterpart being Suicidal Tendencies

carhartt

REEBOK
TOMMY GEAR
TOMMY GEAR

TOMMY TANG'S

PISS ANT PISS ANT PISS ANT PISS ANT

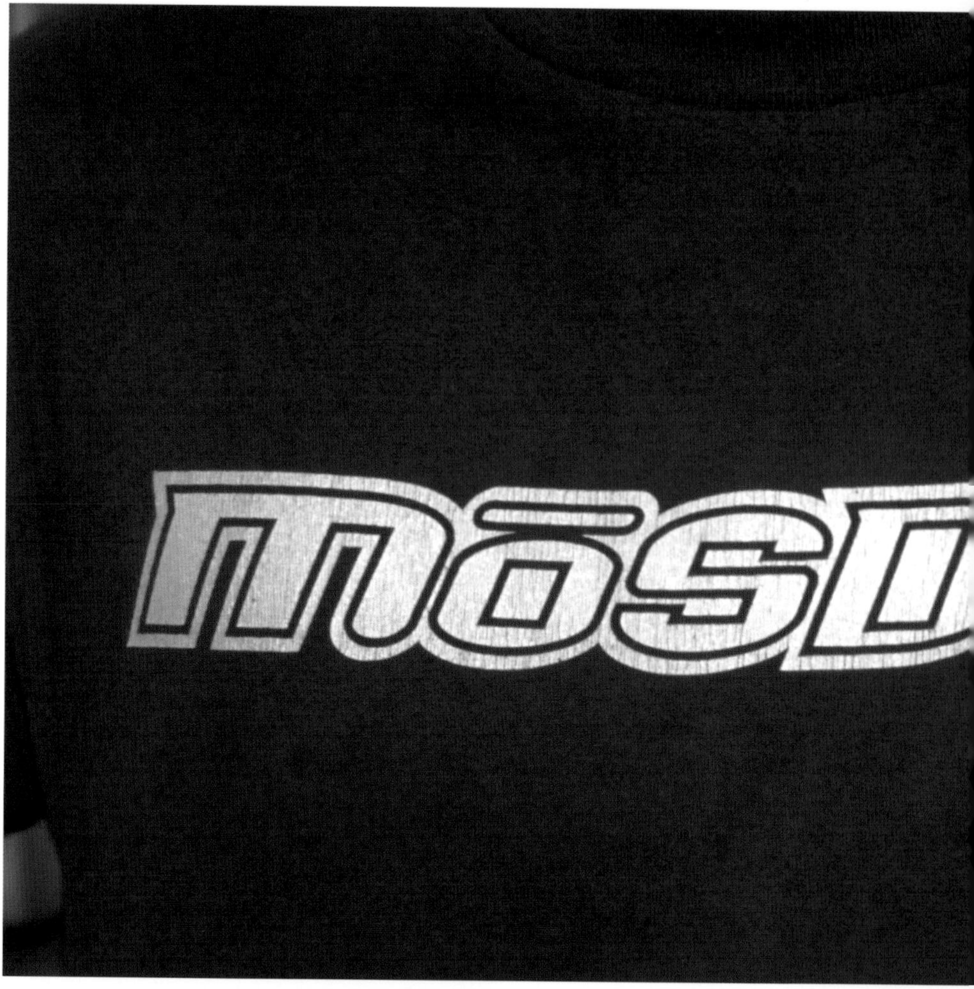

BLAST
BOARD KULTURE, ACTION & REACTION

HYSTERIC

and Deftones. On one such model, Fuct described itself as "Twice as evil as Hitler, more fun than Elvis." Logos beamed out from T-shirts and XXL sweatshirts, while disproportionately large jeans made bodies look all out of proportion. Skateboarding and surfing laid down the guiding principles of streetwear. Shawn Stussy started by affixing his name to graffiti for surfboards. After that he wrote it on T-shirts. Nowadays, this is one of the standard streetwear brands.

Streetwear

Clothes designed for sports and work have, over the years, been adapted to asphalt, and previously exclusive name brands have now clinched a broader public. Out of this has emerged a fashion movement called streetwear. It's a far-flung and somewhat vague trend, where casualness rules at the expense of elegance. Board sports, hip hop, high tech—every style interprets streetwear in its own way. Within this genre, the T-shirt has carved out a choice niche for itself, alongside sweatshirts, sneakers and baggy pants. Brands of jeans like Levi's, Dickies and Carhartt, and sports footwear specialists like Adidas and Puma were quick to climb on the bandwagon. T-shirts bearing a company logo have become classic items. Labels produced by graphic designers have also turned the T-shirt into a favorite medium. Gimme Five, the Japanese company behind Hysteric Glamour; the Londoners running Savage; and the various hip hop brands have given this undershirt back its creative, and at times subversive, dimension within an urban landscape.

SPARKS
JAPAN TOUR
Sponsored by theWinneyCo

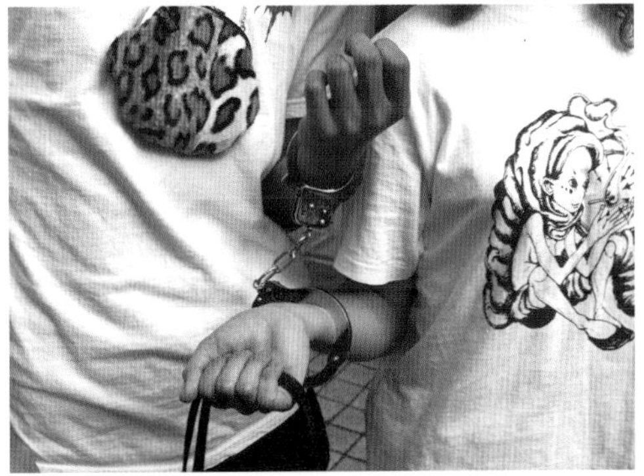

FUCT™
superstitious sports division Bond interna
superstitious sports division Bo
STUSSY
DEFENDER OF STYLE
BAP
"APE SHALL NEVER KILL
EVISU UNCHAINABLE MANIACS
SELF DEFENCE CLUB

CASE INVADERS
KULTE
LOTUS EATERS
100% FLIP.
BAD BOY
ENTERTAINMENT
Twins
11

Pages 350 and 351: Young Japanese teenagers sporting an eccentric look, 2001.

Pages 351 to 353: Various creations of the Bruno Collin collection.

From left to right, above, opposite and next pages: New York bike messengers photographed by Philippe Bialobos: William, Silver, Joseph, Brenton.

Pioneers of street style

It is obviously "New York's messengers who have invented a very typical streetwear style, significantly influencing today's fashion," writes art historian Valerie Steele in her foreword to the book *Messengers Style* (Assouline, 2000). Being a messenger in New York City is more than a job—it's a kind of philosophy of life combining a need for freedom and a fondess for asphalt. These street riders are looking for comfort as much as a style that is now turning into their brand image. Their desire for authenticity comes across in their quest for individuality—punk trends, sporty looks, grunge, paramilitary, they all overlap in a world that conveys an often surprising creativity, and has influenced more than one fashion designer. With their knowledge of every kind of high tech textile innovation, these messengers in Manhattan and one or two other mega-cities are true mines of urban information and personal style.

turbo
HOP FOR RESPECT
GREGOR

FOX

GEAR TM

TREZEGUET
VERON
RAUL
TOLDO
VERON
CARLOS
BECKHAM
SCHOLL
CRESPO
SALAS

Sportswear

In Constantinople's hippodrome, in those bygone days, Byzantine onlookers would sport the colors of their favorite teams. This is par for the course, these days, in every kind of stadium, where sports club T-shirts, along with scarves and flags, are like silent exhortations transmitted by supporters to their idols. As at rock concerts, they are just another way of adulating the stars performing on stage. The T-shirt and its cousin the athletic shirt have actually become essential gear in almost every kind of sport as the supreme top. It is worth remembering that in the 1930s, American universities affixed their names to the T-shirts of their sports teams. Each discipline had its particular model. But these most appropriate details were no match for the rocketing star status of individual players. In the 1940s, we find T-shirts and jerseys bearing the image of the champion baseball player Joe DiMaggio. Twenty years later, T-shirts with French footballer Michel Platini's face were all the rage, even in the most remote islands of Indonesia. All this was just another striking consequence of the highly-funded media bubble of sport—a bubble which started to gain its exponential momentum a couple of decades ago in the early 1980s. Today, sportswear companies fight fiercely over the champions who will show off their products to the tune of millions of dollars. Nike, like Adidas, started out as a footwear manufacturer, but nowadays it has its

Opposite: An assortment of soccer T-shirts.

CBF
BRASIL
10

T-shirts printed with the logos of the NBA, the Chicago Bulls and the NY Knicks. Nike has chalked up several other fine coups, too: the Michael Jordan T-shirt—Jordan being touted as the greatest basketball player of all time—and the Aurivere de Reynaldo T-shirt, which, it just so happens, didn't actually seem to bring the Brazilian footballer any luck. During the 1998 World Cup, French footballer Zinedine Zidane revealed an Adidas T-shirt bearing the number "10" to two billion TV viewers. In no time, this model would become one of the most pirated T-shirts ever: in the 1998 season, Adidas sold 450,000 T-shirts of the French football team. And this figure only just beats the annual sales of Liverpool Soccer Club replicas.

Above: A Yankees T-shirt.

Opposite: Supporters of the Nakanogo Japanese baseball team.

NAKANOGO
NAKANOGO
9

U.S.
BOSS
RACING
TEAM

FUBU
SPORTS

Above: Members of a tour are identified by their T-shirts.

Opposite: A New York Guardian Angel in 1984.

Next pages: In 1996, in the Metrodome Stadium in Minneapolis, evangelist Billy Graham drew a throng of believers wearing T-shirts with this man of the cloth's face on them.

The T-shirt as uniform

Initially an undergarment for the armed forces, the T-shirt also managed to cultivate its function as a uniform in civilian life, where its messages unambiguously spell out its social functions, real or imaginary. Within tough institutional professions, the T-shirt must above all meet the requirements of comfort. Like military units, New York firemen wear FDNY—Fire Department New York—T-shirts during their training sessions. These particular items have become notorious, and were quickly sold out in souvenir shops after the destruction of the World Trade Towers. The T-shirt also tends to tone down the formality and austerity of any uniform—uniforms having become gradually more and more unpopular. The T-shirt can convey a certain authority, but it blends in, like camouflage in the cityscape. In the New York subway, volunteer Guardian Angels used to wear grey T-shirts bearing the word "Guardian," a word intended to both reassure passengers and deter anyone considering committing a crime.

GUARDIAN

Above: Little kids' T-shirts act as ambassadors for environmental and wildlife protection.

Opposite: Pokemon star Picachu.

Merchandising

As part and parcel of the whole merchandising thing, the T-shirt found grist for its mill in the movie theatres. In the early 1970s—the heyday of Pop Art—Disney indulged in a bit of hype for its characters by selling Mickey Mouse, Donald Duck, Goofy and other T-shirts—a dazzling success, and one that lasted, too. Today, wearing a Bart Simpson or Pokemon T-shirt lends the wearer a certain caché on the playground. But the Hollywood-T-shirt marriage was to yield better still. In the 1980s, when the United States was still reeling from *Jaws*, Americans gawked at those young, voracious Wall Street whizzkids flaunting the gaping jaws of Steven Spielberg's infamous shark on their T-shirts—which turned out to be one of the biggest selling garments the world has ever seen.

A few years later, the cult film *Star Wars*, with its legendarily astronomical budget, ruined its director, George Lucas. By great good fortune, however, he didn't sell the rights to the film's imagery. And the film was such a runaway success that Luke Skywalker, Darth Vader and Princess Leia T-shirts were all it took—along with the other merchandising fetishes and mascots—to make his fortune.

Since then, where T-shirts are concerned, anything goes. From the

Pokémon ™
Attrapez-les tous! ™
TM & © 2000 NINTENDO

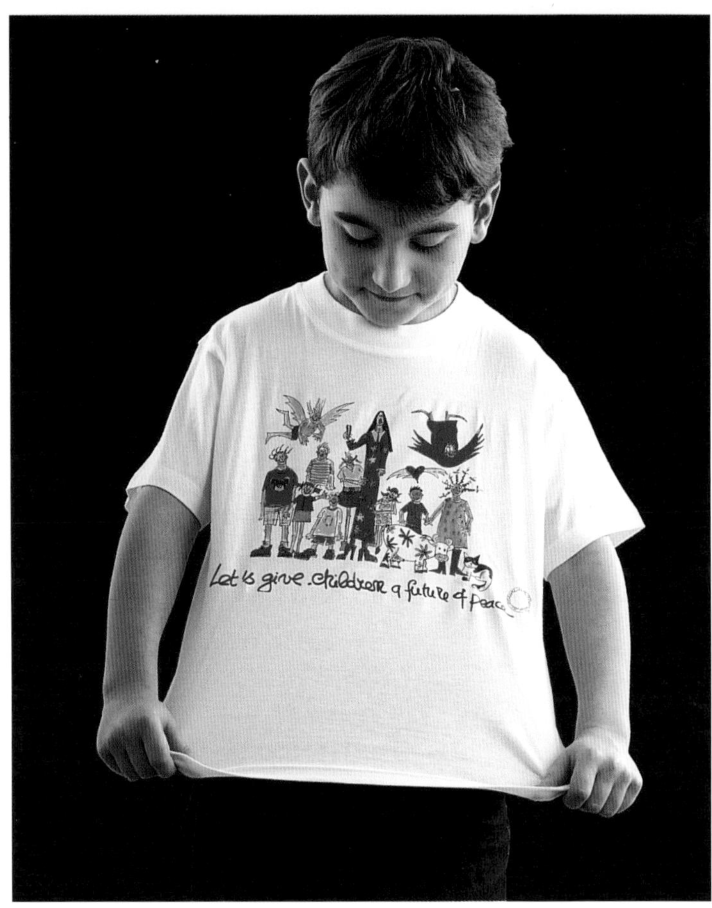

Opposite: Heroes of the South Park cult comic strip.

Next pages, left: As a comic strip character who made it to the big screen, Super Man's famous "S" has been emblazoned on millions of T-shirts.

Next pages, right, top and bottom: Pokemons in agnès b.'s versions. Center: Wallace and Gromit.

opening of the Xüly Bet store to the Forum at Les Halles in Paris, to the "Fuck Me I'm Famous" Baths night, by way of a magazine launch, or the fkgb.com website, the T-shirt can now be seen commemorating every kind of party. And for people who like to hang on to them, these T-shirts are great souvenirs, reminders of good times had by all. People who go on wearing them are in effect saying "I was there," and people who no longer put them on can at least use them as nightshirts.

Theme T-shirts

These days no excuse is needed to come out with a T-shirt. Used as a promotional tool par excellence, T-shirts mark cultural or, more straightforwardly, sales and marketing events. They are

KICK ASS!

EVERYWHERE
I WEAR
CHANEL
EYEWEAR

Above: The T-shirt introduced to launch the Chanel line of glasses.

Opposite: From Hawaii to Paris, by way of Singapore, the Hard Rock Café has spawned T-shirts all over the planet.

usually freebies, and have the charm of those soon-put-aside trinkets, tchotchkes and souvenirs that fill peoples lives. Just like the events they celebrate, they are by their very nature ephemeral. In the 1970s, John Lennon advertised Yoko Ono's new book *Grapefruit* by wearing a T-shirt printed with the scandalous cover of the Japanese artist's buttocks in close-up. More recently, Frigide Barjot (editor of the French tabloid *Voici*) brought out a T-shirt with the title of her amusing book called: *Educating My Husband/J'élève mon mari*. The movie industry also uses this textile medium to inform the press about new releases. *Trainspotting*, *Chicken Run* and *Tanguy* all used T-shirt advertising. It is a practice frequently employed by record companies who use T-shirts to promote new albums and singles, and to commemorate anniversaries, like the 100th birthday of EMI. Many

Hard Rock

S RESTE
TOUT L'ÉTÉ
partir de 23h00
rs sauf Dimanche et Lundi
e 75009 PARIS Tel : 53 21 07 33
LE BUS
Every Tuesday
LADIES NIGHT
Free

DECEMBER
PRICE
THE MAGAZINE FO
Esquire
ree to the first 5 winners
f our quiz on the 60's
n official Esquire softball shir
ust in time for Christmas)

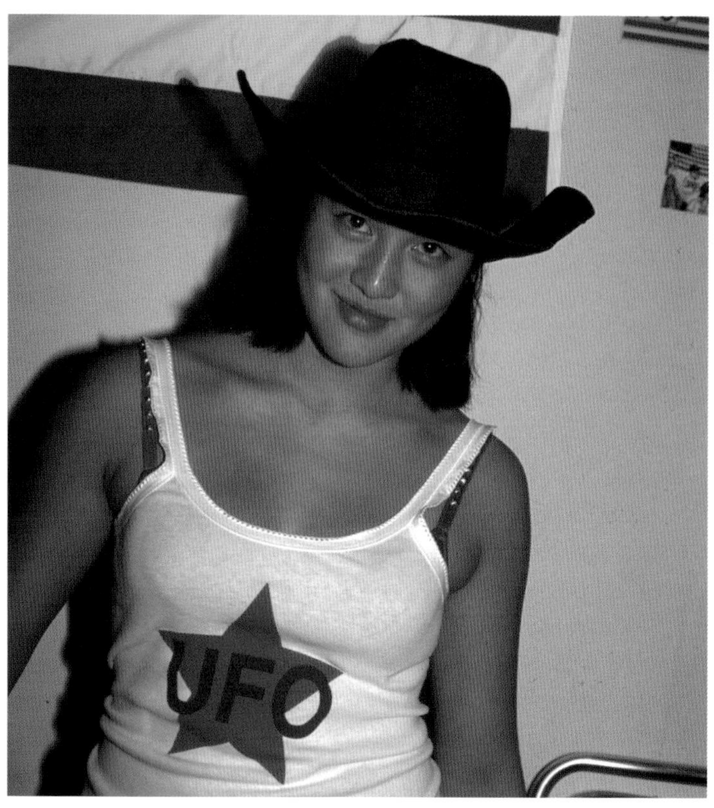

Previous pages, left: Promotional T-shirt for Paris night club Le Bus

Above: UFO T-shirt.

Opposite, clockwise from top left: Promotional T-shirts for the release of Pedro Almodovar's *All About My Mother*, Ted Demme's *Blow* with Johnny Depp, the Colette Concept Store in Paris, and the book *La Mode en peinture* [Fashion in Painting].

music festivals have now turned into annual gatherings complete with their souvenir T-shirts. In 1992, the Sacramento Jazz Festival celebrated its jubilee with a T-shirt.

Whether for an angling contest in Canada, or the opening of a health club in Dallas, T-shirts are part and parcel of all kinds of celebrations and festivities. In the fashion world, they're often used as invitations to the shows. By Chloé, for the spring-summer 2001 collection in the form of a "banana" tank top, and by Nina Ricci for the winter 2002 collection. Such T-shirts inevitably become collectors' items. T-shirts are also used to mark the opening of boutiques, like designer Xüly Bet's store at the Forum des Halles in Paris. But, above all, T-shirts have a night-owl's streak about them. At private parties, it's never too late for this night-clubbers uniform to be out advertising. And it shows up for parties given by *Interview* magazine, or *Jalouse*, or even for the launch of a new newspaper. But clubs also use T-shirts for their own ends. The Bus Palladium used them to advertise free

TODO
SOBRE
MI
MADRE
ALL
ABOUT
MY
MOTHER

BLOW

colette
RULES

CANNES 2000
CINEMA
AGAINST AIDS

ainspotting

Previous pages, left: The model Stephanie Seymour wearing an Amfar HIV/AIDS T-shirt at the 53rd Cannes Film Festival in 2000.
Next pages, right: T-shirt edited at the launch of U.K. blockbuster *Trainspotting*.

Above: DKNY jeans T-shirt.

Opposite: Raggamuffin T-shirt.

Following pages: T-shirt "No pain, No gain."

admission for girls on special evenings, and the Bains Douches printed up one model with the name of their VIP night: "Fuck Me I'm Famous."

T-shirts harbor a host of memories, bringing back happenings in high society circles and enabling those still wearing these T-shirts to proclaim that they were once part of the in-crowd.

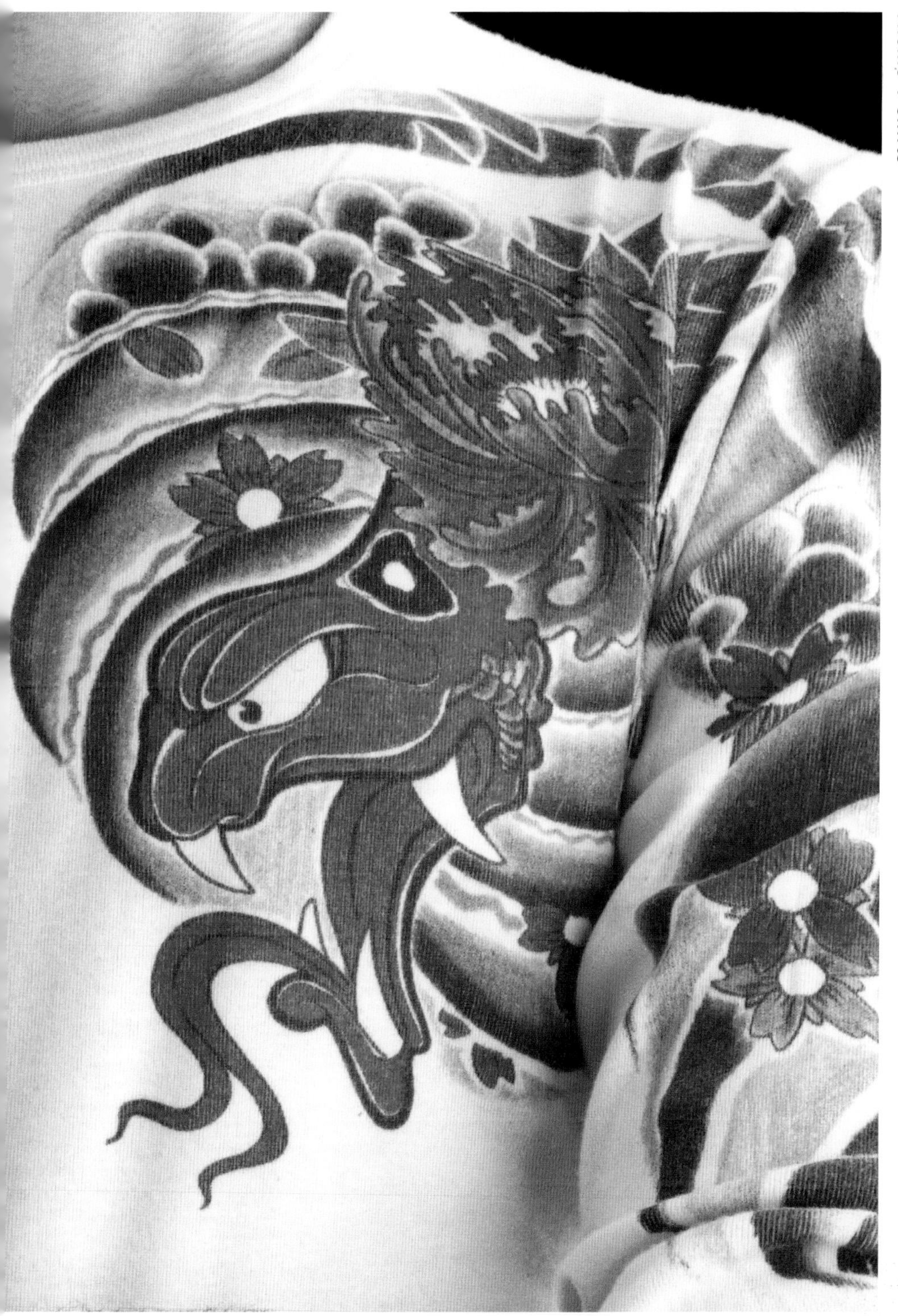

The khaki T-shirt

Before the T-shirt became a fully-fledged garment in its own right, it was ushered in at the end of the 19th century as the official underwear of the U.S. Navy. In 1942, the army gave it its classic form and duly called it the "T-Type Shirt." This undershirt, originally still in the pristine, spick-and-span white of underwear, then assumed more military hues to remain inconspicuous in the jungles of the South Pacific islands. From 1944 on it sported the khaki camouflage pattern, which blended perfectly with a tropical landscape—a few months earlier, the German army had printed its own uniforms with the same design. Until then, the T-shirt was unknown in Europe, which discovered it through the GIs. In no time at all, this comfortable and revolutionary garment would become part and parcel of army uniforms. It accordingly adopted the regulation color: khaki. This color, derived from the Persian word *khak* meaning dust, earth or mud, was being used at the beginning of the 20th century "for the personal wardrobe of Indian soldiers who dyed their clothes with natural pigments to disguise how dirty they were," explains Stefano Tonchi, in the catalogue for the Uniforms exhibition, held at the Pitti Imagine Uomo show in 2001. Since those days, the khaki military T-shirt has served in all wars, including the Vietnam War. As a loathsome object for any self-respecting pacifist, it was nevertheless a trophy for many war veterans who kept on wearing it once they'd left the service. And it was sometimes an object of fascination for young recruits: "Even the young men of West Point wear T-shirts in camouflage patterns (1987), linking the postwar

1

POLICIA NACIONAL
UPF

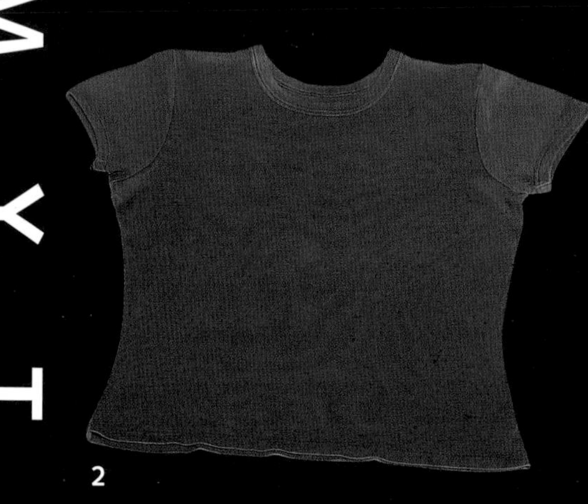

2

military to its history of jungle combat and suggesting the full-scale transference of military," wrote Richard Martin in his book *The Jocks and the Nerds*. Since then, guerrillas and para-military factions have appropriated camouflage and khaki T-shirts. From the Tamil Tigers to members of the American White Power movement, everyone puts on the uniform of their particular struggle. Just like the trench coat which was worn by British officers in the First World War, these military undershirts have made their way into the civilian wardrobe. Diverted from their original function, they have become fashion objects that help their wearers merge with the urban jungle. In Japan, the A Bathing Ape brand has turned its fighting ape, set against a camouflage-patterned backdrop, into its theme of choice. In Paris, Jean-Charles de Castelbajac has come to the fore as the specialist of this motif. For summer 2001, he used camouflage for his tank tops as well as in his china collection, while Comme des Garçons diverted it into T-shirts, demoting Op Art patterns with plastified camouflage stripes.

Previous page: Special unit of the Panama police in a jungle operation on the Chico river, 1999.
2: Vintage T-shirt.

3: Customized T-shirt.

4: Singer Pierpoljack in London, 2000.

3

of
Lane

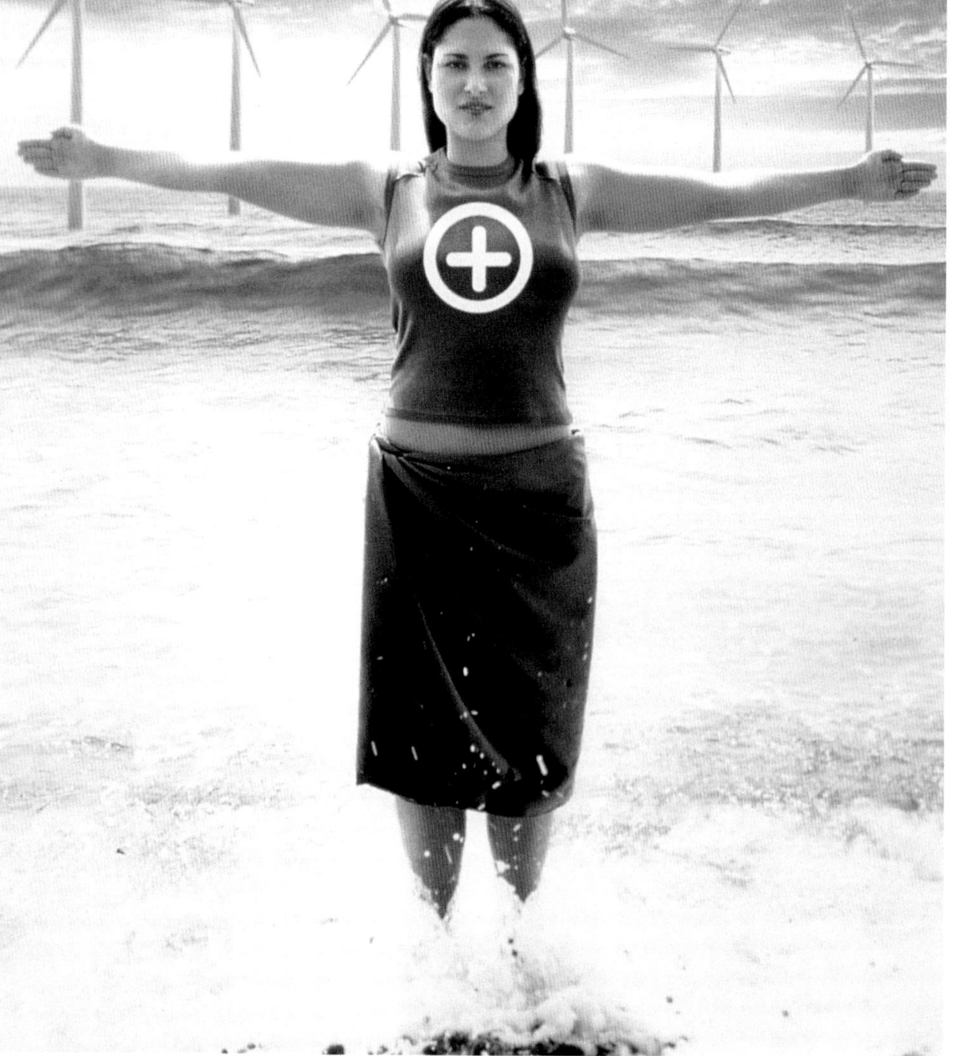
CHOOSE
POSITIVE ENERGY
turn on to a brighter future
discover green power

Conclusion

The T-shirt has never been content merely to embellish the person wearing it; it also strives to express more internal qualities. As technological innovations come ever faster and more furiously, it has learned how to protect, protest and communicate. In an age when everyone is concerned with their health and well-being, this garment can also serve as a kind of cocoon designed to protect the body from external attacks. With microfibers, the T-shirt merges with the skin by imitating its soft, supple texture and, also like skin, actually breathes. Woven without seams, it molds any kind of anatomy and accentuates the body's curves. But it also makes the most of high-tech fibers to fight pollution, stress, bacterias and harmful solar rays. Antibacterial and antimicrobial fabrics, in their ongoing struggle against germs, have gradually infiltrated the world of underwear to rid us of unpleasant smells. Sunburn, the number one foe of vacationers, has been successfully

Opposite: The Body Shop/Greenpeace. 2001 campaign for environmental preservation.

combatted by anti-UV ray T-shirts. Borrowed from cycling gear, the sun-block T-shirt is knitted with a yarn enriched with titanium dioxide, which enables it to filter harmful rays four times more effectively than a conventional garment. And to deter mosquitoes, the T-shirt can also be impregnated with an insecticide.

Today, however, urban stress is one of the scourges of modern life, greatly exacerbated by electromagnetism. After designer Elisabeth de Senneville's antimagnetic T-shirt, a Japanese firm called Gunze came up with a model called the "Pace Protector," specially designed to protect people fitted with pacemakers from those harmful emissions. The number one Japanese underwear manufacturer made this garment with silvery nylon thread, meant to block 92% of such waves.

Influenced by dietary supplements and cosmetics, textiles are teaming up with cosmetics, and even with medicines, to come up with new ways of promoting health and well-being. Elisabeth de Senneville has designed scented T-shirts, where the fragrances are enclosed in microcapsules released when they come into contact with the skin's warmth. To keep the epidermis constantly moisturized, all you have to do is replace these fragrance capsules with soothing lotions. Better still, scientists working for the Japanese Fuji Spinning Company have developed a T-shirt incorporating vitamin C. This revolutionary fiber, known as V-up, contains a chemical product which turns into a galvanizing dosage—the equivalent of two lemons—when it touches the skin. This is a therapeutic process which calls to mind those antidepressant Japanese T-shirts impregnated with Prozac.

Textiles can also be caring. Smart fabrics are thus far still limited to the medical domain, where they are being used to make bed linen that stimulates the circulation, pain-killing head-bands, and T-shirts capable of taking the temperature of the body and measuring blood pressure. Even at this early stage, the Smart Shirt has already gone beyond the prototype. Originally developed by the U.S. Navy, this undershirt is capable of providing information about wounds suffered by soldiers—indicating the state of the wounded person's health, the point of impact of the bullet, and so on, thus helping rescue and medical units decide which casualties to treat first on the battlefield. Sensors woven into the fabric continually monitor vital signs—heartbeat, breathing rate, body temperature. Thanks to a processor fitted at the bottom of the T-shirt, these data can then be transmitted by cell phone or satellite. In the non-military world, this T-shirt is already being used by chronically ill people, the elderly and even premature infants, vulnerable to the risk of SIDS (sudden infant death syndrome). Be it as the real thing or as a prototype, the T-shirt is definitely not through with us yet.

Books
Andrew Tucker, *London Fashion*, Thames & Hudson, 1998.
Tommy Hilfiger with David A. Keep, *All American: A Style Book*, Universe, 1997.
Le Siècle rebelle, dictionnaire de la contestation au XXe siècle, Larousse, 1999.
Helen Walters and Tim Fletcher, *100% cotton: T-shirt Graphics*, Laurence King Publishing, 2001.
Magelonne Toussaint Samat, *Histoire technique et morale du vêtement*, Bordas, 1990.
Alice Harris, *The White T*, Harper Style, 1996.
La marginalité à l'écran, CinémAction, Corlet Télérama, 1999.
Philippe Bialobos, *Messengers Style*, Assouline, 2000.
Gene Krell, *Vivienne Westwood*, Assouline, 1997.
Naomi Klein, *No Logo*, Picador, 2002.
Laurence Benaïm, *L'Année de la mode 1988-1989*, La Manufacture, 1989.
Farid Chenoune, *Des modes et des hommes : deux siècles d'élégance masculine*, Flammarion, 1993.
Richard Martin and Harold Koda, *Jocks and Nerds: Men's style in the Twentieth Century*, Rizzoli International Publications, 1989.
Ted Polhemus, *Streetstyle: From Sidewalk to Catwalk*, Thames & Hudson, 1994.
Valerie Steele, *Fashion and Eroticism*, Oxford University Press, 1985.
Valerie Steele, *Fifty Years of Fashion: New Look to Now*, Yale University Press, 2000.
Ruhrberg, Shneckenburger, Fricke, Honnef, *Art of the 20th Century*, Taschen, 2000.
Edmonde Charles-Roux, *Le Temps Chanel*, Chêne Grasset, 1979.
Neil Grant, *James Dean in His Own Words*, Crescent Books, 1991.
Joshua Sims, *Rock/Fashion*, Omnibus Press.
Jane Dorner, *Fashion in the forties & fifties*, Arlington House Publishers, 1975.
Philippe Parreno, *Snow Dancing*, GW Press.
Vicki B. Carnegy, *Fashion of a decade; the 1980's*, Facts on File, 1990.
Sharon Churcher and Steven S. Gaines, *Obsession: The Lives and Times of Calvin Klein*, Carol Publishing Group, 1994.
Colin McDowell, *Jean-Paul Gaultier*, London Cassel, 2000.
Maurice Farge and Barry Rubin, *The Wash and Wear Canvas, T-shirt Tripping in the 70s*, Lester and Orpen Limited, 1974.
Roland Barthes, *The Pleasure of the Text*, Noonday Press, 1980.
Gilles Lipovetsky, *L'Ere du vide : essais sur l'individualisme contemporain*, Gallimard, 1983.
Michel de Certeau, *L'Invention du quotidien*, Gallimard, 1990.
Les dieux d'Hollywood, Atlas, 1995.
Kazan par Kazan : entretiens avec Michel Ciment, Ramsay, 1985.
Claude Fauque and Sophie Bramel, *Une seconde peau, fibres et textiles d'aujourd'hui*, Editions Alternatives, 1999.
Anne Bony, *Les Années 80*, Editions du Regard, 1995.
Anne Bony, *Les Années 90*, Editions du Regard, 2000.
Colin McDowell, *The Man of Fashion*, Thames & Hudson, 1997.
John De Greef, *Sous-vêtements*, Booking International, 1989.
Marie Simon, *Les Dessous*, Chêne, 1998.
Alison Carter, *Underwear, the fashion history*, London B.T Bataford, 1994.

Catalogues

A-Poc Making Issey Miyake & Dai Fujiwara, Vitra Design Museum, 2001.
Vote: the 1992 elections in T-shirts, National Museum of fashion, Fashion Institute of Technology, July 13-September 12, 1992.
Uniform: Order and Disorder, Milano, Charta, 2000.
T-shirt, T-show, Galeira Studi o Marcioni di Milano, April 1984, Electa Carlo Pirovano.
Mutations/Mode, 1960-2000, Musée Galliera, Paris Musées, 2000.

Articles

Malcom McLaren, "Elements of Antistyle," *The New Yorker*, September 22, 1997.
Richard Martin, "Identity: George Platt Lyne's Photograph of Carl Carlsen," *Dress*, 1995.
Richard Phalon, "Walkin Bilboards," *Forbes*, December 7, 1992.
Jean-Michel Normand, "La Vogue du maillot de foot survit au 'phénomène Mondial'," *Le Monde*, October 18, 1998.
Anne-Laure Quilleriet, "Maillot rayé pour tous," *Le Monde*, January 15, 1997.
Pascal Galinier, "Athlètes et sponsors : le couple roi du 'sport business'," *Le Monde*, February 8, 2000.
"Le T-shirt peinture sur soi, les tentations," *Libération*, October 12 to 18, 2001.

Acknowledgments

The author expresses her warmest thanks to Martine and Prosper Assouline, Christian Dior, Sonia Rykiel, Jean-Charles de Castelbajac, Amnesty International, Act Up, Jacques Brunel, Laurence Benaïm, Anne-Laure Quilleriet, Véronique Bataille, Christophe Chiappa, Clémentine Fauret, Hélène Antoine, Malik, Margot Delafon, Elisabeth Brunel, Sonia Rachline, Charlotte and Michael, Victoire de Taillac, Nicole Chopin, André, Gerald Cohen, BMCS, Didier Claude of the store Boys Bazar and Stéphane Nappez, Mathilde Dupuy d'Angeac for their generous help and contribution.

The publisher wishes to thank Bruno Collin & *Wad* magazine, Ralph Lauren, Dolce & Gabbana, A-POC Issey Miyake, Emporio Armani, Gucci, agnès b., Yohji Yamamoto, Jean-Paul Gaultier Parfums, Colette, Comme des Garçons, Galerie Emmanuel Perrotin, Galerie Jousse Entreprise, César and Marion Bounoure, La Périphérie, Pressing, Jérôme Bel, René Walker, Mercredi, Captain Transfert, Galerie Jennifer Flay, Galerie Air de Paris, Frédéric Beigbeder, APC, Body Shop, Benetton, Tati, Lattitude Sud, Flammarion 4, Petit Bateau, Galeries Lafayette, Charlotte Brunel, Philippe Sebirot, Véronique Bataille, Alexandre Assouline, Sébastien Ratto-Viviani, Light House & Peter Lindbergh, Peter Knapp for thier contribution to this book.

4-5 © Assouline; 7 © Pièce à conviction, Paris; 10 © Pablo Corral V/Corbis; 15 © Lipnitzki-Viollet; 16 © Boyer-Viollet; 17 Courtesy U.S. Navy; 18 © Rue des archives, Paris; 19 © AKG, Paris; 20 © Courtesy U.S. Navy; 21 © Collection Viollet; 23 © Sunset Boulevard/Raymond Boyer; 24 © Assouline; 27 © The Bettmann archive; 28 Eliot Elisofon/*Life* Magazine © Time Inc., reprinted by permission; 29 © Les archives du 7e art, Paris; 31 © 100% Cotton; 33 © Magnum USA/Dennis stock/MP; 34-35 © Magnum/René Burri/MP; 36 © Magnum/Patrick Zachmann/MP; 37 © Françoise Huguier; 38-39 © Friedmann Hauss/A-Poc/Issey Miyake; 40-41 © Petit Bateau; 43 © Keibun Miyamoto/Retna Ltd USA/MPA Stills France only; 44-45 All rights reserved; 46 © Assouline; 48 © Irina Voronkonskii; 49 © Assouline/Philippe Sebirot; 51 © UPI Bettmann; 52 © Rue des archives, Paris; 53 © Assouline/Philippe Sebirot/collection Charlotte Brunel, style Véronique Bataille; 54 © Magnum; 55 © Assouline; 56 © AKG; 57 © Rue des archives/CS/FF; 58-59 © Sunset Boulevard/Raymond Royer; 61 © Les archives du 7e art, Paris; 62-63 © Les archives du 7e art, Paris; 65 © Rue des archives, Paris; 66 © Les archives du 7e art, Paris; 68-69 © Les archives du 7e art, Paris; 70-71 © Les archives du 7e art, Paris; 72 © Les archives du 7e art, Paris; 73 © *Starfix*; 74 © Les archives du 7e art, Paris; 75 © Raymond Cauchetier; 76-77 © AKG, Paris; 79 © Halla; 80 © Assouline/Philippe Sebirot, style Véronique Bataille (top left), © Rue des archives (bottom left); 81 © Java (left), © *Elle*/Scoop © Les archives du 7e art, Paris (top right); 83 © 2000 Stone/Dale Durfee; 84-85 © Les archives du 7e art, Paris; 86 © Magnum/Burt Glinn/MP; 87 © Friedmann Hauss/A-Poc/Issey Miyake; 88-89 © Rue des archives/Everett, Paris; 90 © *Photo* Magazine/John Derek; 91 © Nathan Benn/Corbis; 92 © Assouline/Philippe Sebirot, style Véronique Bataille; 91 © MPA/Stills/Michel Bourquart/Stills Press; 95 © AKG/ Bruce Cartwright, Paris; 96-97 © Les archives du 7e art, Paris; 98 © Assouline/ Philippe Sebirot/collection Bruno Collin/*Wad* magazine, Paris, style Véronique Bataille; 99 © Pierre & Gilles/Courtesy Galerie Jérôme de Noirmont, Paris; 100 © Rue des archives, Paris; 101 © MPA/Stills; 102-103 © *Wad* magazine, Paris; 104-105 © Rue des archives, Paris; 106 © Allan Tannenbaum; 107 © Magnum/LeonardFreed/MP; 109 © Assouline/Philippe Sebirot, style Véronique Bataille/Captain Transfert; 110 © Planet/F. Giacobetti (top left), © All rights reserved (bottom); 111 © Rue des archives/Agip, Paris (top), © Vo Trung Dung/Corbis/Sygma (bottom); 112-113 © Magnum/Leonard Freed/ MP; 114-115 © Assouline; 116 © Tore Kristiansen/Rue des archives, Paris; 117 © Johan Copes Van Hasselt/Corbis; 118-119 © Assouline/Philippe Sebirot, style Véronique Bataille; 120 © Corbis/David & Peter Turnley; 121 © Magnum/Marc Riboud/MP; 122-123 © Courtesy Galerie Jousse Entreprise/ Gianni Motti, Paris; 124-125 © Magnum/Abbas/MP; 126 © Leif Skoogfors/Corbis; 127 © Peter Turnley/Corbis; 128-129 © Assouline/Philippe Sebirot/collection Charlotte Brunel, style Véronique Bataille; 130-131 © Assouline/Philippe Sebirot/collection Charlotte Brunel, style Véronique Bataille; 132 © Corbis-Sygma/Ciniglio Lorenzo/Corbis; 133 © Retna USA/ MPA Stills; 134 © *Wad* magazine, Paris; 135 © Assouline/Philippe Sebirot/collection Bruno Collin, style Véronique Bataille; 136 © Miladinovic Voja/Corbis-Sygma; 137 © Ciniglio Lorenzo/Corbis; 138 Assouline; 139 © Assouline/ Philippe Sebirot/collection Charlotte Brunel, style Véronique Bataille; 140 © *Wad* magazine, Paris; 142 © Nathalie Bottalico/Magalie agence Profil; 143 © Starface/Kevin Mazur/Wireimage; 144 © Philippe Bialobos; 145 © Assouline/ Philippe Sebirot/collection Bruno Collin, style Véronique Bataille; 147 © Tod Gipstein/Corbis; 148 © Hulton-

Deutsch/Corbis; 139 © Assouline/Philippe Sebirot/collection Bruno Collin/*Wad* magazine, style Véronique Bataille; 150-151 © Assouline/Philippe Sebirot, style Véronique Bataille/Captain Transfert; 152 © Assouline/Philippe Sebirot/collection Bruno Collin, style Véronique Bataille, Colette, Tati; 154 © Rue des archives, Paris (left), © Corbis/Steve Raymer (right); 155 © *Wad* magazine, Paris; 156 ©Steve Raymer/Corbis; 157 © Nathalie Bottalico; 158 © MPA/Stills (left), © Assouline/Philipe Sebirot/collection Bruno Collin *Wad* magazine, style Véronique Bataille; 159 © Frédéric Beigbeder; 160 © Assouline/Philippe Sebirot/collection Charlotte Brunel, style Véronique Bataille; 161 © Java/Luc Papa; 162 © Roman Soumar/Corbis; 163 © Magnum/Bruno Barbey/MP; 164 © APC; 165 Corbis Sygma/John Van Hasselt; 166 © Assouline/Philippe Sebirot, style Véronique Bataille; 167 © *Wad* magazine, Paris; 168-169 © Assouline; 171 © Assouline/Philippe Sebirot, style Véronique Bataille; 172 © *Vogue* Italy/Java; 173 © Magnum (bottom); 175 © AKG/private collection, Paris; 176 © Assouline/Philippe Sebirot, style Véronique Bataille/Colette; 177 © Roxanne Lowit; 178 Production Flammarion 4 © ADAGP; 180 © Assouline/Philippe Sebirot/collection Bruno Collin, style Véronique Bataille; 181 © Pressing; 182-183 © Galerie Emmanuel Perrotin; 185 © Richard Porteau/Alain Sechas/collection Frac Poitou-Charentes; 186 © Assouline/Philippe Sebirot, style Véronique Bataille/ agnès b.; 187 Production Flammarion 4 © ADAGP; 188 Production Flammarion 4 © ADAGP; 189 Jean-Pierre Khazem © Courtesy Galerie Emmanuel Perrotin, Paris; 191 Nicole Tran Ba vang © Courtesy Galerie Emmanuel Perrotin/ADAGP, Paris; 192 © André Walker; 193 © Assouline/Philippe Sebirot, style Véronique Bataille/agnès b.; 194 © Assouline/Philippe Sebirot, style Véronique Bataille; 196-197 © Mutsumi Tsuda; 199-200-201 © Fruit of the Loom, London; 202-203 © Archives du 7e art, Paris; 204 © Peter Knapp/Assouline; 205 © Peter Knapp/*Elle*/Scoop; 206 © Hulton Getty/Photogram Stone Images, Paris; 207-208 © Rue des archives/Agip, Paris; 209 © Courtesy Assouline; 210-211 © Paul Erhardt/*Elle*/Scoop; 212 © agnès b.; 214 © Assouline/Philippe Sebirot/collection Bruno Collin/*Wad* magazine, style Véronique Bataille; 215 © Gilles Bensimon/*Elle*/Scoop/Assouline; 216-217 © Peter Lindbergh; 218 © Assouline/Philippe Sebirot, style Véronique Bataille; 220 © Assouline/ Philippe Sebirot/Collection Bruno Collin/*Wad* magazine, style Véronique Bataille; 221 © Assouline/ Philippe Sebirot/collection Charlotte Brunel, style Véronique Bataille; 223 © Jacques Olivar/*Marie-Claire*; 225 © Calvin Klein; 226-227 © Java/Frédérique Dumoulin; 228 © F. Dumoulin/Java, © G. Marineau/ Starface, F. Dumoulin/Java, © F. Dumoulin/Java; 229 ©Java/Luc Papa; 230 © APC; 231 © Java/Frédérique Dumoulin; 232 © Java/Luc Papa; 234 © Java/Frédérique Dumoulin; 235 © Mario Testino/Dolce & Gabbana; 237 © Dolce & Gabbana; 238 © Roxanne Lowit; 239 © Java/Frédérique Dumoulin; 240 © Foc Kan; 241 © MPA/Stills/Eric Catarina; 242-243 © Christian Lacroix; 244 © Java/Frédérique Dumoulin; 245 © Java/Guy Marineau; 246 © Monica Feudi (left) © J.-François José (right); 247 © Java/Frédérique Dumoulin (left) © Java/Frédérique Dumoulin (right); 248 © Friedmann Hauss/A-Poc/Issey Miyake; 249 © A-Poc/Issey Miyake; 250 © Assouline/Philippe Sebirot, style Véronique Bataille; 251 © Java/Frédérique Dumoulin; 252 © Assouline/Philippe Sebirot, style Véronique Bataille; 253 © All rights reserved; 254 © Courtesy Galerie Emmanuel Perrotin/Jean-Pierre Khazem; 256 © Java/Frédérique Dumoulin (top left), © Les archives du 7e Art (bottom left), © Bruno Barbey/Magnum; 257 © Frédérique Dumoulin/Java, Jean-Paul Gaultier Parfums; 259 © Troy Word; 260 © Giorgio Armani; 261 © Roxanne Lowit; 262 © Rue des archives, Paris;

263 © Rue des archives/Agip, Paris; 264 © Foc Kan; 265 © Jean-Marie Perrier/*Elle*/Scoop; 266-267 © Miguel-Rozales; 268 © Dominick Conde/Star File/Stills Press; 269 © All action/MPA/Stills; 270 © Assouline/Philippe Sebirot, style Véronique Bataille/agence Mercredi; 271 © *Wad* Magazine, Paris; 272 Chris Rainer/Corbis; 273 © Owen Franken/Corbis; 274 © collection Helen Wellington; 275 © Assouline/Philippe Sebirot, style Véronique Bataille/ Colette; 276-277 © Assouline/Philippe Sebirot, style Véronique Bataille/ Colette; 278 © *Wad* magazine, Paris; 279 © *Wad* magazine, Paris; 280-281 © Assouline/Philippe Sebirot/collection Bruno Collin/*Wad* magazine, style Véronique Bataille; 282-283 © Assouline/Philippe Sebirot/collection Charlotte Brunel, style Véronique Bataille; 284-285 © *Wad* magazine, Paris; 287 © Galeries Lafayette/Avant Première; 288, 290 to 293, 295 © Assouline; 289 © Assouline; 294 © Martine Camilleri; 297 © Pressing; 299 © Arsfutura/Olaf Breuning; 300 © Foc Kan (left), © Christian Dior (right); 301 © Foc Kan (top), © 100% Cotton (bottom); 303 © Neal Preston/Corbis; 304 © Rue des archives/Everett, Paris; 305 © Assouline/Philippe Sebirot/collection Bruno Collin/*Wad* magazine, style Véronique Bataille; 306 © Assouline/Philippe Sebirot, style Véronique Bataille/Captain Transfert; 281 (from top to bottom) © MPA/Stills, © Bourquart/MPA/Stills, © Foc Kan; 308 © Hulton-Deutsch Collection/Corbis; 310 © MPA/Stills; 311 © Assouline/Philippe Sebirot/collection Bruno Collin/*Wad* magazine, style Véronique Bataille; 312 © E. Catarina/Stills; 313 © Redferns/Roberts/ MPA/Stills; 314 © Denis Darzacq/Stills; 315 © Bob Gruen/Stills/Star File; 316 © Les archives du 7e art, Paris; 317 © Courtesy Assouline; 318-319 © Rue des archives, Paris; 320 © AKG Paris; 322 © Rue des archives/Everett; 324-325 © Lynn Goldsmith; 326 © Lynn Goldsmith/Corbis; 327 © Catarina/Corbis; 328-329 © Star File/Kaplan/Stills; 330 © Stills © Bourquart/Stills; 331 © Isard/MPA/Stills, Paris; 332-333 © Magnum/MP; 334-335 © Pascalito/ Stills; 337 © F. Albert/Stills; 338-339 © *Wad* magazine, Paris; 340 © F. Albert/Stills; 341 © *Wad* magazine, Paris (top left), © All Action/Stills (top right), © All Action/MPA/Stills (bottom left), © *Wad* magazine, Paris (bottom right); 342 © *Wad* magazine, Paris; 343 © MPA/Stills; 344 to 349 © *Wad* magazine, Paris; 350 © Magazine Fruits, 2001, Japon; 351 © *Wad* magazine, Paris and Assouline/Philippe Sebirot, style Véronique Bataille/Captain Transfert; 352-353 © *Wad* magazine, Paris; 354-355-356-357 © Philippe Bialobos; 358 © Assouline; 359 © Assouline/Philippe Sebirot/collection Charlotte Brunel, style Véronique Bataille; 360 © Assouline/Philippe Sebirot/T-shirt and style Véronique Bataille; 361 © *Wad* magazine, Paris; 362 Assouline/Philippe Sebirot/collection Charlotte Brunel, style Véronique Bataille; 363 © Burt Glinn/Magnum; 364-365-366 © *Wad* magazine, Paris; 367 © Magnum/Eve Arnold; 368-369 © Magnum © Abbas/MP; 370 © DR/Spree, Paris; 371 © Assouline; 372 © Assouline/Philippe Sebirot, style Véronique Bataille/Spree, Paris; 373 © Burquart/Stills Press/David Gallager; 374 © Assouline/Philippe Sebirot, style Véronique Bataille/Captain transfert; 375 © Assouline/Philippe Sebirot/collection Charlotte Brunel, style Véronique Bataille and Captain Transfert; 376 © *Wad* magazine, Paris; 377 © Guy Le Querrec/Magnum, Photo Ray Lema; 378 © Foc Kan; 379 © *Esquire*; 380 © *Wad* magazine; 381 © Assouline/Philippe Sebirot, style Véronique Bataille, agence Mercredi, Colette; 382 © Arnal/Catarina/Charriau/MPA-Stills; 383 © *Wad* magazine, Paris; 384-385 © *Wad* magazine, Paris; 387 © René Burri/Magnum; 388 © Assouline/Philippe Sebirot/collection Charlotte Brunel (top), style and customized T-shirt Véronique Bataille (bottom); 389 © Eric Catarina/Stills; 390 © The Body Shop.